I0794998

IMAGES
of America

EAU CLAIRE COUNTY

IMAGES
of America

EAU CLAIRE COUNTY

Frank Smoot and the Chippewa Valley Museum

ARCADIA
PUBLISHING

Copyright ©2005 by Frank Smoot and the Chippewa Valley Museum
ISBN 978-0-7385-3395-7

Published by Arcadia Publishing
Charleston, South Carolina

Printed in the United States of America

Library of Congress Catalog Card Number: 2005923939

For all general information contact Arcadia Publishing at:
Telephone 843-853-2070
Fax 843-853-0044
E-mail sales@arcadiapublishing.com
For customer service and orders:
Toll-Free 1-888-313-2665

Visit us on the Internet at www.arcadiapublishing.com

Contents

ACKNOWLEDGMENTS

Many of the images in this book came from the archival collection of the Glenn Curtis Smoot Library and Archives at the Chippewa Valley Museum (CVM). It holds about 14,000 photographs, at least 5,500 of them taken in the county. CVM Librarian Eldbjorg Tobin offered her perpetual patience and uncanny knowledge of that collection. Other photographs came from our good friends, both institutions and people. The Eau Claire *Leader-Telegram* was very generous (a special shout out to Don Huebscher and Steve Kinderman, and the award-winning photographers under their commands), as was Ellen Loken of the Fall Creek Historical Society. Sandra Boettcher found a treasure trove of photos from her father Roger "Buzzy" Hahn's estate and helped organize an event for Augusta locals to identify them. Carol Benning, Curt Bestul, Brian Blakeley, The Chippewa Valley Convention and Visitors Bureau, Jenny Ebert, Marty Fisher-Blakeley, Karl Holbrook, George Johnson, Eleanor Jones, Jane Justesen, Patrick Levkin, Fritz Litchfield, Bev Peterson, Alice (Larson) Pingel, Marsha Robinson, Joan Scharlau, Norma Severson, and Lois Thomas all contributed photos to the project. Lila Brummond and Bert Chatterson furnished aid. CVM Director Susan McLeod offered advice, consent, a steady hand, and a bit of the whip. Catherine Rollman suffered my odd hours. Arcadia editors Jessica Belle Smith and Elizabeth Jobe carried the book on part of its journey, and Ann Marie Lonsdale brought it on home.

INTRODUCTION

Several ample books share the history of Eau Claire County, in greater or lesser part. Judge William F. Bailey's *History of Eau Claire County Wisconsin* runs 920 pages, and it stops in 1914, 90 years ago. Not to be outdone, George Forrester's *Historical and Biographical Album of the Chippewa Valley Wisconsin* runs 950. Lois Barland's two-volume set—*Sawdust City* and *The Rivers Flow On*—total 499 pages of dense two-column text. Charlene Gillette's *West of the Chippewa: A Town of Union History, Eau Claire County, Wisconsin* weighs in at 522 pages, and its central subject is just one of the county's 13 townships, although it also does a nice job of outlining the foundations of U.S. territorial controls and Wisconsin statehood.

Other books, while more svelte, are content-rich. Gene Miller's *Fairchild … When You and I Were Young*, Patricia Henke and Steve Wise's *Sights and Sounds of the Valley: A History of Fall Creek*, Gerald Hagen's *A History of Altoona*, Jane Hieb's *Eau Claire*, and Tim Pfaff's *Settlement & Survival: Building Towns in the Chippewa Valley 1850-1925* (published by the Chippewa Valley Museum Press) each tells a slice of the story. The Chippewa Valley Museum's latest book *Farm Life* spends most of a half-dozen pages discussing just one of the county's 82 one-room schools. There are other books as well. Slow readers could spend years inside those pages. This is not to mention the 23,000 websites that mention Eau Claire County.

Since the county's history is so ably explained elsewhere, this book aims instead to catch a small glimpse of the county's soul. We started with these questions: What is Eau Claire County, and, more broadly, What is a county, this historical human incorporation? It's more than this book could ever tell, of course, but we summoned up nine answers, which became our chapters: What is Eau Claire County? A Spot on the Globe; A Landscape, Sometimes Harsh; Natural Resources to Hunt and Harvest; Structures and Infrastructure; Services, Public and Private; A Place for Work and Commerce; A Place to Learn; A Place to Live and Play; and, A Place for Friendship and Fellowship.

This book makes almost no mention of any celebrities who have passed through or stayed a while, although the county has had a few: the Lederer sisters, Dear Abby and Ann Landers, stage star Rose King, '40s film star Carole Landis, film *and* stage star Laila Robins, and pianist Geoff Keezer. Even hapless O.J. Simpson housemate Kato Kaelin took a semester or two at the local university before heading for Brentwood, California, and his date with accidental notoriety. The three who have made the cut here may not often find themselves on the same list: writer Waldemar Ager (author of *Christ before Pilate: An American Story*, *On the Way to the Melting Pot*, and *Sons of the Old Country*, among other books), home run king Henry "Hank" Aaron, and former pro wrestler Jim Gagnon. Generally, Eau Claire County is neither a Mecca nor a breeding ground for celebrity. But people appear in almost every picture in these pages. This is the key to the tenth and overarching answer to the question: What is Eau Claire County? Eau Claire County is its people. This book is dedicated to them.

Similarly, this portrait of the county doesn't seek to find the county's most famous tavern, manufacturer, or school. On a few occasions—with ice cream parlors, for example—we used several evocative photos to try and paint a portrait over time. (Ice cream parlors were all over, this being the heart of America's Dairyland.) Other times, we've had to let one business or locale serve for many: We hope that Lincoln Street in Fall Creek will remind folks of their main drags; that the Register of Deeds office doesn't mind speaking up for other branches of government bureaucracy; and that horseshoe players will testify for the fine softball, soccer, and curling teams in these parts. Whatever your favorite restaurant, fishing hole, or organization might be, we're sure it's just as good or better than the one we've chosen here.

As the county approaches its sesquicentennial in 2006 and gets ready for its next chapters, it can reflect back on a childhood well spent.

— Frank Smoot, Eau Claire, 2005

Notes:

CVM stands for the archival collection of the Chippewa Valley Museum. CVM has operated as a regional history museum in scenic Carson Park, Eau Claire, Wisconsin, since 1974. The museum discovers, collects, preserves, and interprets Chippewa Valley history from the time of its earliest inhabitants some 10,000 years ago to the present day. Area residents founded the museum, which operates as a professional institution strongly based in its community. CVM is accredited by the American Association of Museums. Currently, CVM is open 1-5 p.m., Tuesday-Sunday, with extended summer hours. Admission fees are waived from 5-8 on Tuesday evenings. For more information on open hours, exhibits, programs, publications or educational services, contact CVM: Chippewa Valley Museum, P.O. Box 1204, Eau Claire WI 54702, (715) 834-7871, www.cvmuseum.com. The CVM images in this collection, along with many others, are available for perusal at the Glenn Smoot Library and Archives inside the museum building. Copies may be made for a fee.

FCHS stands for the archival collection of the Fall Creek Historical Society. The FCHS Museum is located at E11940 County Road J, Fall Creek, WI 54742, 11 miles from Eau Claire, (715) 877-3108. Built in historic Randall Park right on Highway 12, the museum houses many items relating to Fall Creek's history, but will be of interest to anyone.

Some of the Eau Claire *Leader-Telegram* images in this book, along with many others, are also available for perusal and purchase at http://photogallery.cvol.net/default.asp.

One

A Spot on the Globe

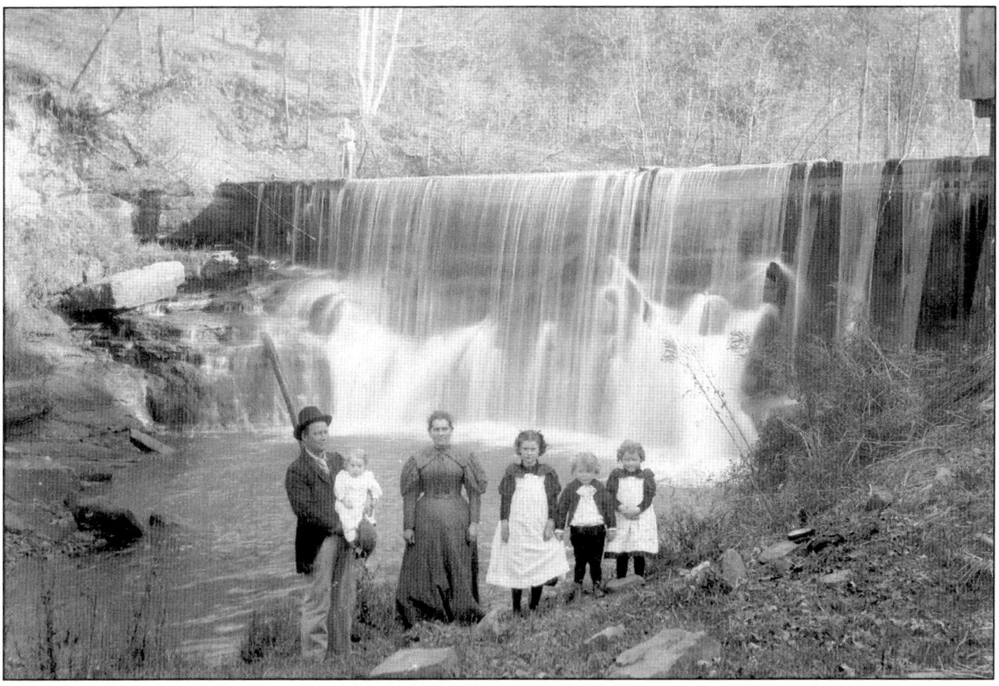

This is the dam at Otter Creek Milling Company, Town of Otter Creek. The Milling Company was owned by Robert Clark and his family from about 1896 to 1909. From left to right are Robert Clark holding Florence Clark, Robert's wife Emma Wilke Clark, Grace Clark, C.L. Clark (an adopted relative who died young), and Ruth Clark. Fred Wilke is standing on the dam. (CVM.)

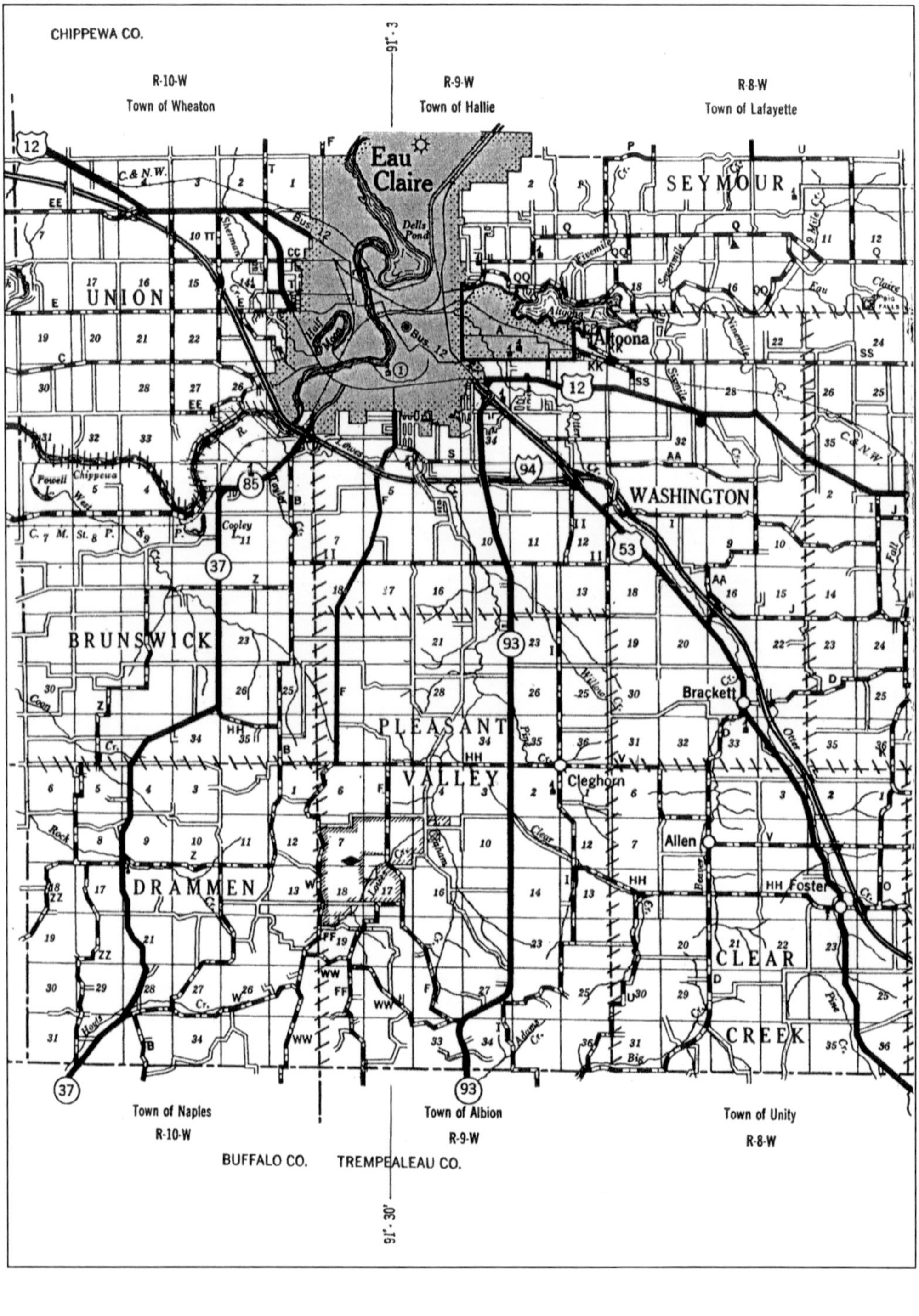
CHIPPEWA CO.
R-10-W
Town of Wheaton
R-9-W
Town of Hallie
R-8-W
Town of Lafayette
Eau Claire
Dells Pond
Altoona
SEYMOUR
UNION
WASHINGTON
BRUNSWICK
PLEASANT VALLEY
DRAMMEN
CLEAR CREEK
Cleghorn
Brackett
Allen
Foster
Cooley L.
Powell L.
Half Moon
Chippewa
C. & N.W.
Town of Naples
R-10-W
Town of Albion
R-9-W
Town of Unity
R-8-W
BUFFALO CO.
TREMPEALEAU CO.
91° - 3
91° - 30'

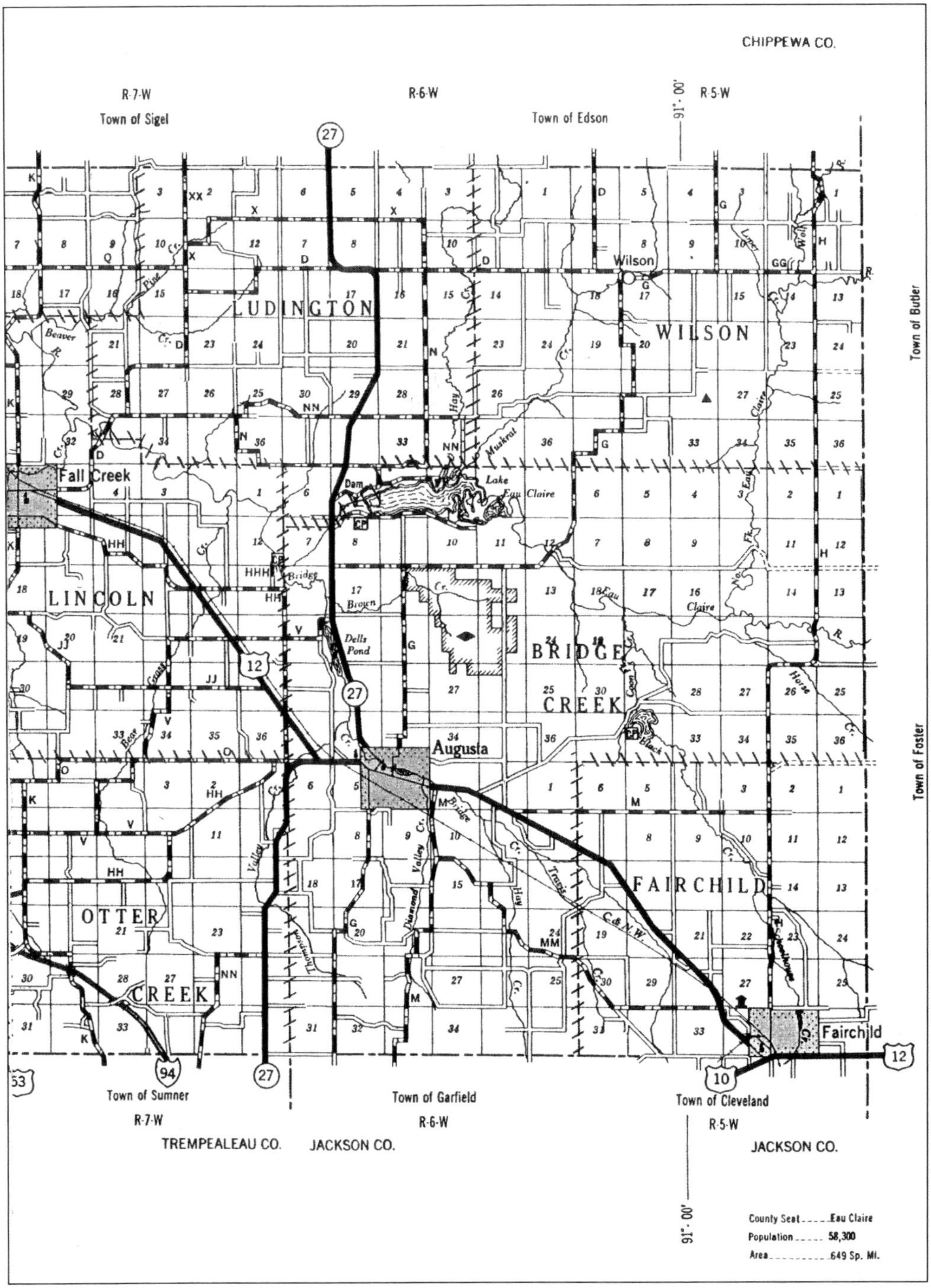

Eau Claire County map, *c.* 1960. (CVM).

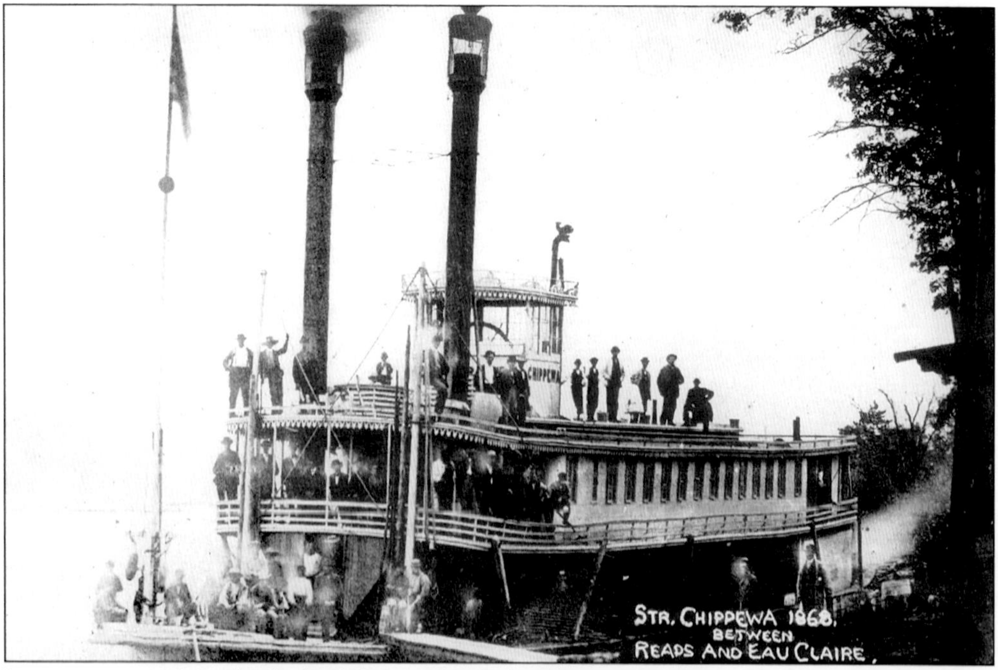

Immigrants stand on the deck of the river steamer *Chippewa*, between Read's Landing and Eau Claire, 1868. In 1855, Eau Claire's population stood at 100; by 1860, it was over 1,000; by 1880, it was over 10,000. (CVM.)

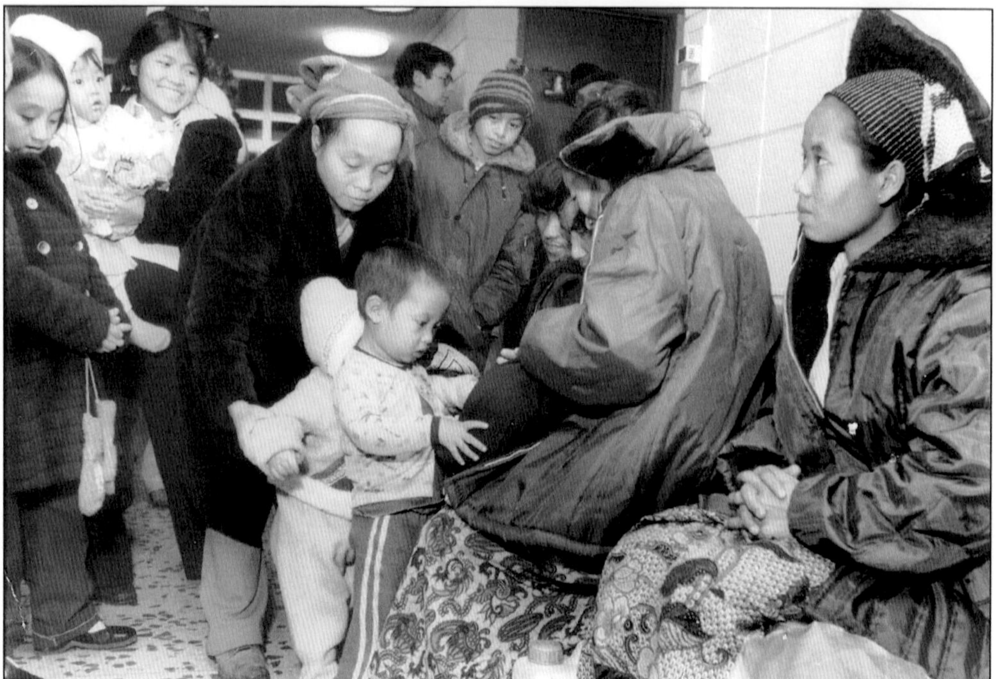
The Vang family arrives at the Eau Claire Regional Airport, December 1979. (Photograph by John Lindrud. CVM.)

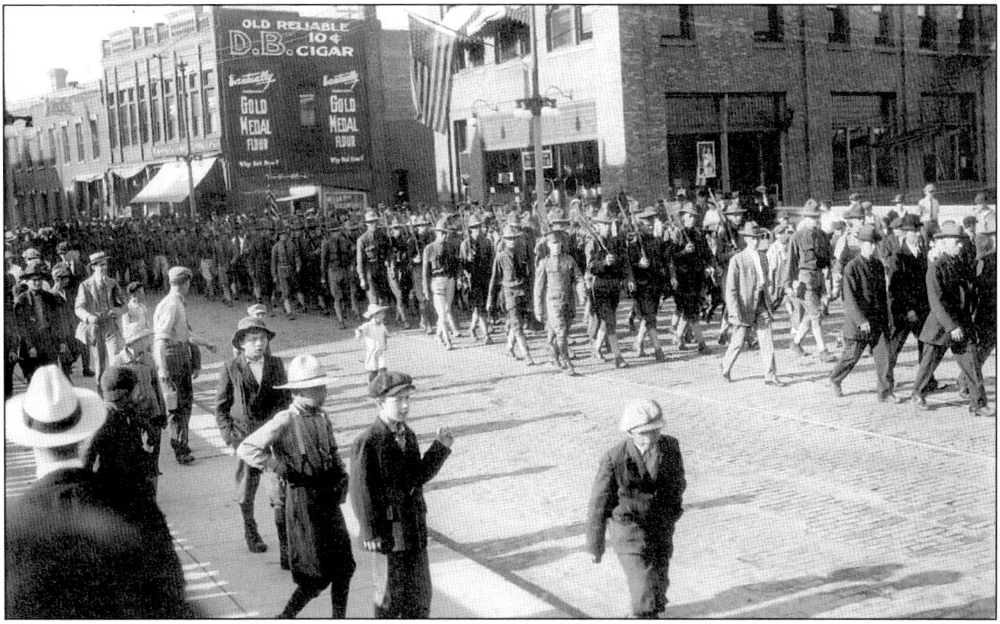

A crowd lines the sidewalk to watch Company E marching toward the Omaha railway station in Eau Claire, August 1917. Company E was bound for Camp Douglas and later action in World War I. (CVM.)

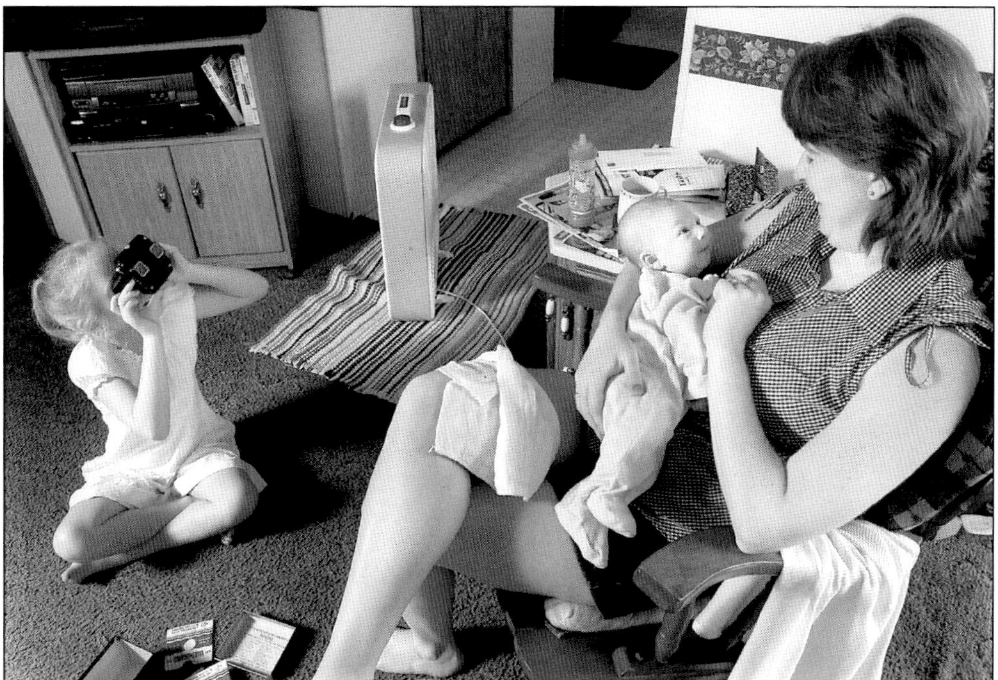
Michelle MacGlashin held her 4-week-old son Keghan, while her 5-year-old daughter Samantha played with a Viewmaster in Fairchild, July 2003. MacGlashin's husband Scott, who was in the Middle East with the National Guard, missed the birth of his son. (Photo by Dan Reiland. Courtesy of the Eau Claire *Leader-Telegram*.)

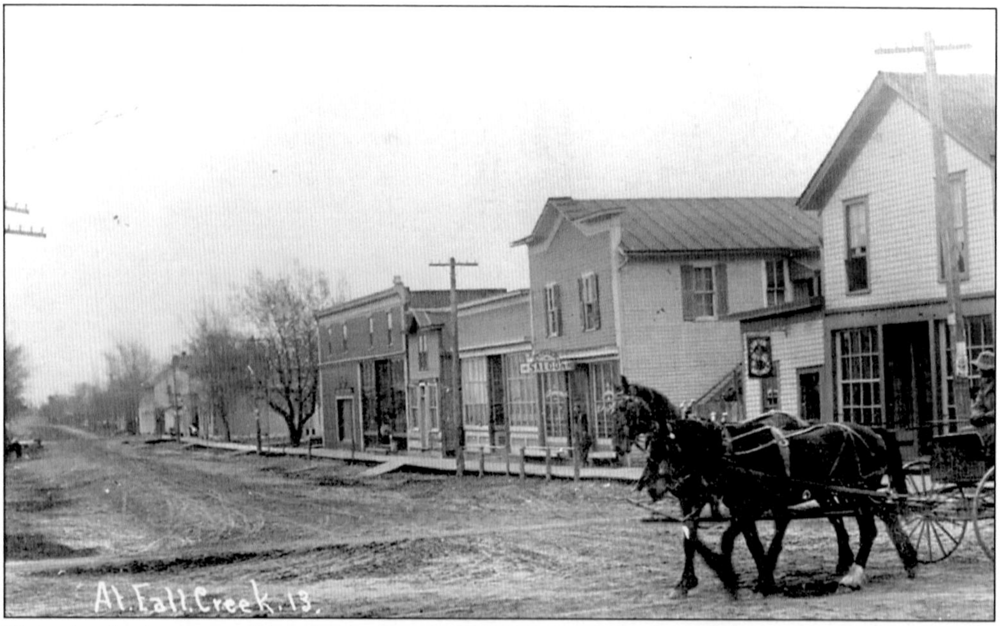

This view looks east on Lincoln Avenue in Fall Creek, 1913. (FCHS.)

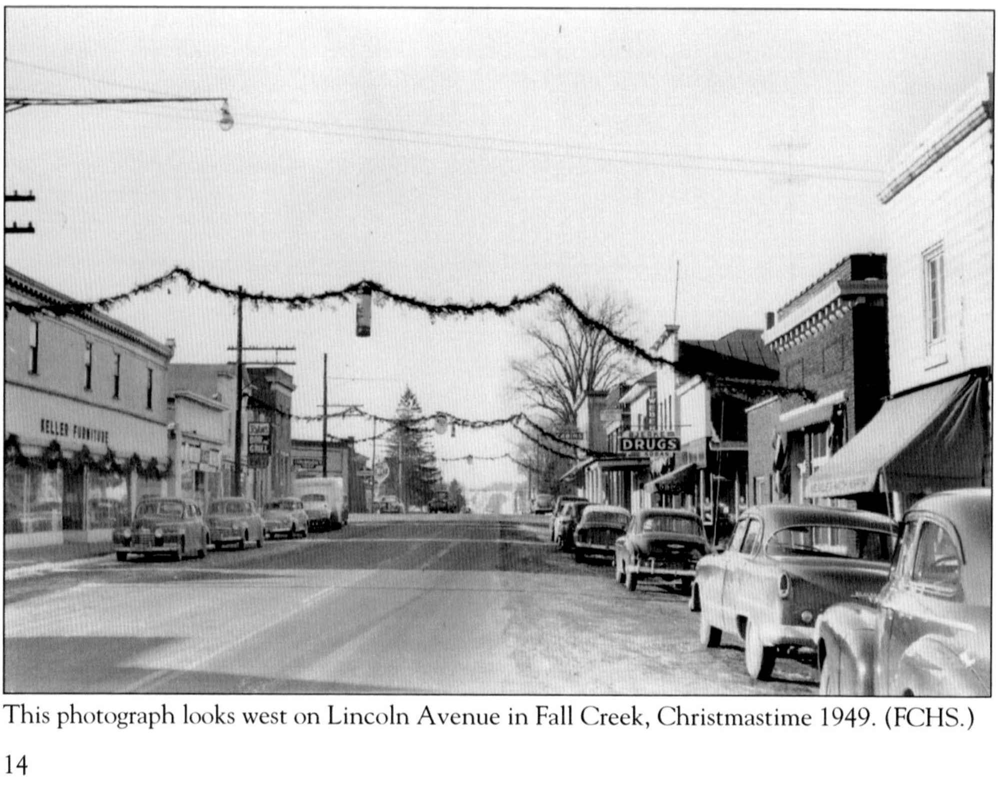

This photograph looks west on Lincoln Avenue in Fall Creek, Christmastime 1949. (FCHS.)

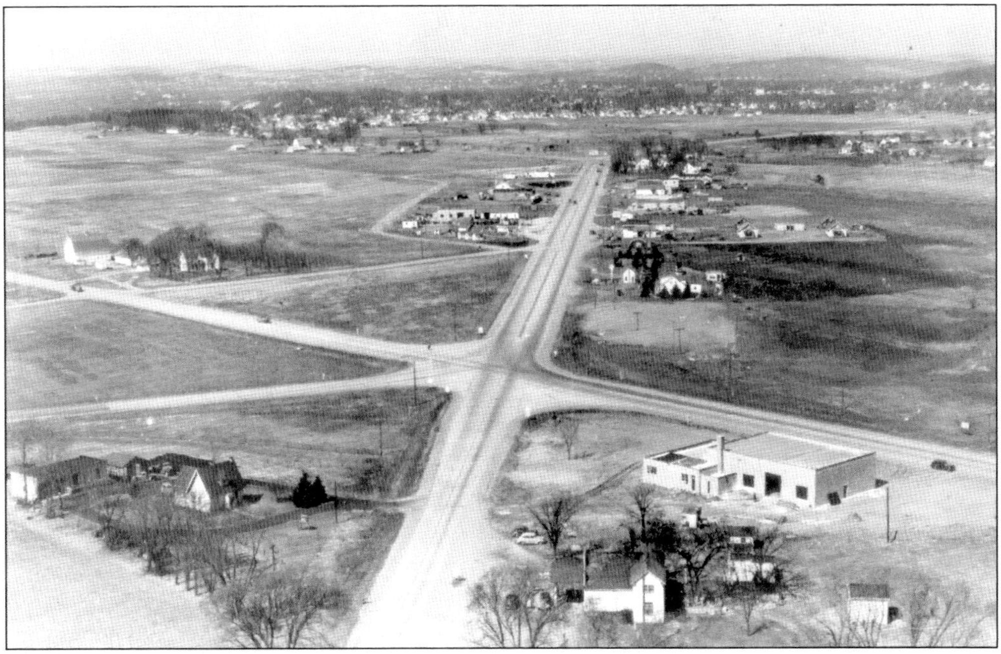

This aerial view shows the crossroads of Clairemont Ave and State Highway 53 in early spring 1946. Litchfield Auto is the flat-roofed building lower right. Just below it (to the south) is McElroy's Tavern. (Photograph courtesy of Fritz Litchfield.)

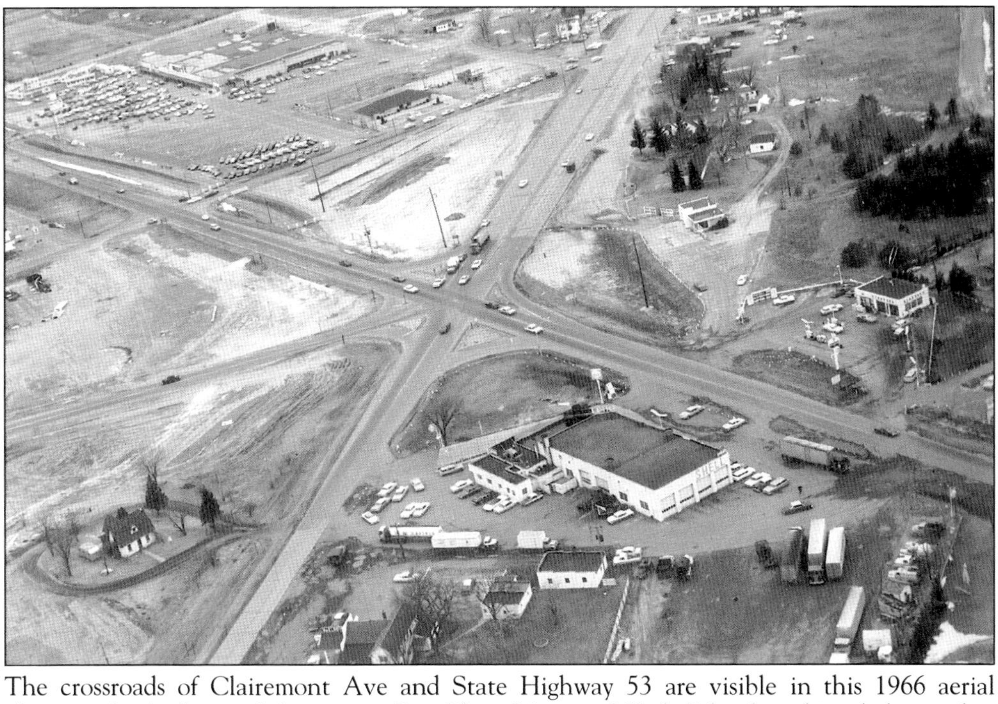

The crossroads of Clairemont Ave and State Highway 53 are visible in this 1966 aerial photograph. At the top left corner is Eau Claire Memorial High School, and just below and to the right, the new Kmart store. As with the photo above, Litchfield Auto and McElroy's Tavern can be seen at lower right. (Photograph courtesy of Fritz Litchfield.)

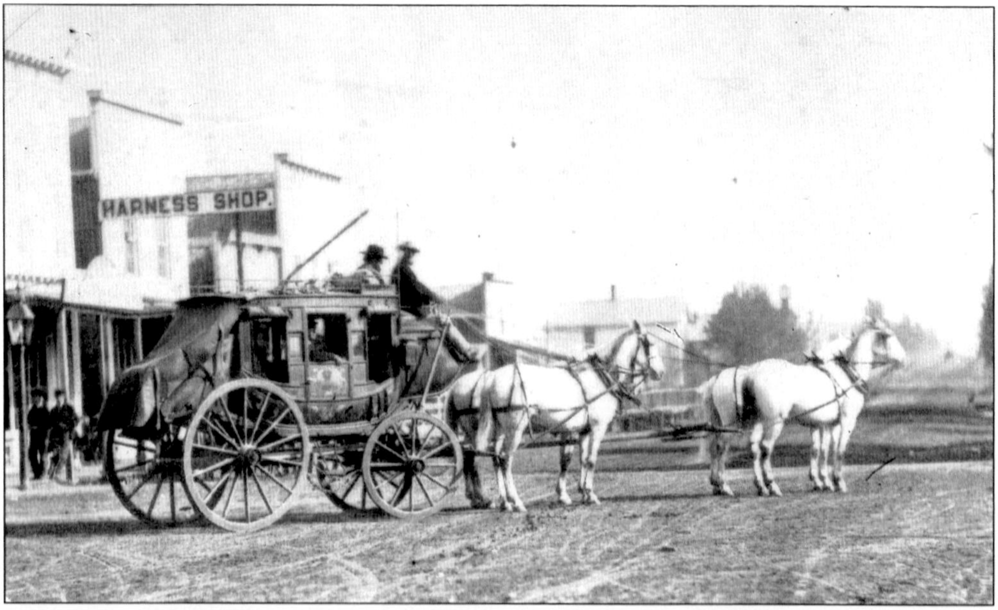

"Last stage coach (Bill Price's line) from Eau Claire to Black River Falls." This photo was taken at Sparta, 1863. (CVM.)

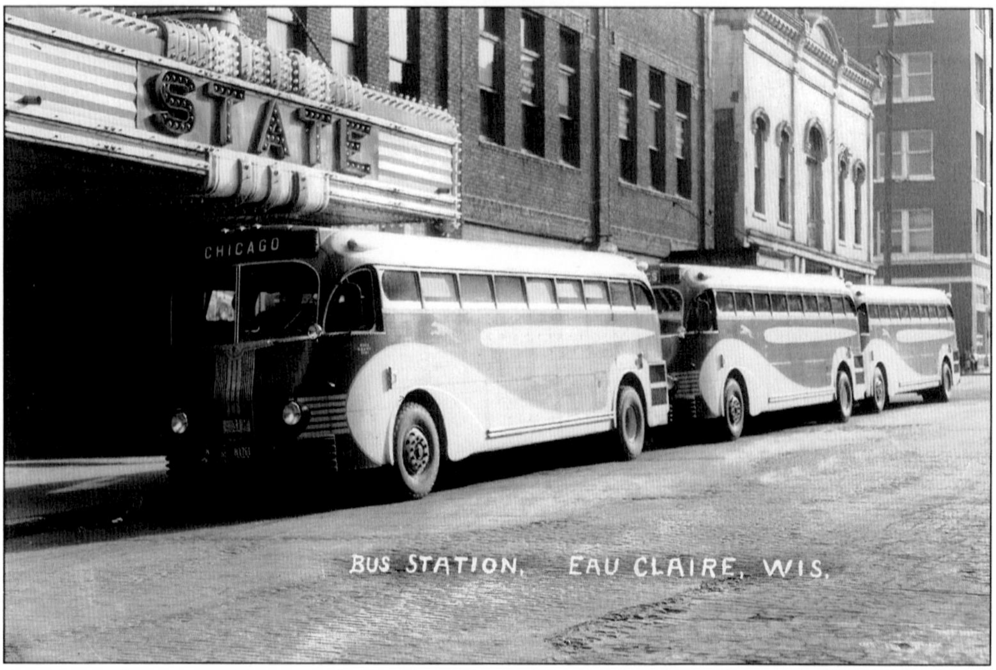

Greyhound buses wait in front of the State Theater on Eau Claire Street, Eau Claire, 1950s. In 1966, the Greyhound depot moved into a new building on Farwell and Railroad Streets on the banks of the Eau Claire River. Bus service left downtown in 2000. In 2005, the station sat west of the city near the Hwy 124 and Interstate 94 interchange. (CVM.)

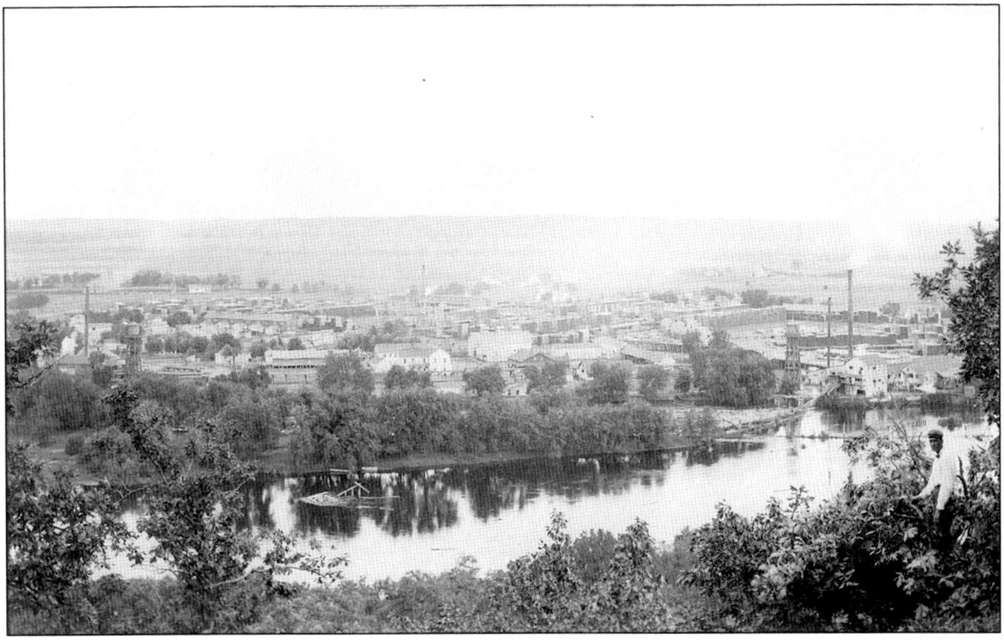

This is the Village of Porter's Mills, Town of Brunswick, in the 1870s or 1880s. By 1901, the once-thriving town had all but vanished after the peak of the lumbering boom. The last house in what was Porter's Mills was razed in 1995 by the Federal Emergency Management Agency (FEMA) after a 1993 Chippewa River flood. Other vanished or all-but-vanished Eau Claire County towns include Anthony, Hadleyville, Ludington, Nix Corner, Noresville, Otter Creek, Rodell, and Strader. Allen is very tiny, but, as its residents would proudly tell you, it's still there. (CVM.)

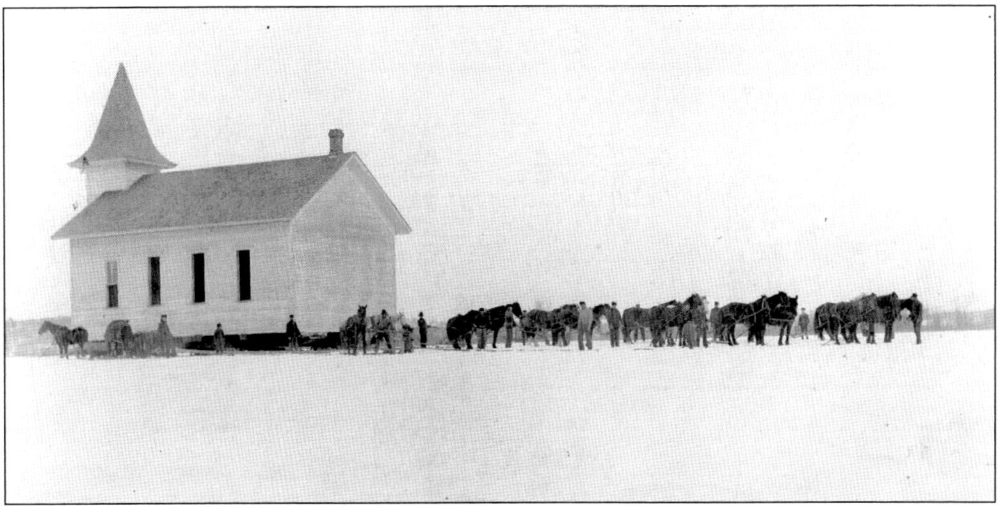

Many men and horses were needed to move the Methodist Evangelical Church from Porter's Mills to its new home near the G.A. Wright farm, March 1901. The Eau Claire *Leader* covered the event, writing, "The last spark of religion that existed here [at Porter's Mills] has, we regret to say, been cruelly extinguished by the redoubtable Capt. John Tinker, who with creaking windlasses, wicked screwjacks and worse levers and rollers rolled the one church we had out of the one-time flourishing town down the prairie three miles south to Badman Corners, where we hope it will prove instrumental in making good men and good women." (CVM.)

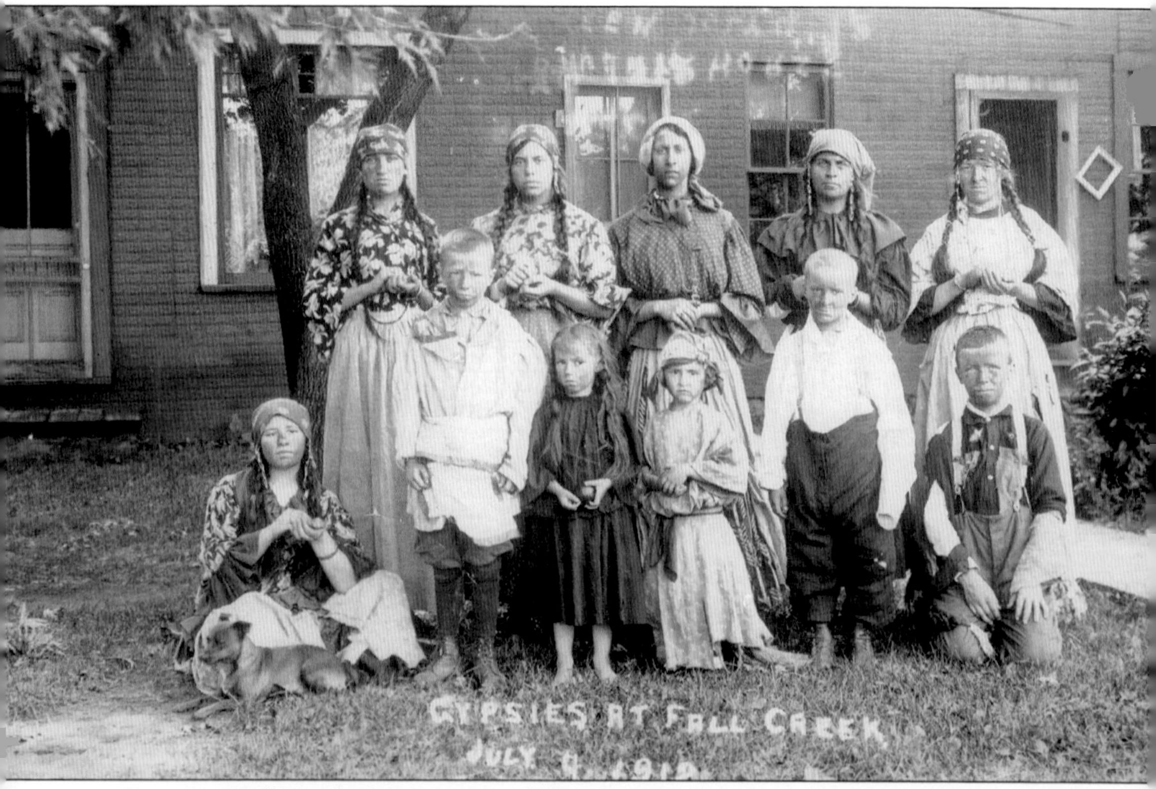

"Gypsies at Fall Creek, July 4, 1912." Gypsy or Gipsy is a slang name for the people known as the Roma, sometimes also called Romany or Romani, after their language. (The name Gypsy derives from Egypt, based on an inaccurate conception of their origin.) The Roma are a traditionally nomadic people whose numbers worldwide are estimated to be between six and seven million. The Roma have clung tenaciously to their identity and folkways. Several area histories make mention of "bands of Gypsies" camped for brief periods during their travels in the first half of the 20th century. (FCHS.)

Two

Land and Landscape, Sometimes Harsh

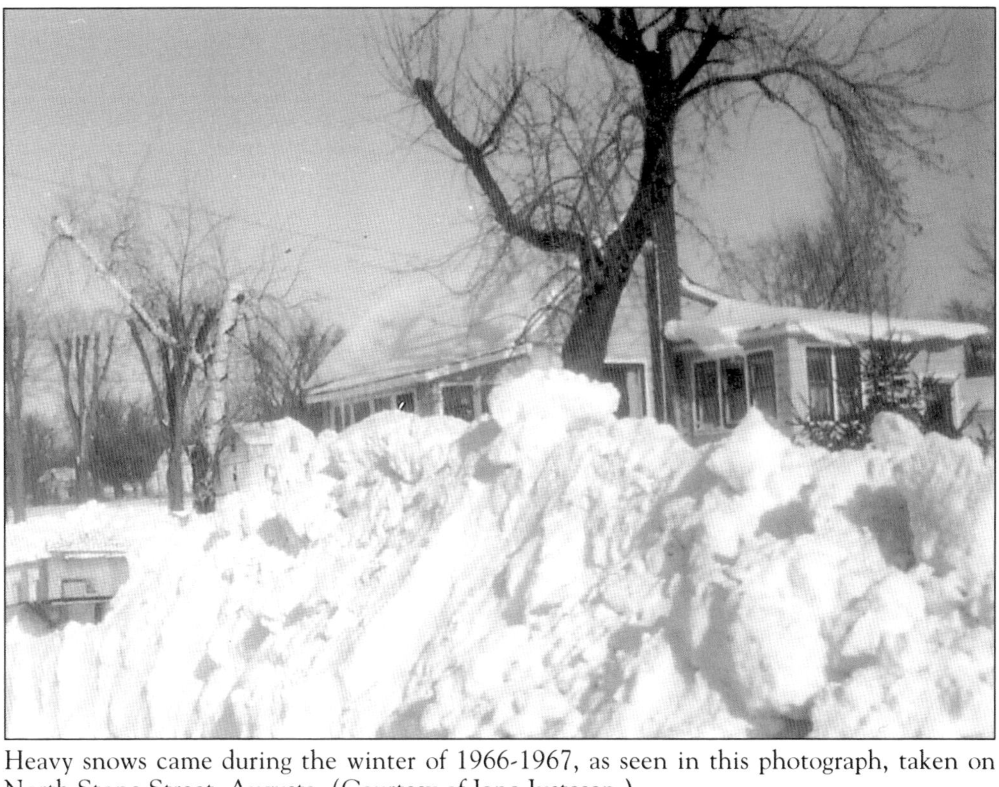

Heavy snows came during the winter of 1966-1967, as seen in this photograph, taken on North Stone Street, Augusta. (Courtesy of Jane Justesen.)

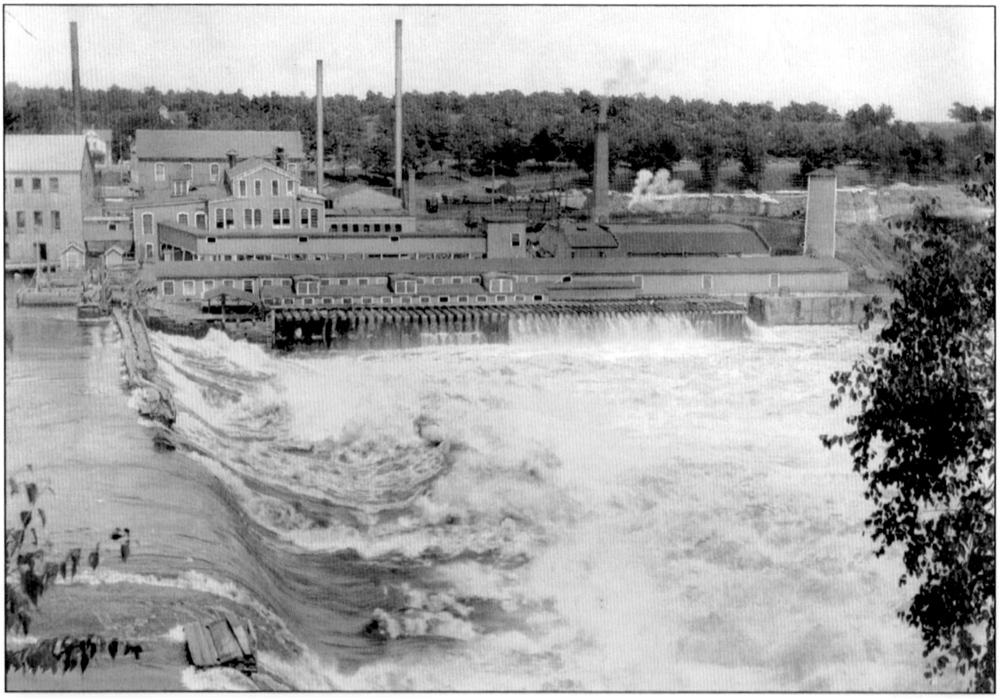

The dam at the Dells Paper Mill, Eau Claire, broke in 1903. (CVM.)

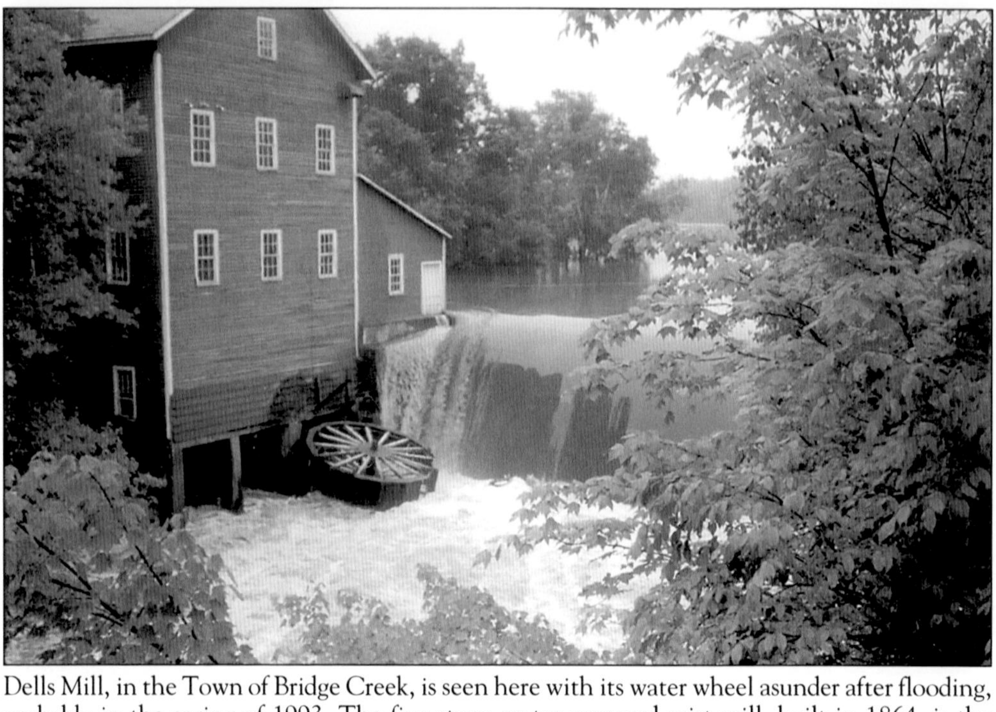

Dells Mill, in the Town of Bridge Creek, is seen here with its water wheel asunder after flooding, probably in the spring of 1993. The five-story, water-powered grist mill, built in 1864, is the oldest Wisconsin mill still in operation. The mill and museum, on County Highway V, is open May through October. (Courtesy of Jane Justesen.)

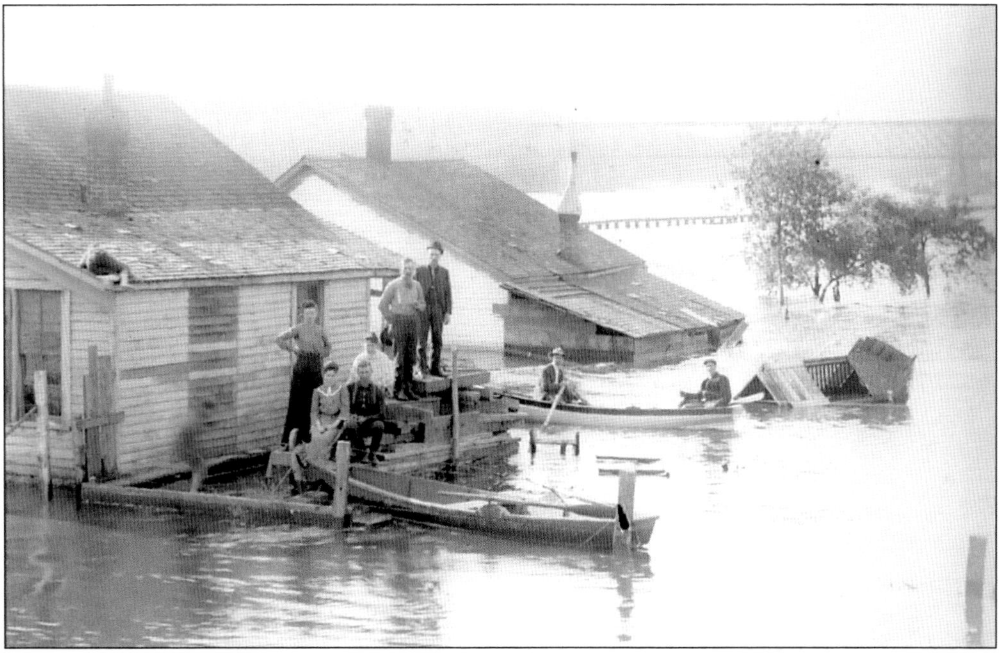

Chippewa River flooding inundated houses along Forest and East Madison Streets, Eau Claire, 1884. The massive flood took out every bridge in Eau Claire and in neighboring Chippewa Falls upstream. The flood gained national attention, and *Harper's Weekly* covered it in an illustrated piece. (CVM.)

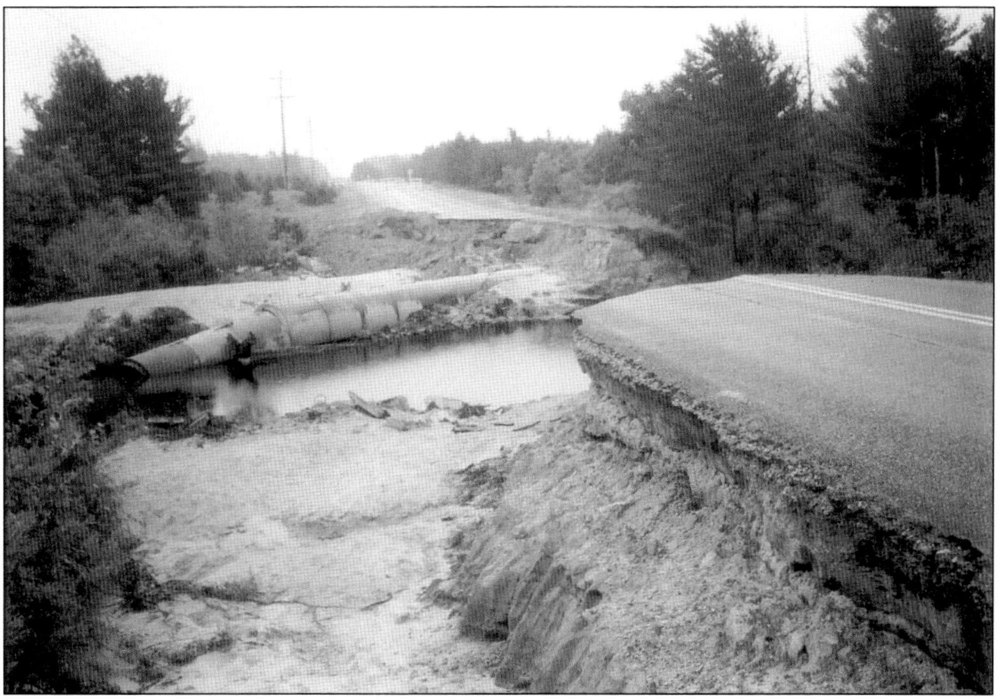

County Highway H was washed out by flooding, probably in the Town of Bridge Creek, during the spring of 1993. (Photo courtesy of Jane Justesen.)

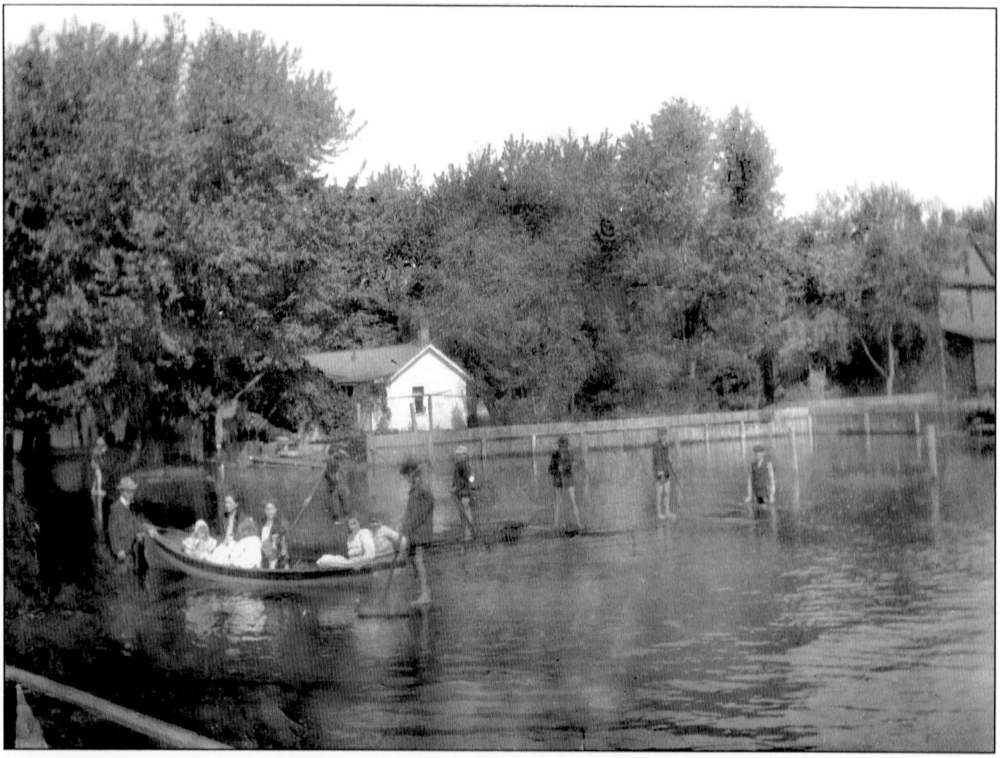

This flood was at Porter's Mills in the Town of Brunswick, 1881. (CVM.)

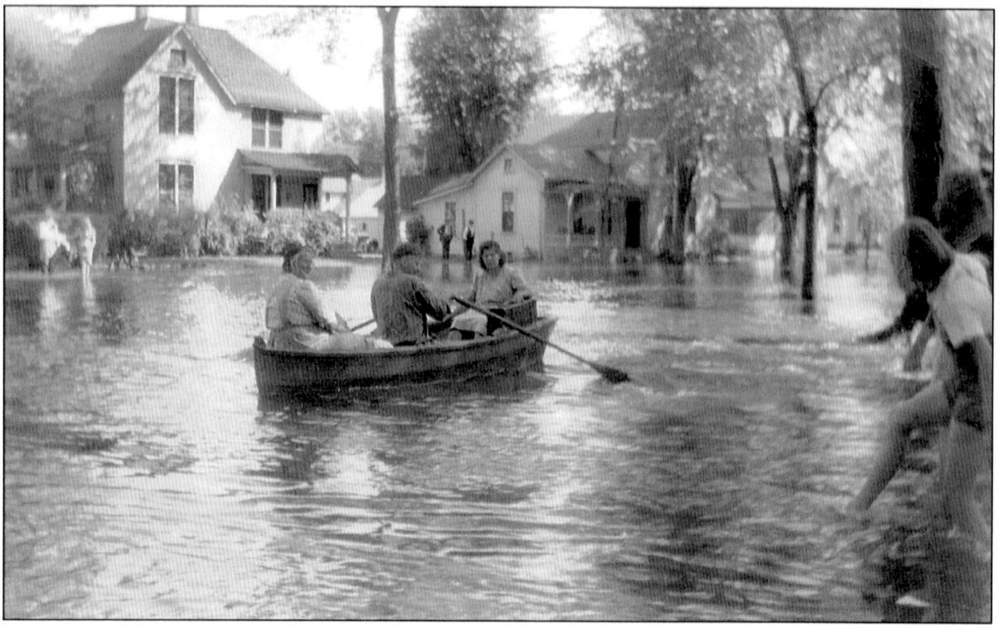

Boaters paddle their way during a flood at the intersection of Second Avenue and Chippewa Street, Eau Claire, September 1941. (CVM.)

Mrs. William W. Bartlett with Mr. and Mrs. Kincaid at Big Falls on the Eau Claire River, Town of Lincoln, sometime between 1915 and 1925. (CVM.)

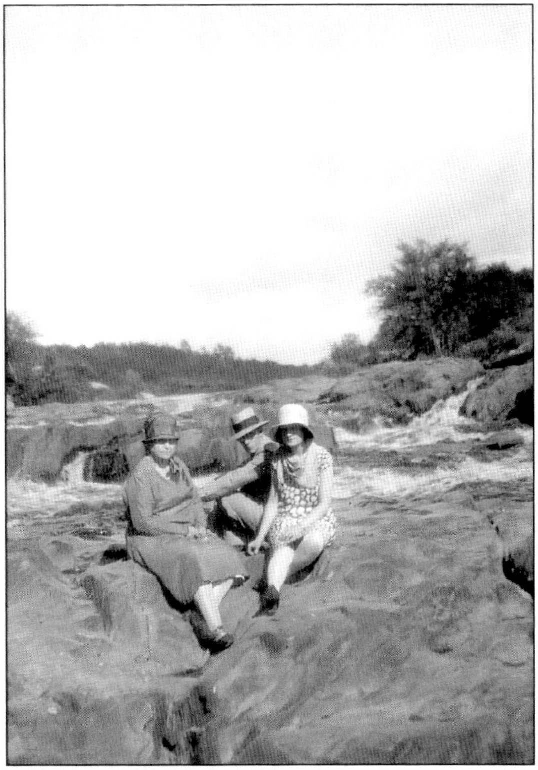

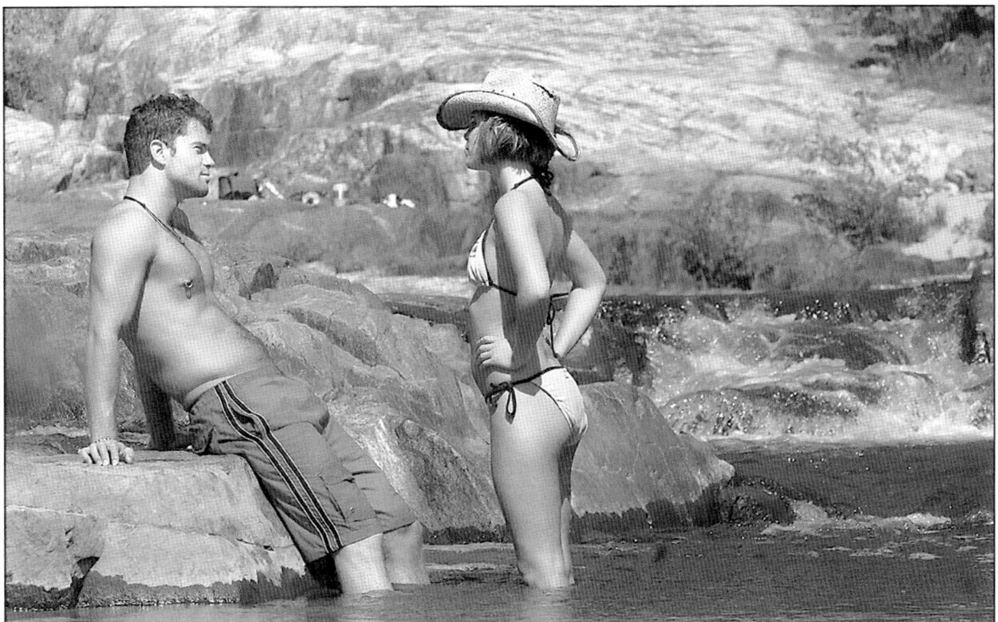

Dan Hozian, a senior at UW-Eau Claire and Nyna Richard, a sophomore at UWEC, carrying on a conversation in the waters of Big Falls County Park, Town of Lincoln, July 2004. (Photograph by Derek Montgomery. Courtesy of the Eau Claire *Leader-Telegram*.)

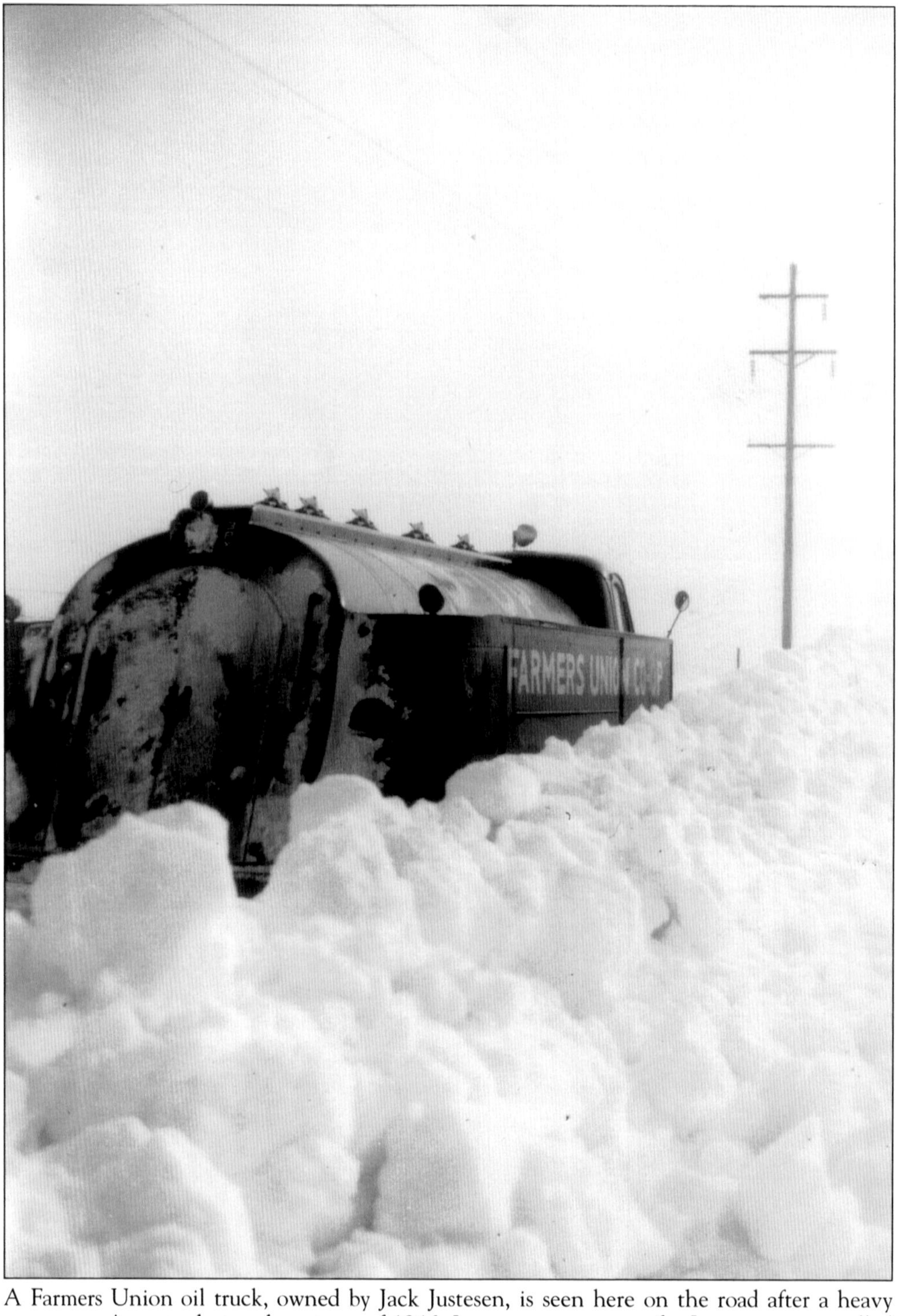

A Farmers Union oil truck, owned by Jack Justesen, is seen here on the road after a heavy snow near Augusta during the winter of 1946. It was very common for Justesen to get called out in such weather after customers' home heating oil had run out or their oil lines had frozen. (Courtesy of Jane Justesen.)

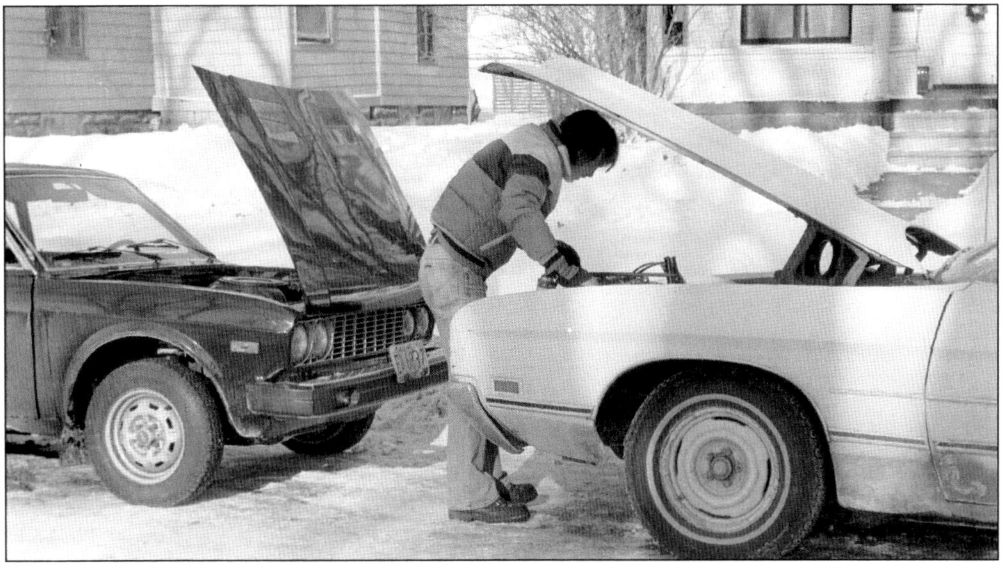

Jump starting a car on a cold day in Eau Claire is all too common. This photograph was taken January 6, 1979. It was -13 Fahrenheit that morning in the city, and that week saw several city temperatures at or near record January lows of below -30 Fahrenheit.(CVM.)

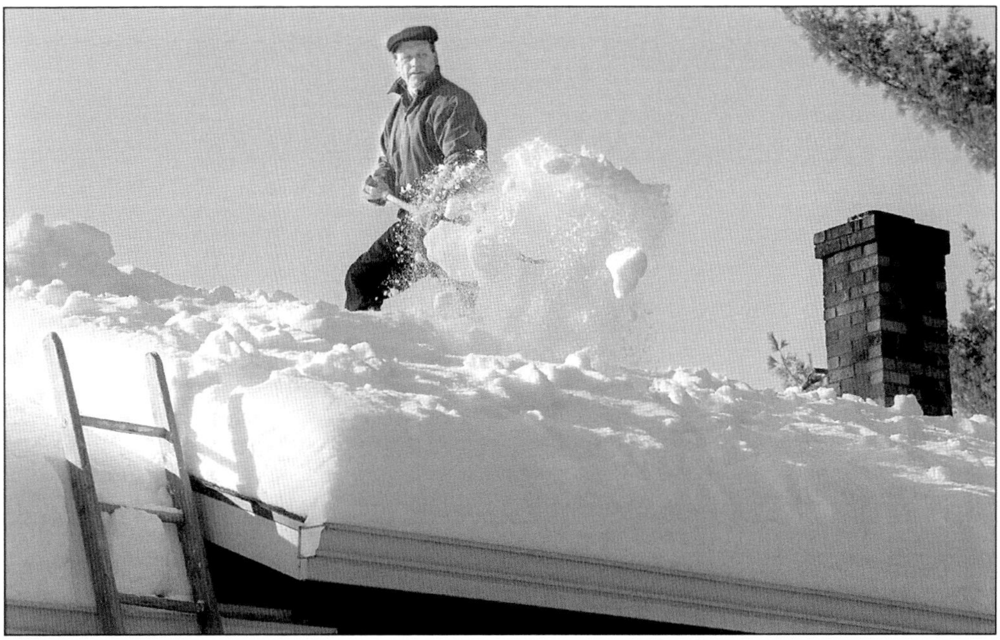

Bill Jaeger shovels snow off his roof to prevent ice damming on his home on Tower Drive, Town of Seymour, *c.* 2002-2004. Jaeger said the shoveling would replace a day of exercise at the YMCA. (Photograph by Dan Reiland. Courtesy of the Eau Claire *Leader-Telegram*.)

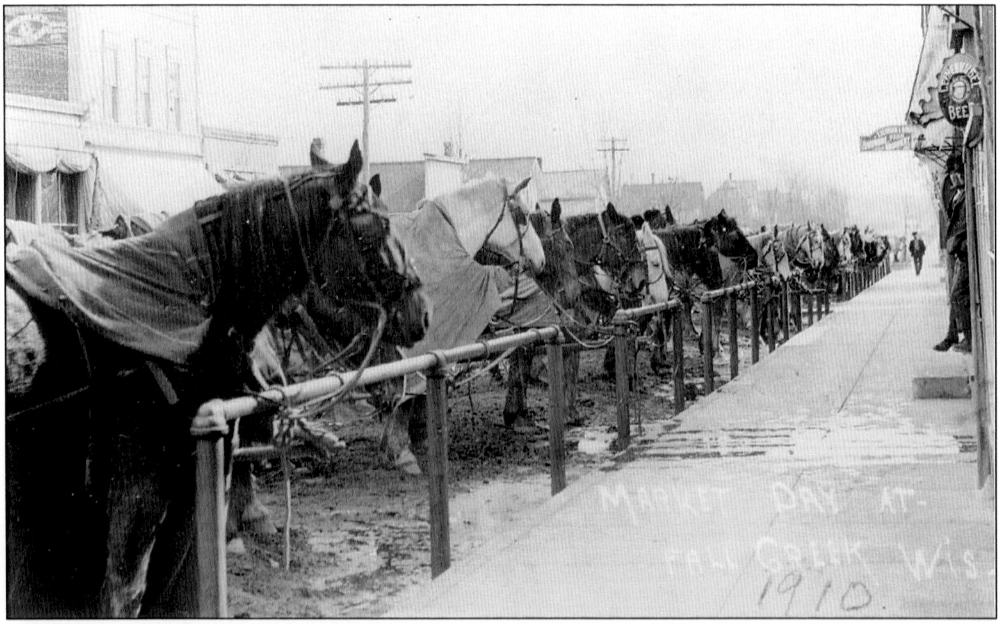

Horses are lined up on a cold Market Day on State Street in Fall Creek in 1910. Many Midwestern agricultural communities had Market Days in spring. Stores offered specials, and communities often held public auctions, where anyone could bring articles to sell, including livestock, machinery, household items, and furniture. (FCHS.)

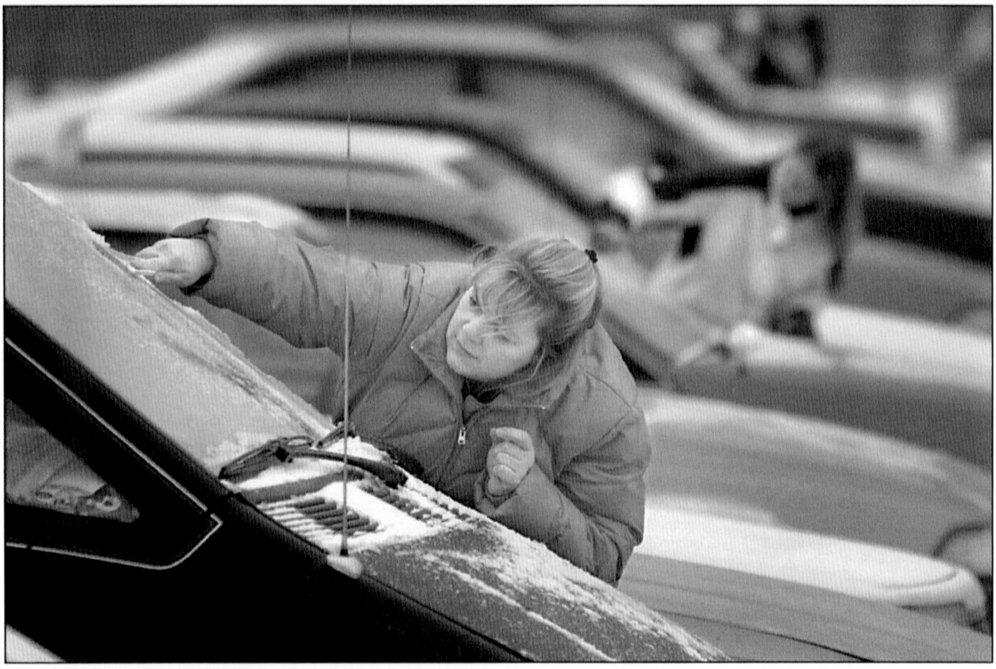

Melissa Larrabee of Altoona joins fellow Chippewa Valley Technical College students in scraping ice from their car windows after classes, main CVTC parking lot south of Highway 12, Eau Claire, March 2003. Larrabee was in her first semester of CVTC's nursing program. (Photograph by Shane Opatz. Courtesy of the Eau Claire *Leader-Telegram*.)

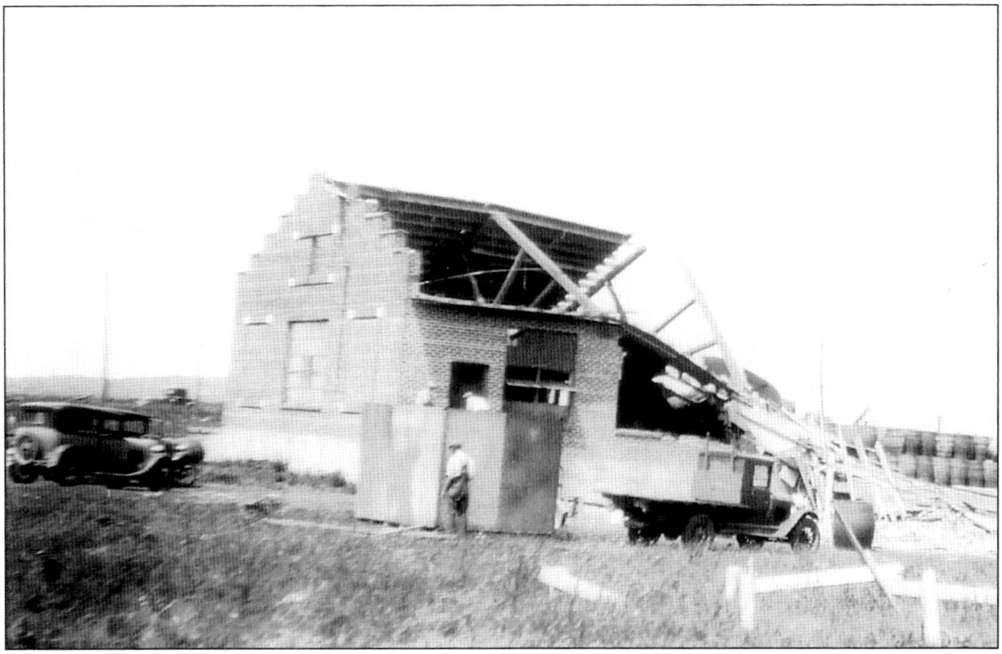

This was the surviving structure of the Reid Murdoch brick pickle plant in the Town of Seymour, after a tornado, June 1930. (CVM.)

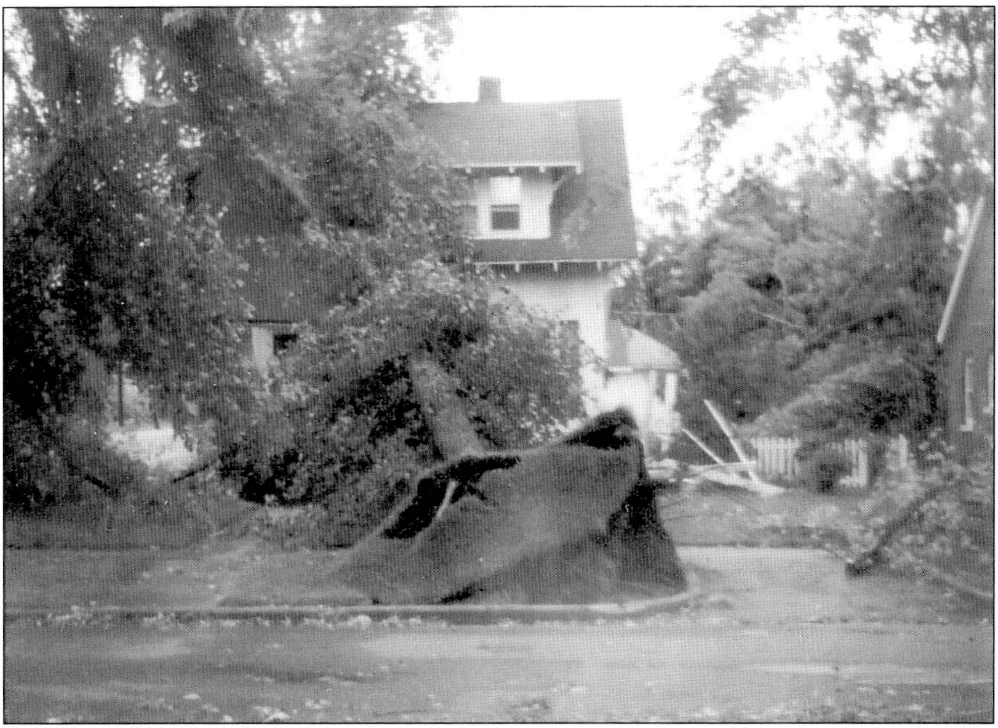

This Elm tree was uprooted by a July 15, 1980 wind shear on Frederick Street, Eau Claire. (Photograph by Adrian Schute. Courtesy of Carol Benning.)

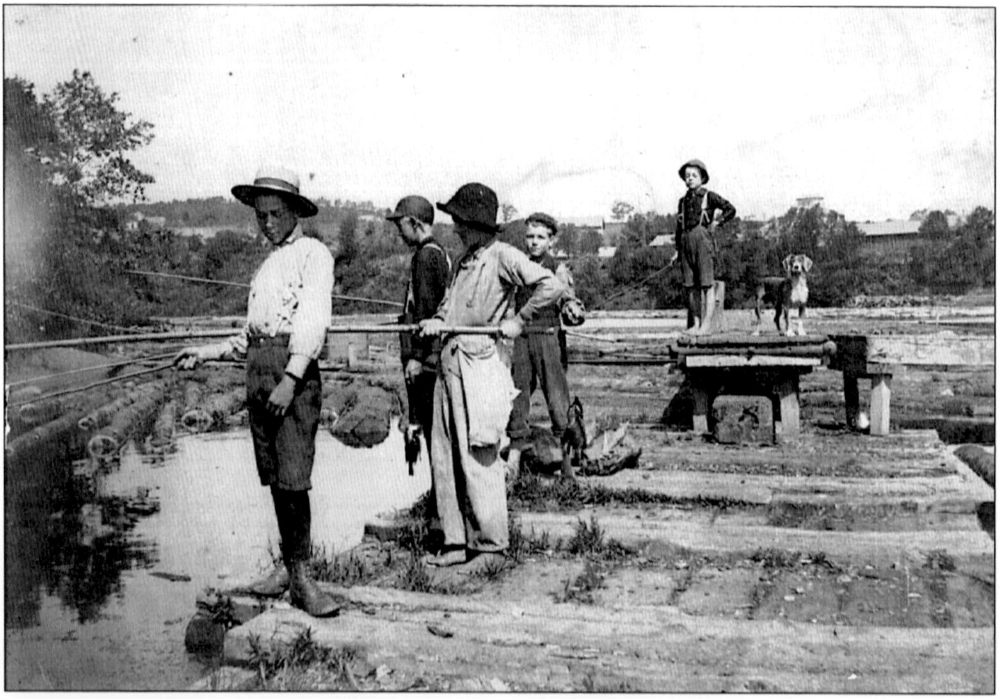

Fishing at Half Moon Lake, Eau Claire, *c.* 1898. (CVM.)

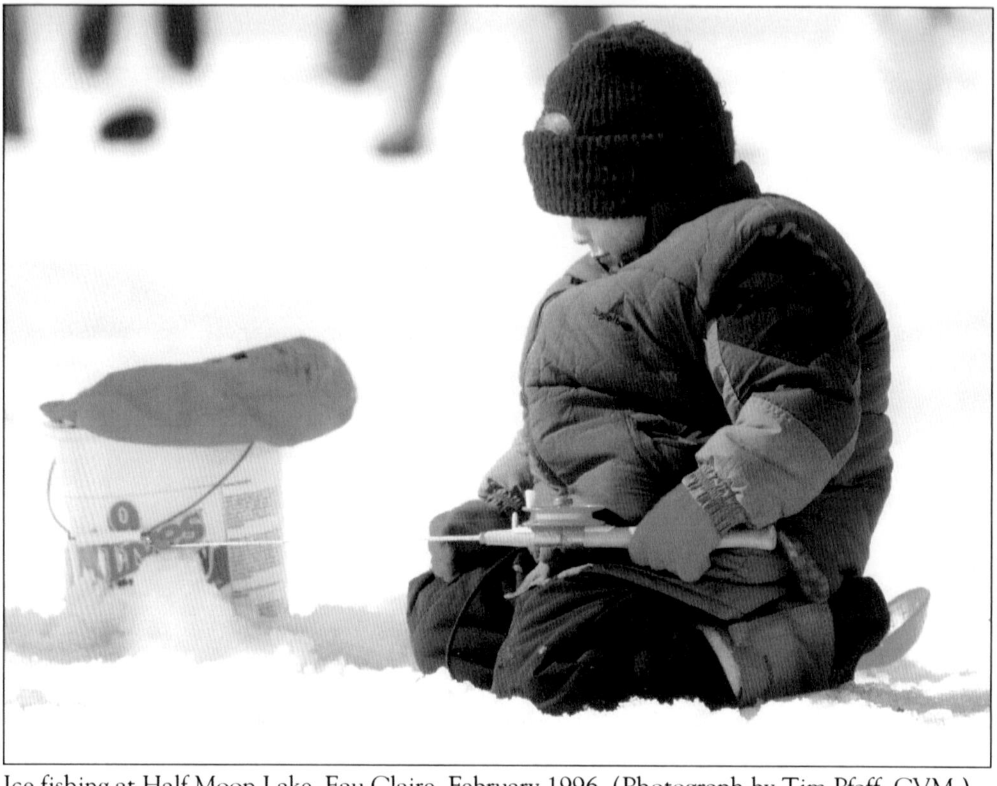

Ice fishing at Half Moon Lake, Eau Claire, February 1996. (Photograph by Tim Pfaff. CVM.)

Three

NATURAL RESOURCES TO HUNT AND HARVEST

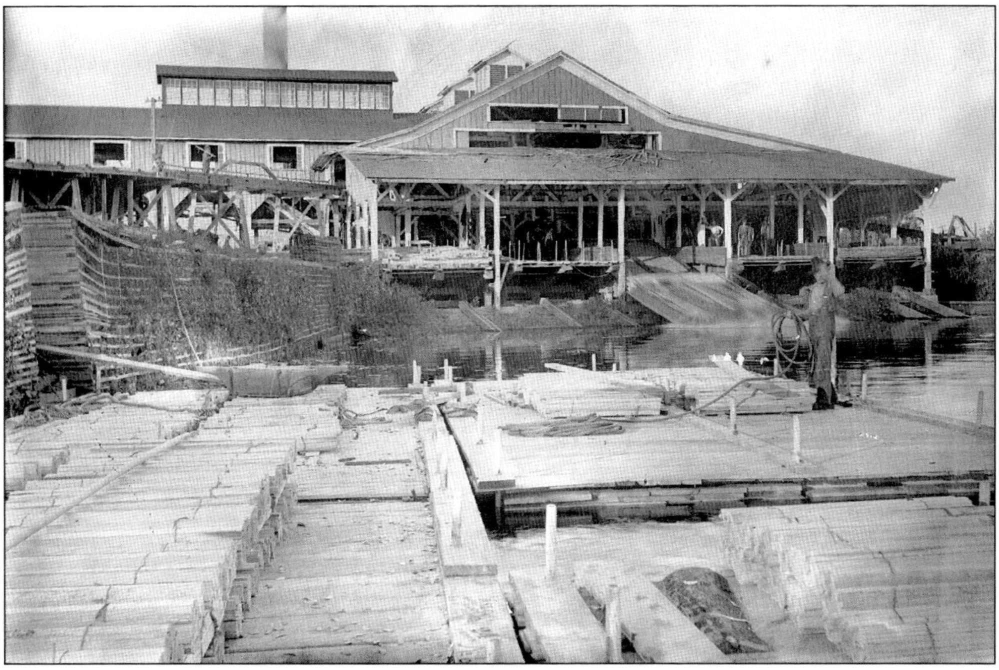

This lumber raft was in back of the Daniel Shaw mill on the bank of the Chippewa River, Eau Claire, c. 1900. Shaw was one of a half-dozen major lumber companies with mills within what is now the City of Eau Claire. In 1879, the Daniel Shaw Lumber Company milled about 25 million board-feet of lumber. By 1900, although the area still produced lumber and wood products, lumbering interests had moved west. (CVM.)

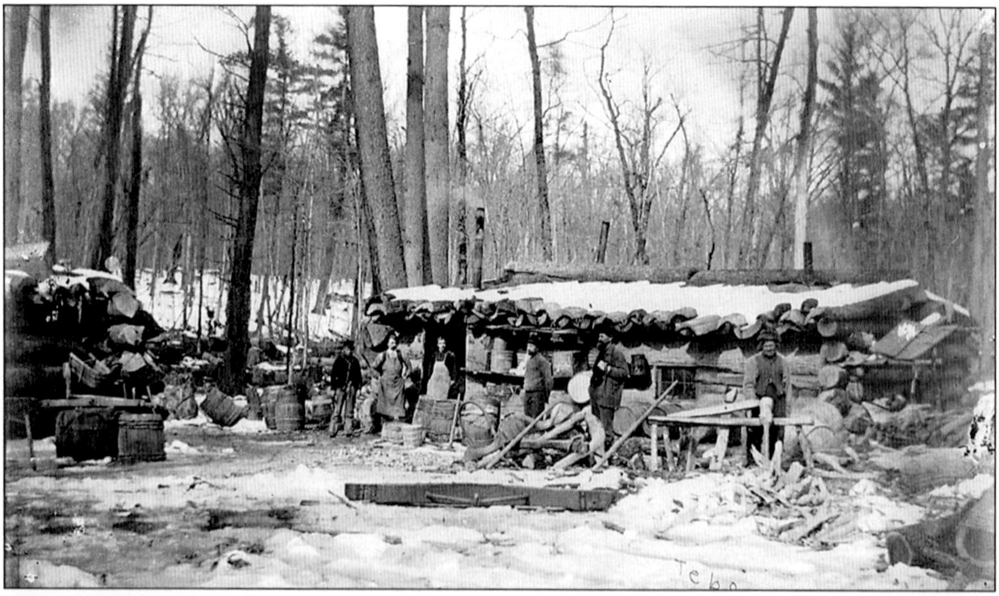

These loggers are at one of Eau Claire Lumber Company's logging camps, North Fork, Eau Claire River, in the winter of 1879-1880. In 1879, the Eau Claire Lumber Company milled 80 million board feet in lumber, shingles, lath, and pickets. Loggers worked in the winter. Snow packed into "ice roads" made the logs easier to drag from the forest. Quite a few loggers farmed during the summer off-season. (Photograph by Tebo & Hanson, Eau Claire. CVM.)

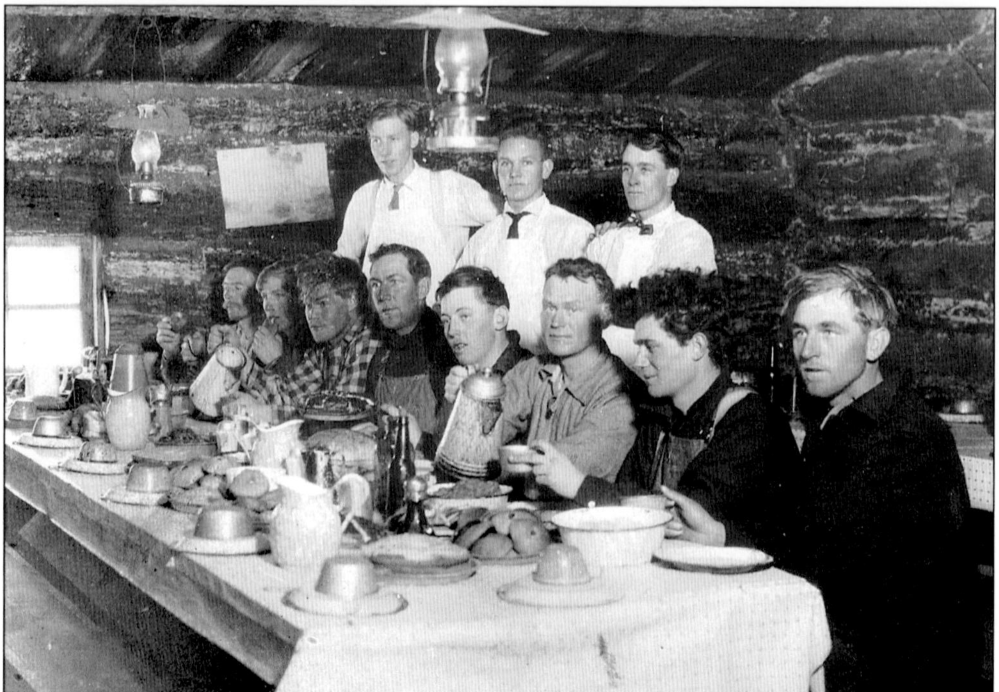

These men are enjoying a meal at the logging camp cook house, 1915. Axel Larson is the cook on the right, while the other men are unidentified. (FCHS.)

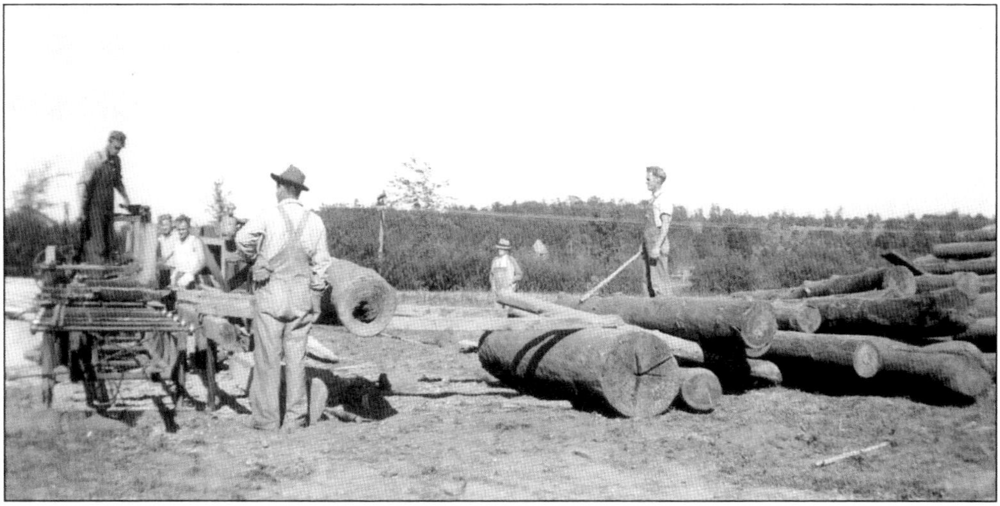

Lumbering-era logs are here being pulled from Dells Pond by the Blakeley family, Eau Claire, c. 1948-1949. The family received permission to raise the logs from the bottom of Dells Pond. In this way, the Blakeleys acquired the lumber to start their building business. Layton Blakeley is one of the two men facing the mill at center left. In the background, second from right, is Layton's grandfather, E.T. Mellville, who moved onto a farm north of Fairchild around 1900. In earlier days, he "went to the woods" in the winter as an ox-team driver for a lumber company. Layton's brother Robert Blakeley stands on a log at right with a peavey hook, a tool for rolling logs. (Photograph courtesy of Brian Blakeley.)

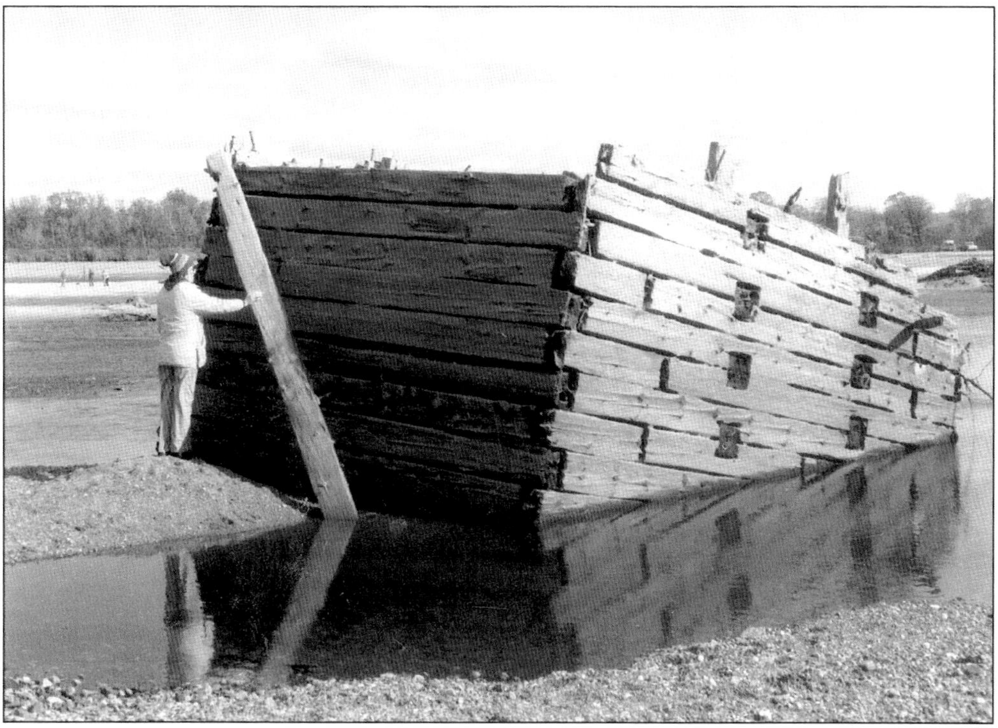

An old, long-forgotten lumber crib is exposed by a drawdown of Dells Pond, Eau Claire, October 1979. (Photograph courtesy of Karl Holbrook.)

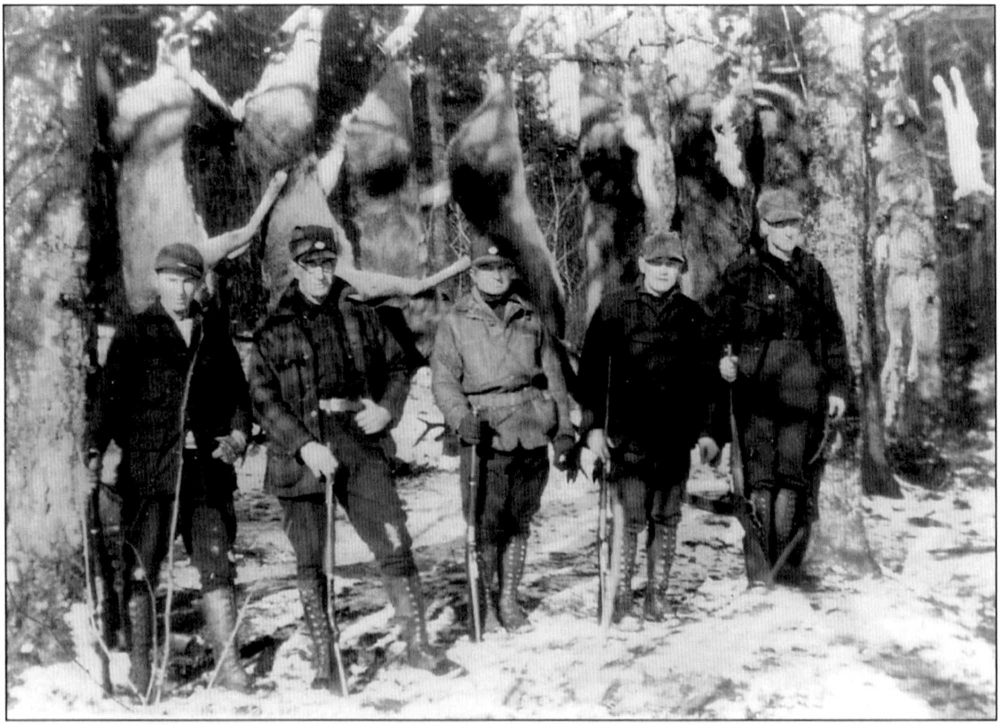

Fall Creek hunters pose during a hunting trip in 1926. Standing from left to right are Ralph Wise, John Meyer, Otto Henning, George Patzwald, and Peter Meyer. (FCHS.)

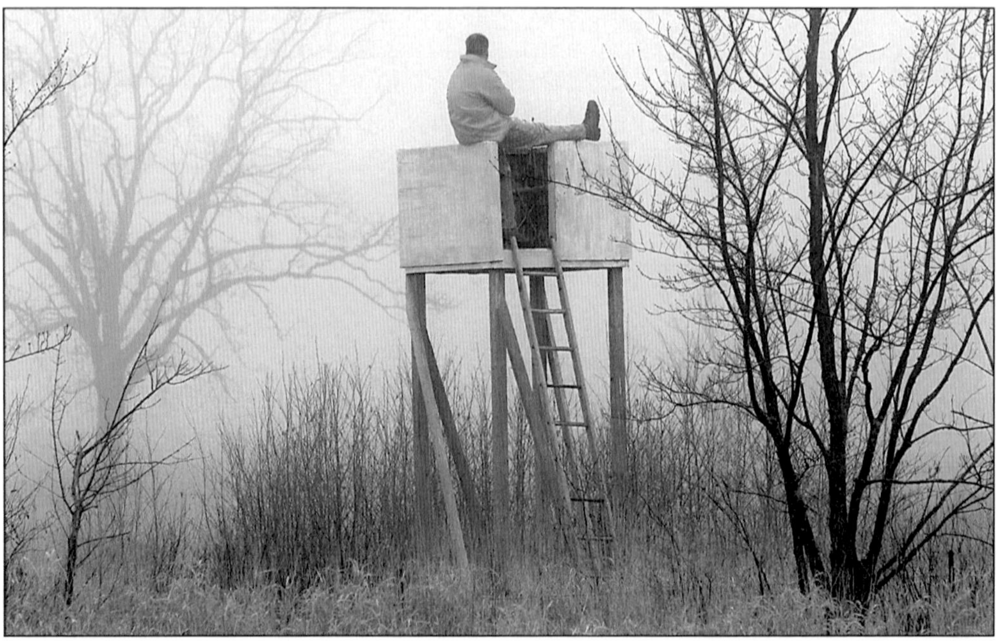

Scott Randall of Augusta peers through early morning fog while looking for deer on the opening day of deer hunting near Augusta in November 2001. Randall was hunting on his father's land. (Photograph by Shane Opatz. Courtesy of the Eau Claire *Leader-Telegram*.)

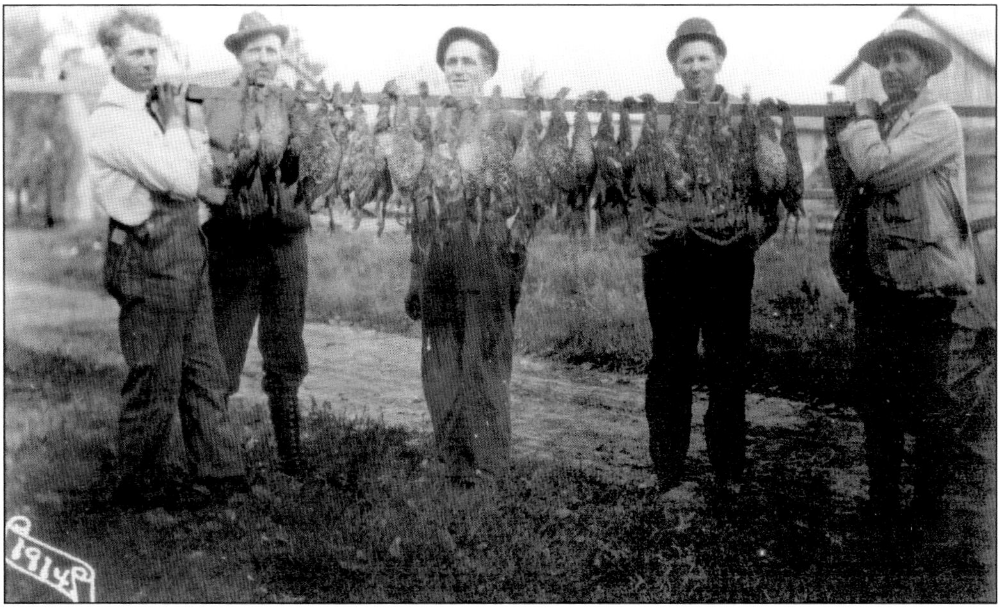

The hunters' catch, prairie chickens, were probably shot near the south fork of Paint Creek, 1914. From left to right are George Hoehn, Otto Schedler, Otto Emanuel, Ed Boernke, and Walter Glenz, all from the Fall Creek area. The prairie chicken has been endangered in Wisconsin since 1979. Recently, individual birds have been seen as close as Clark and Taylor Counties. (FCHS.)

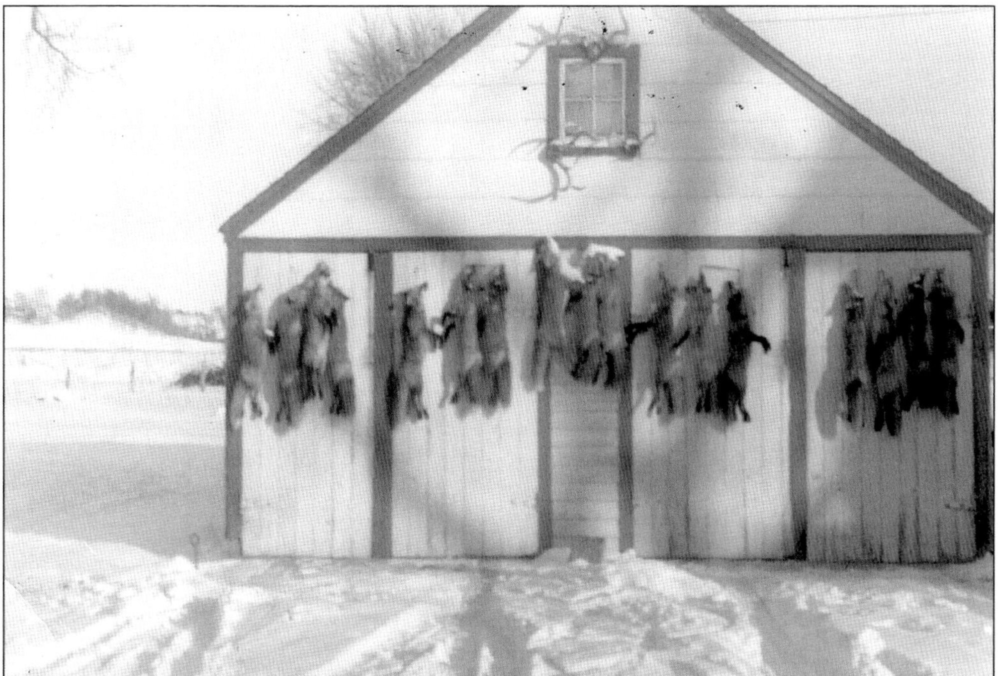

Fred Albrecht's trap-line results, all red fox, displayed on his garage door near Augusta, during the winter of 1955. (Courtesy of Jane Justesen.)

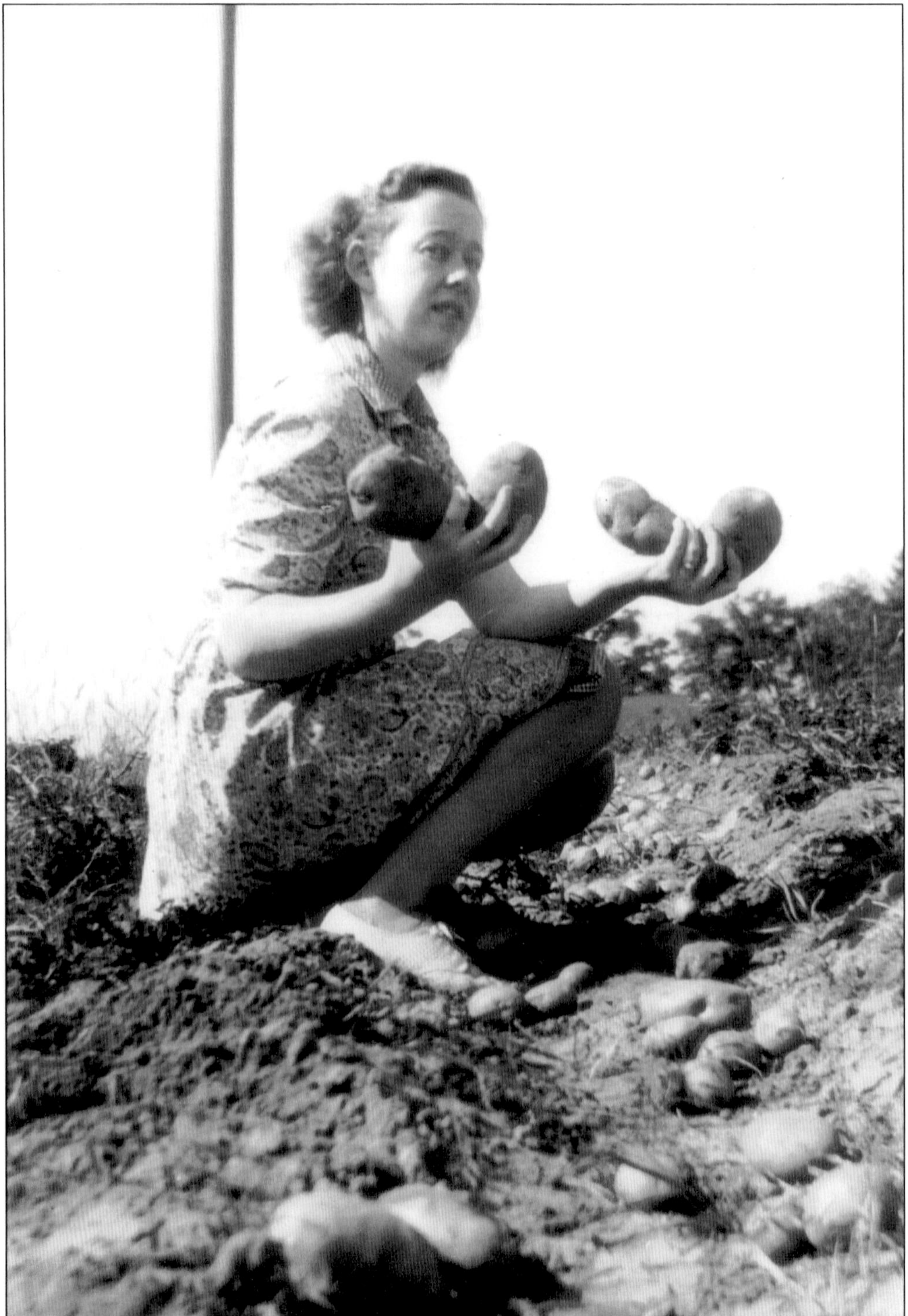

Annie Kramer with her potato crop, Town of Seymour, 1942. (CVM.)

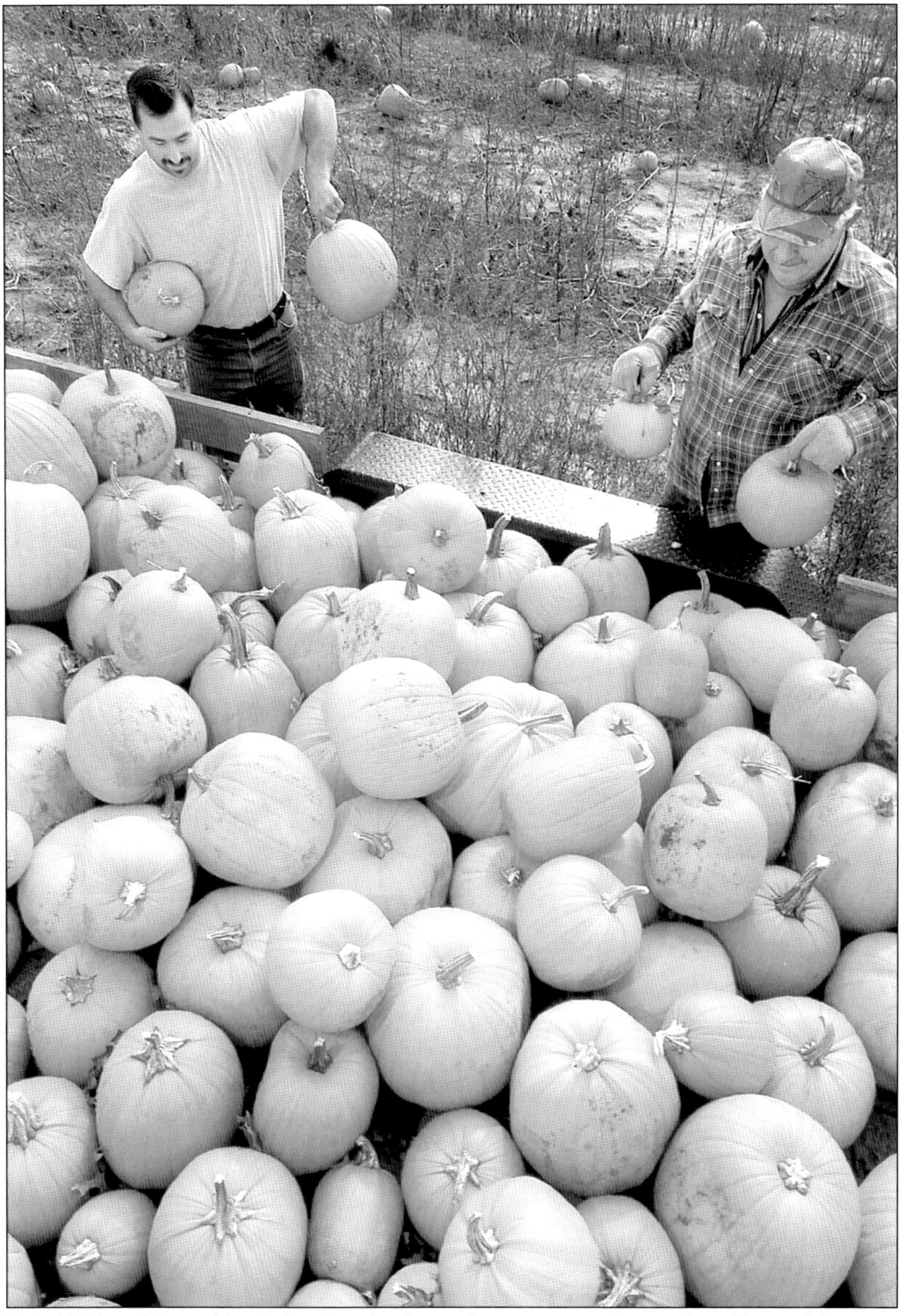

Jerrod Dohm, left, and his father Jerry load pumpkins onto a trailer on their Town of Seymour farm, October 2003. They grew over 6,000 pumpkins that year to sell at local convenience stores. (Photograph by Dan Reiland. Courtesy of the Eau Claire *Leader-Telegram*.)

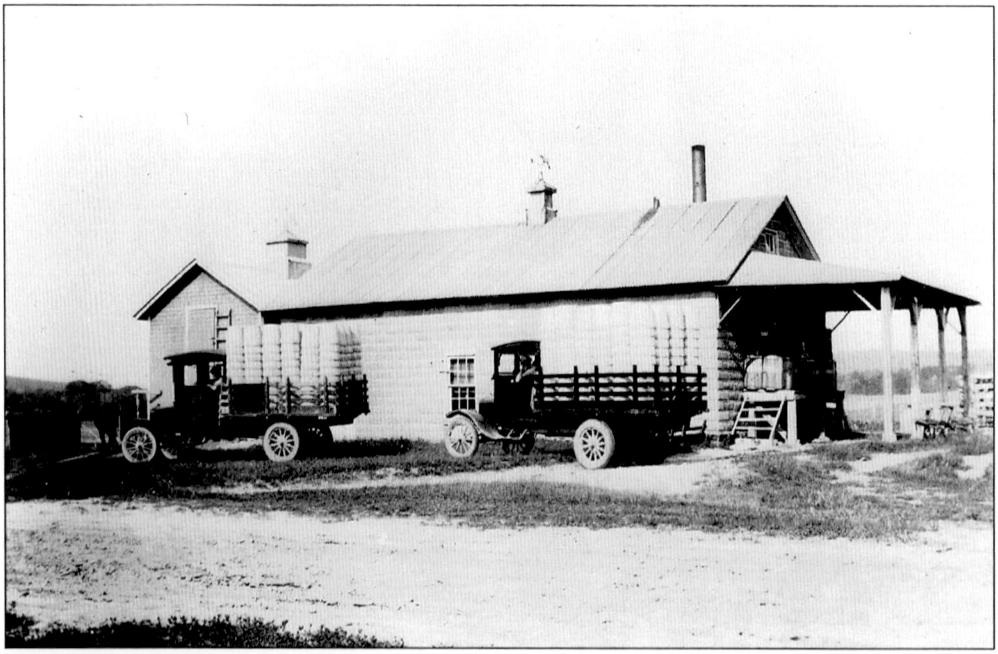

The Ludington Creamery as it looked *c.* the mid-1920s. The Model T Ford trucks are loaded with empty butter tubs. John Meyer is driving one of the trucks. (FCHS.)

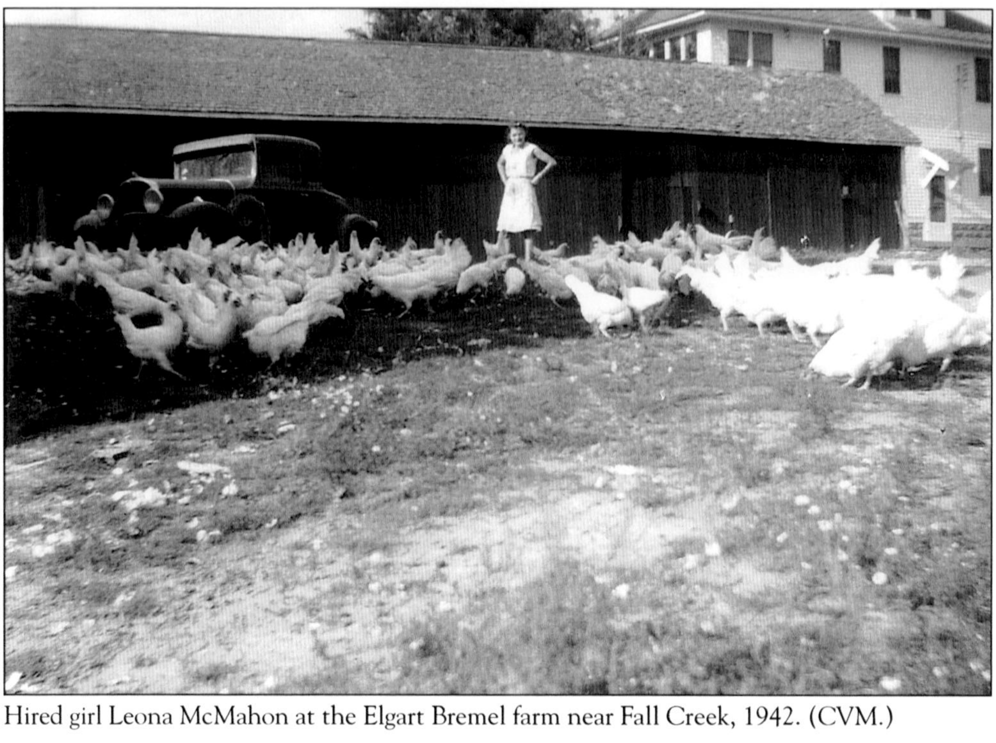

Hired girl Leona McMahon at the Elgart Bremel farm near Fall Creek, 1942. (CVM.)

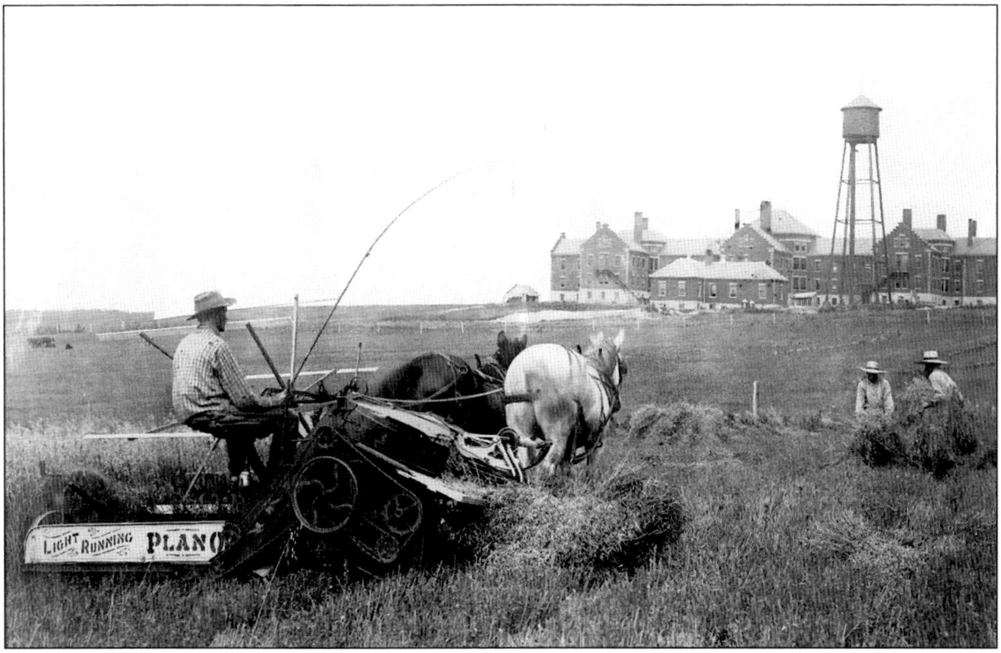

These men are binding grain at the Eau Claire County Asylum, Town of Union, c. 1900. Under staff supervision, patients raised crops and vegetables and maintained working dairy herds. Milk, cream, and butter were sold to local creameries. In 1945, the Asylum and County Home showed a net profit of $25,780, twice that year's national average for farms of all kinds. (CVM.)

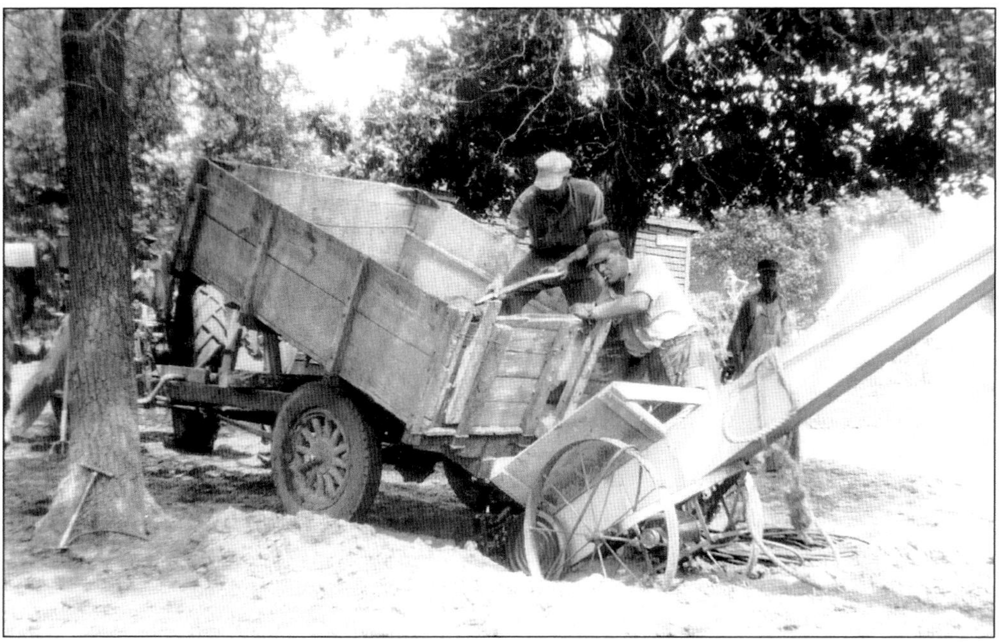

These men are emptying grain into an elevator at Charles McMahon's farm, Town of Pleasant Valley, 1946. In 1950, Eau Claire County's farmers harvested 42,000 acres of oats and 16,000 acres of corn. At the time, most grain was grown by dairy farmers to feed their own milk cows. Today, a much higher percentage is grown for sale. (CVM.)

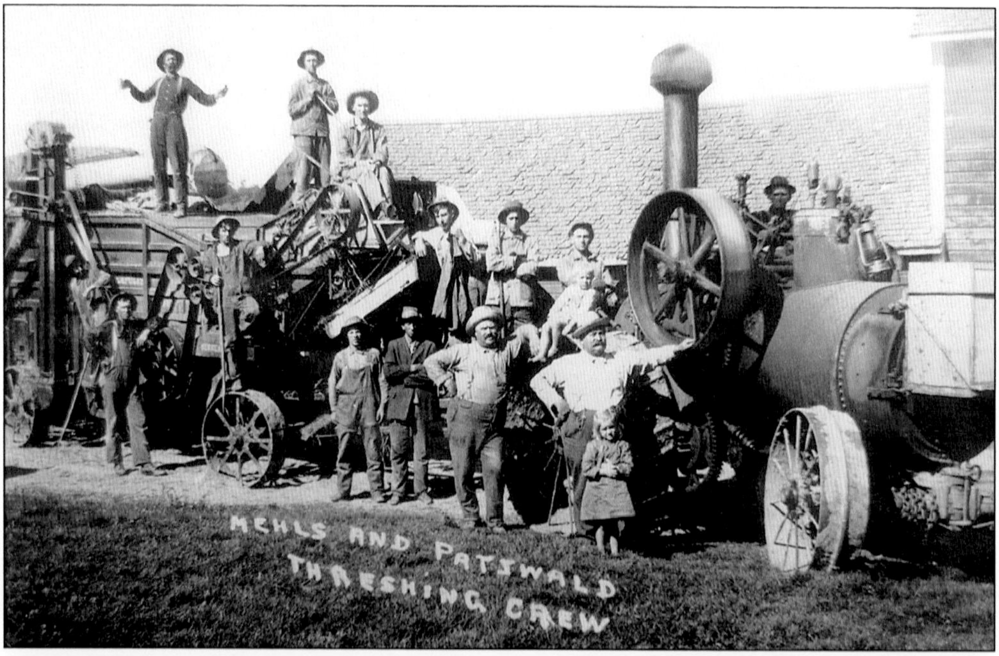

The Mehls-Patzwald threshing crew poses for a photograph *c.* 1918. Standing from left to right are: (in front) Fred Haas, Ed Kuehn, Gus Degner, Frank Redlaczyk, August Patzwald, Helen Redlaczyk; (on the machine) Louis Mehls, Rudy Boernke, Ed Schultz, and Henry Fenske, while the others are unidentified. Fred Greening sits on the steam engine. (FCHS.)

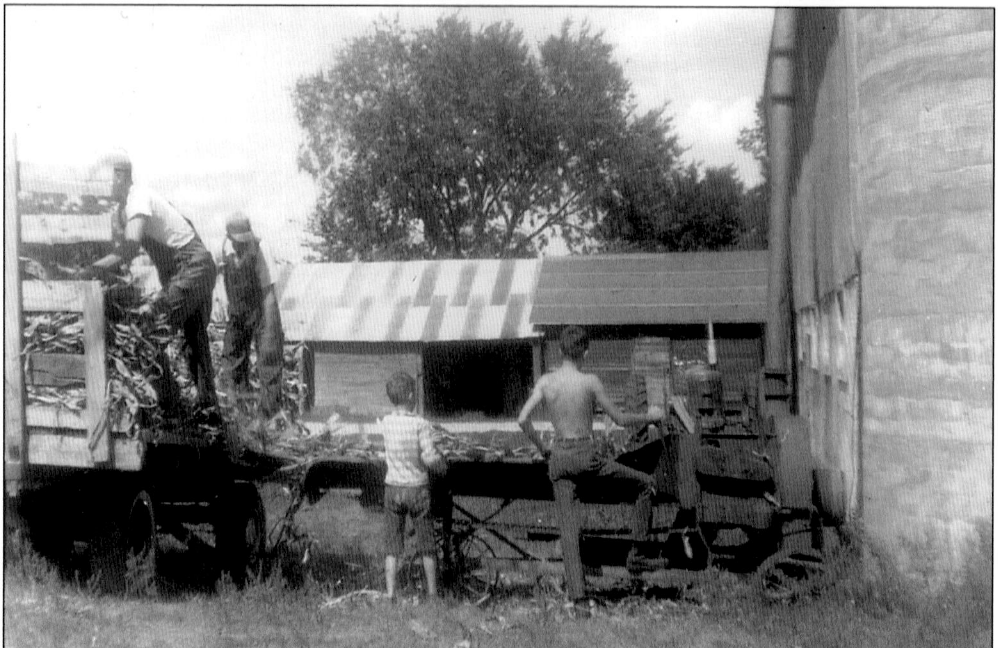

John Winter and an unidentified man are filling a silo on his farm with help from his sons Clinton and Donald, Town of Brunswick, 1968. (CVM.)

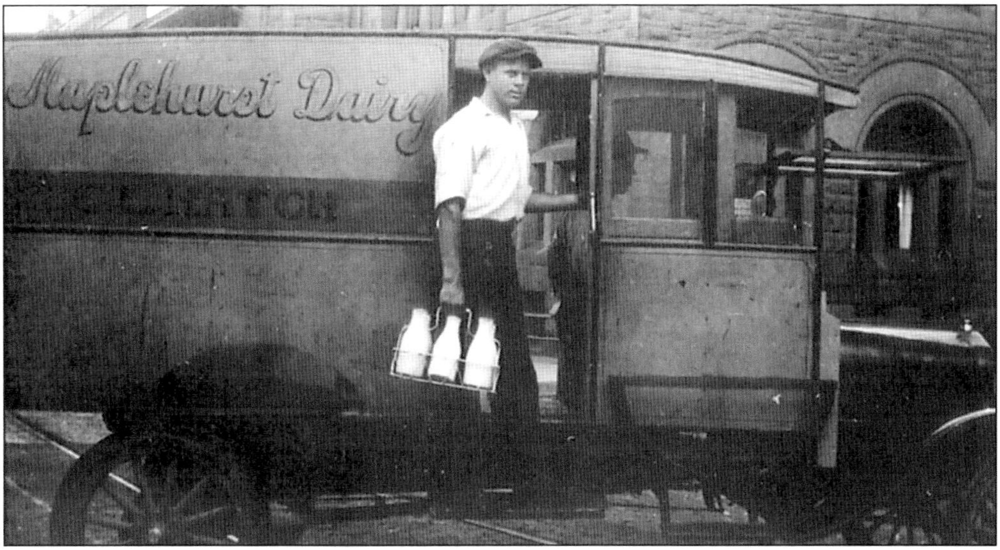

Clinton L. Hatch is seen here on his milk delivery route, Eau Claire, *c.* 1920s. Hatch, an area farmer, bought the Maplehurst Dairy in 1918. His wife Hester drove a milk truck after they added a second route. Maplehurst expanded several times and became Oak Park Dairy in 1929. In 1968, Oak Park Dairy had 16 refrigerated trucks and a tank truck, and serviced 28 door-step delivery routes in and around Eau Claire. The facility, on Rudolph Road in Eau Claire's Putnam Heights neighborhood, later became the Fuller-Speckien Funeral Home. (CVM.)

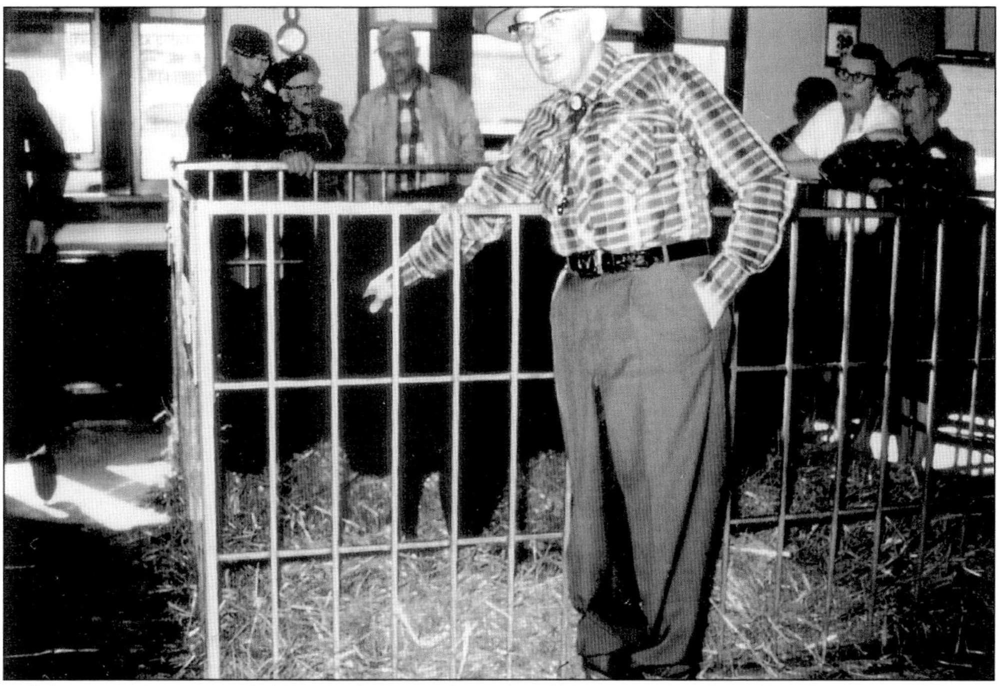

Ralph Wise is pictured here with Someday, the champion steer of the 1965 International Livestock Show. The $10,000 steer was displayed in the State Bank of Fall Creek lobby for an entire day before he was taken on a tour of Europe. The price is equivalent to over $60,000 in year 2000 dollars. (FCHS.)

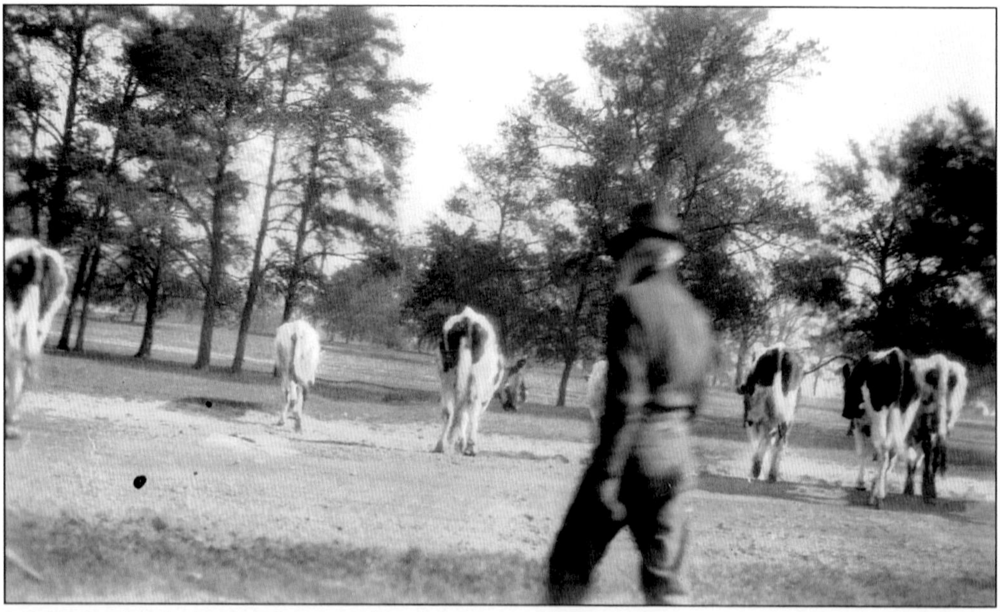

J.C. Barland is driving cattle across Altoona Avenue, Eau Claire, *c.* 1925. The Barland farmstead sat on what is now the 2000 block of Altoona Avenue, in the well-developed area of Regis High School. (CVM.)

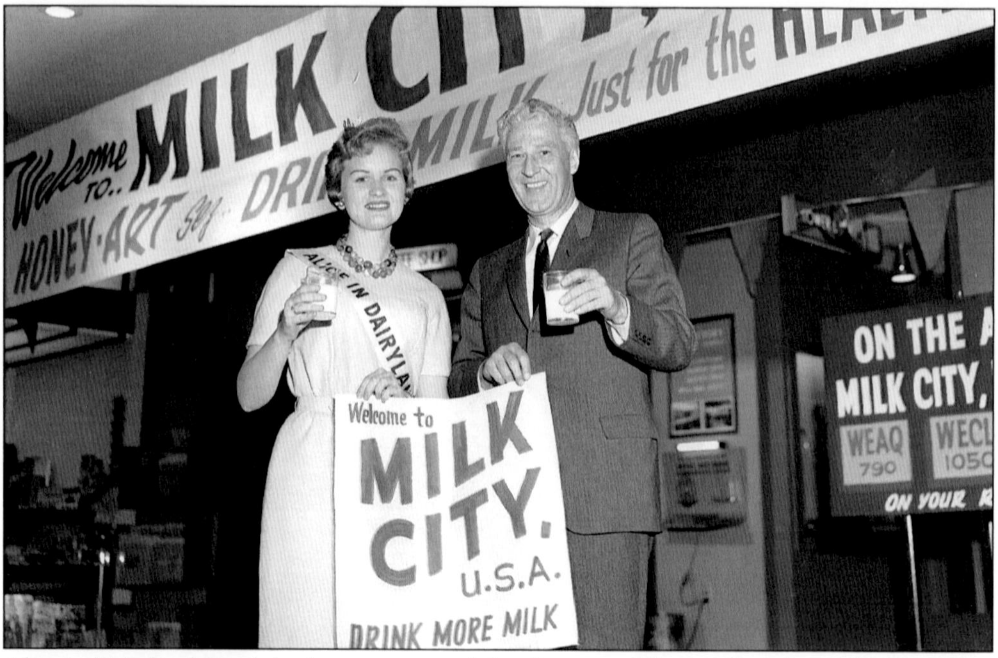

Alice in Dairyland Carol Anderson poses with Lt. Governor Warren Knowles at the Hotel Eau Claire for a "Milk City USA" promotion, Eau Claire, 1962. In the 1960s, regions of the country remote from the Dairy Belt of Wisconsin and Minnesota were facing milk shortages. Congress reacted by passing the Federal Milk Marketing Order, widely known as Eau Claire Rule. It divided the U.S. into 31 regions and paid a bonus to farmers based on how far their cows were from what was then the geographic center of the dairy industry: Eau Claire, Wisconsin. (CVM.)

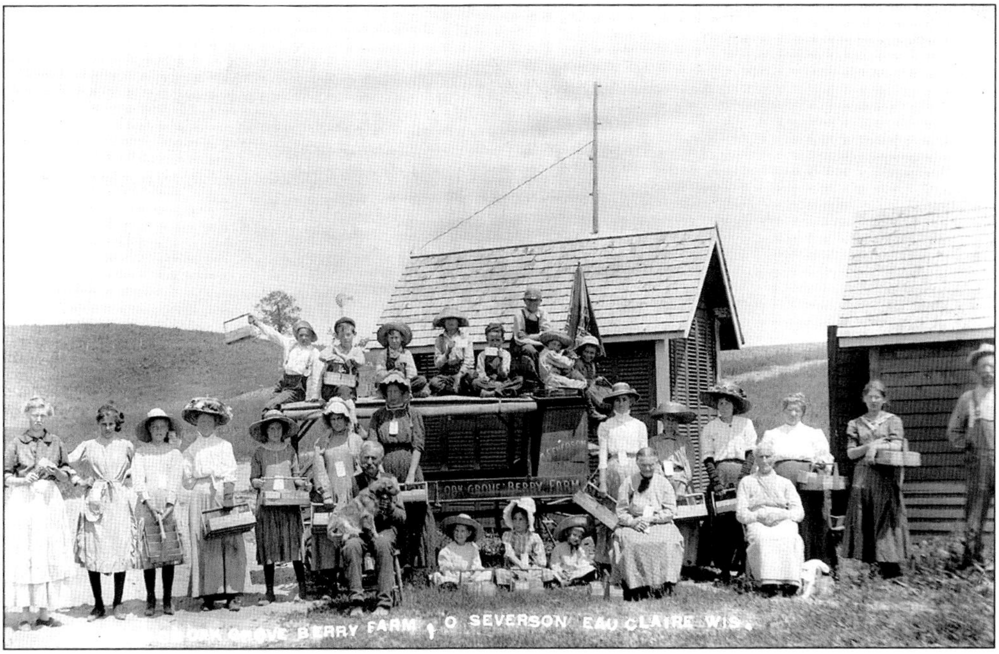

O. Severson's Oak Grove Berry Farm in the Town of Union is seen here *c.* 1915. (Courtesy of George Johnson.)

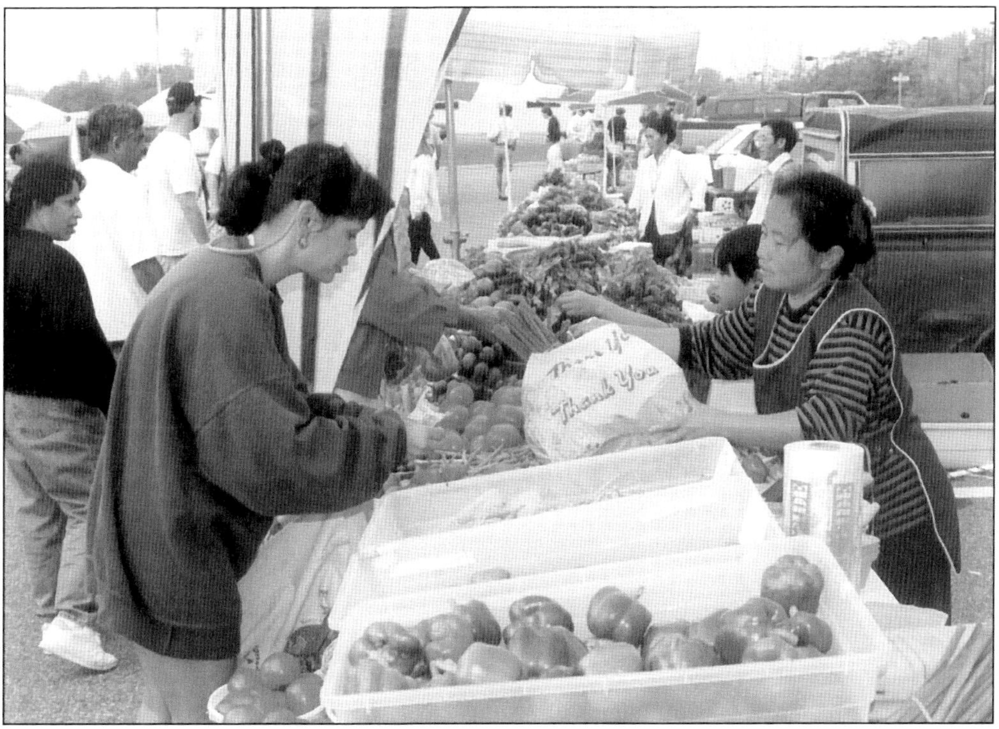

Hmong gardeners are selling summer produce at the Downtown Farmers' Market, Eau Claire, August 1994. (Photograph by Jason Tetzloff. CVM.)

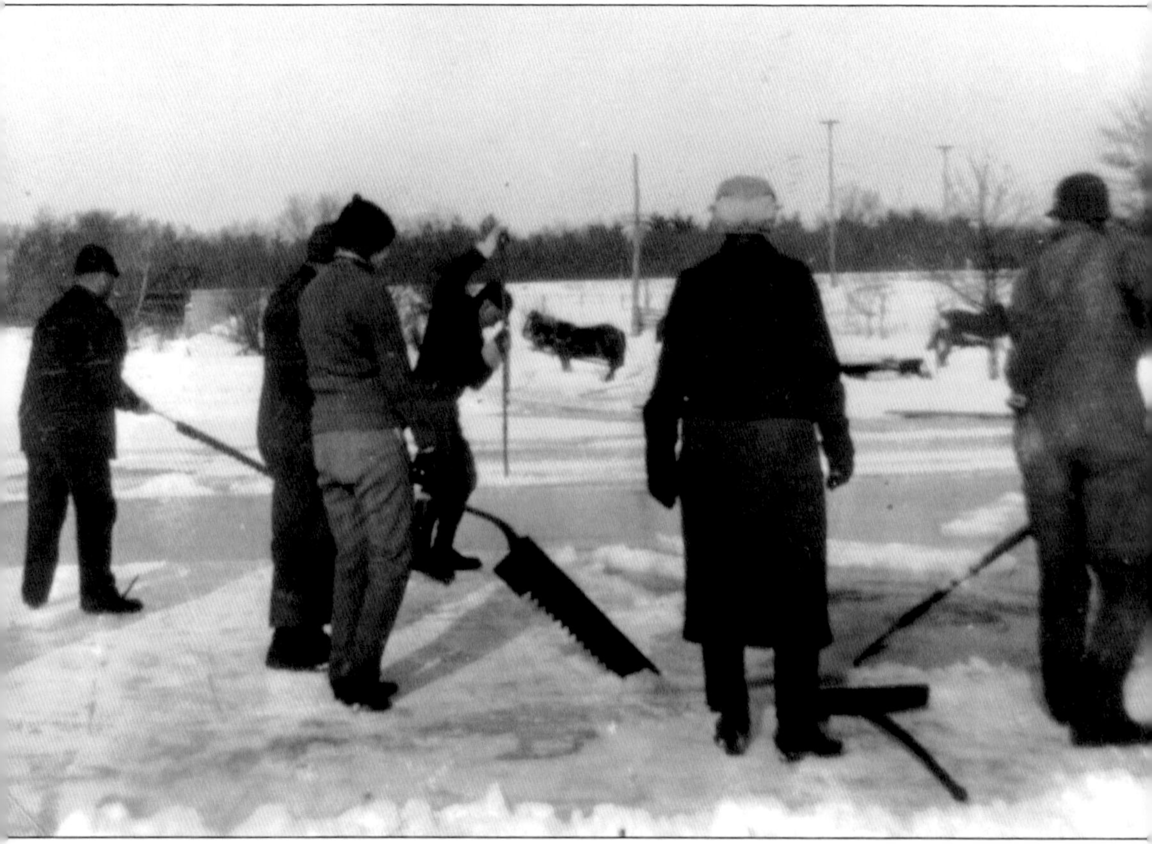

The hard work of cutting ice is captured in this photograph of the Fall Creek mill pond, c. 1930. Before widespread electricity, ice was harvested in the winter and used to refrigerate goods throughout the next year. The ice was often stacked and covered with sawdust. This kept it from melting during the summer. (FCHS.)

Four

Structures and Infrastructure

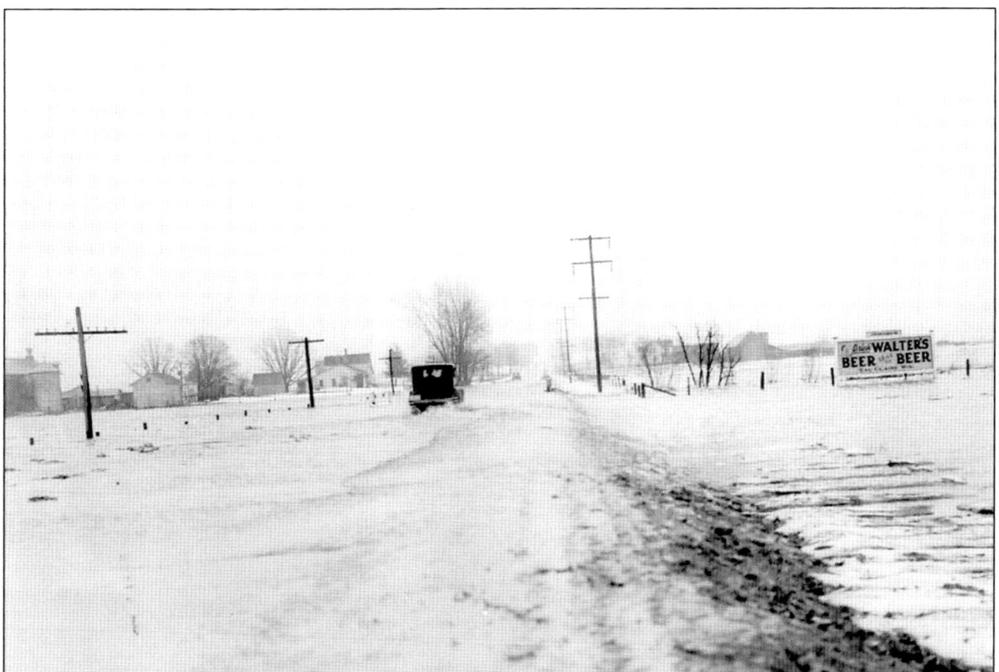

Elk Creek flooded onto Highway 12 near the Eau Claire-Dunn County line in April 1934. In earlier decades, citizens often helped maintain such infrastructure as graded roads and power poles in rural areas. (CVM.)

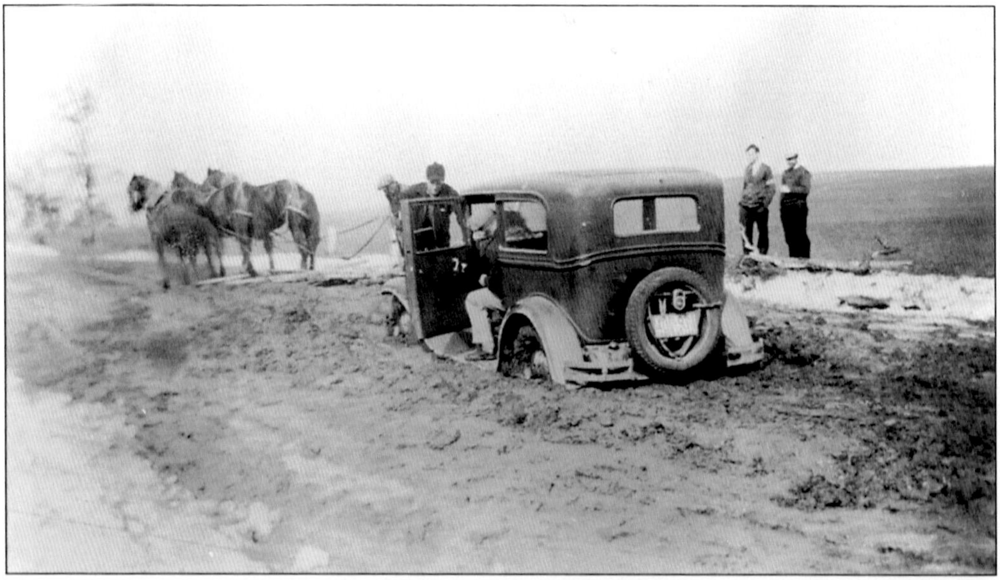

A three-horse team pulled this Model A Ford out of the mud in 1931 (or later). This was a common spring sight before surfaced roads became widespread in Eau Claire County. (FCHS.)

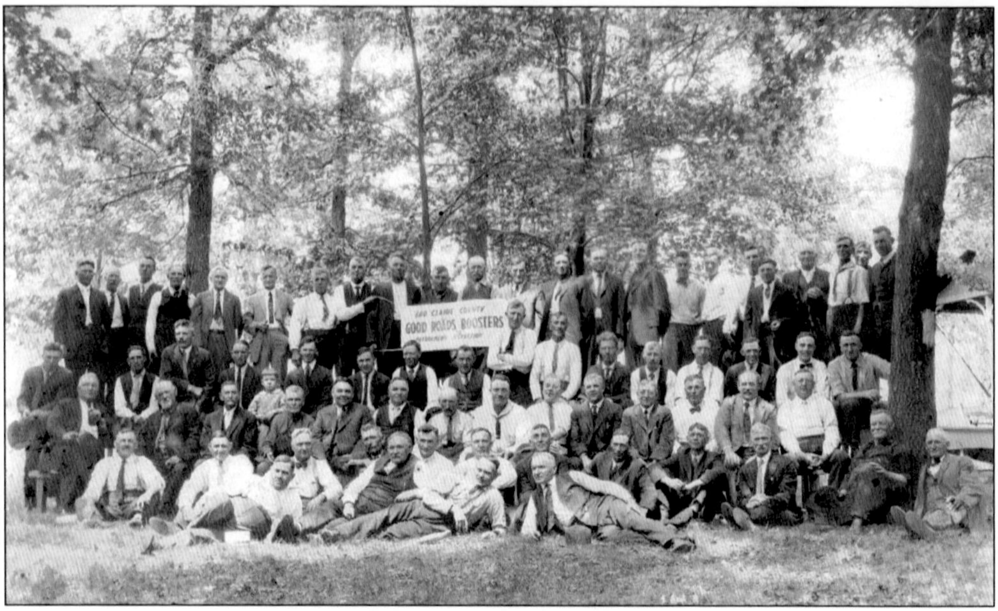

The Eau Claire County Good Roads Boosters, pictured here, were supporting the Good Roads Movement, which had gained momentum across America since the 1890s. In Wisconsin, a defining symbol of the movement was the "Good Roads Bill" of the 1910s. Before its passage, the state's rural roads were cared for by farmers maintaining their own roadways. The bill gave state aid to highways and created a highway commission to secure funds to build and maintain the State Highway System. (CVM.)

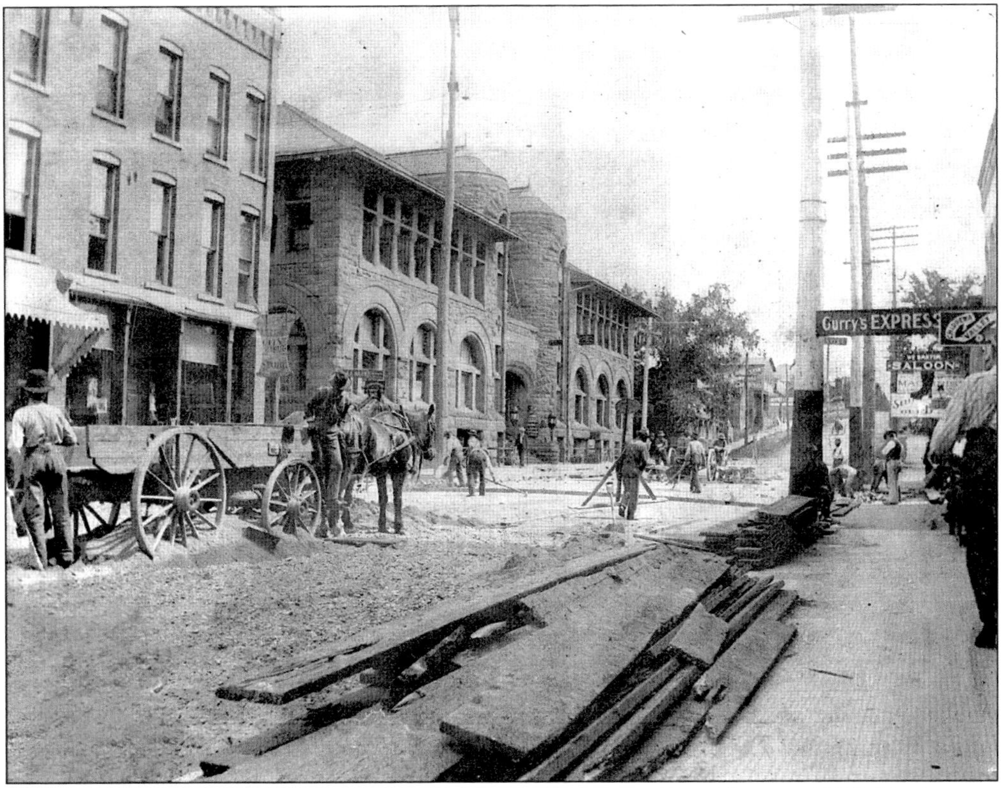

These workers are removing planks from a street in downtown Eau Claire, *c.* 1900. Planks were used as a road surface in the city before bricks, concrete, or asphalt. In fact, Harding Street Hill is still commonly known by locals as Plank Street Hill. (CVM.)

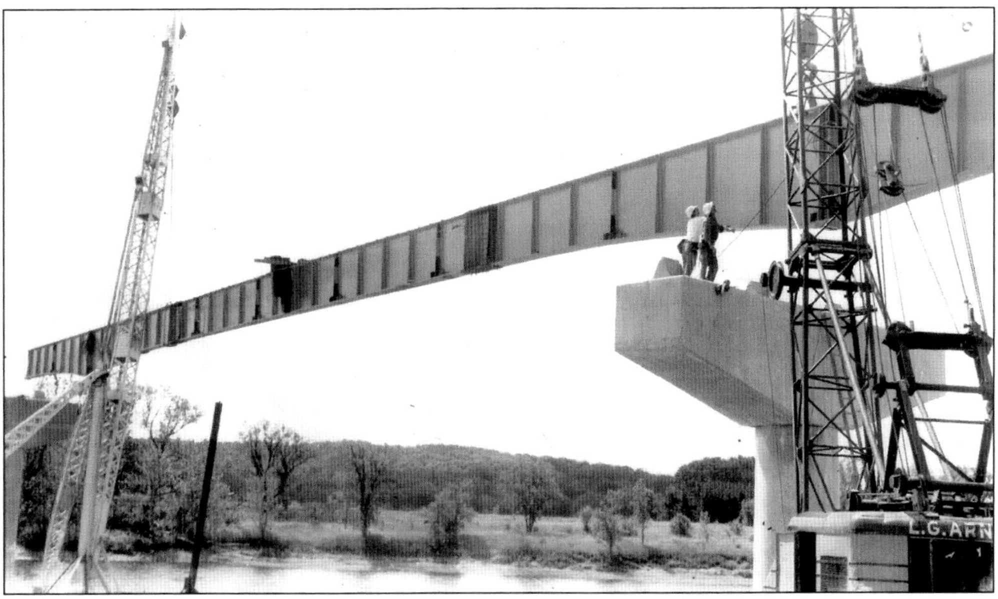

A construction crew is placing girders for an Interstate-94 bridge over the Chippewa River, Town of Union, *c.* 1965. (CVM.)

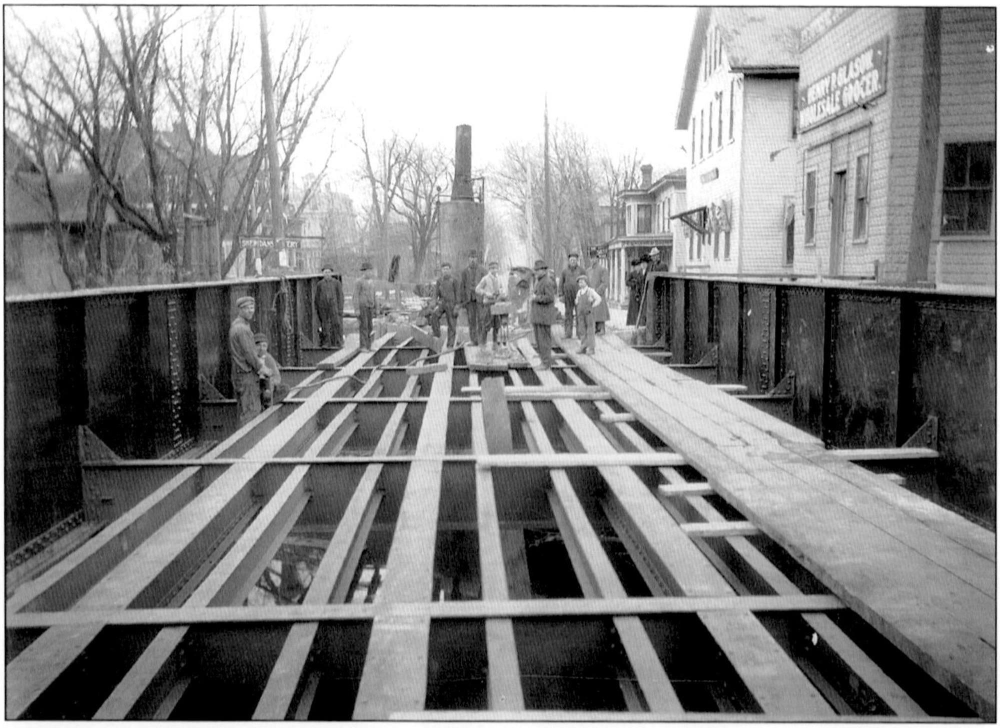

Workmen are putting a deck on the Grand Avenue bridge, Eau Claire, 1915. (CVM.)

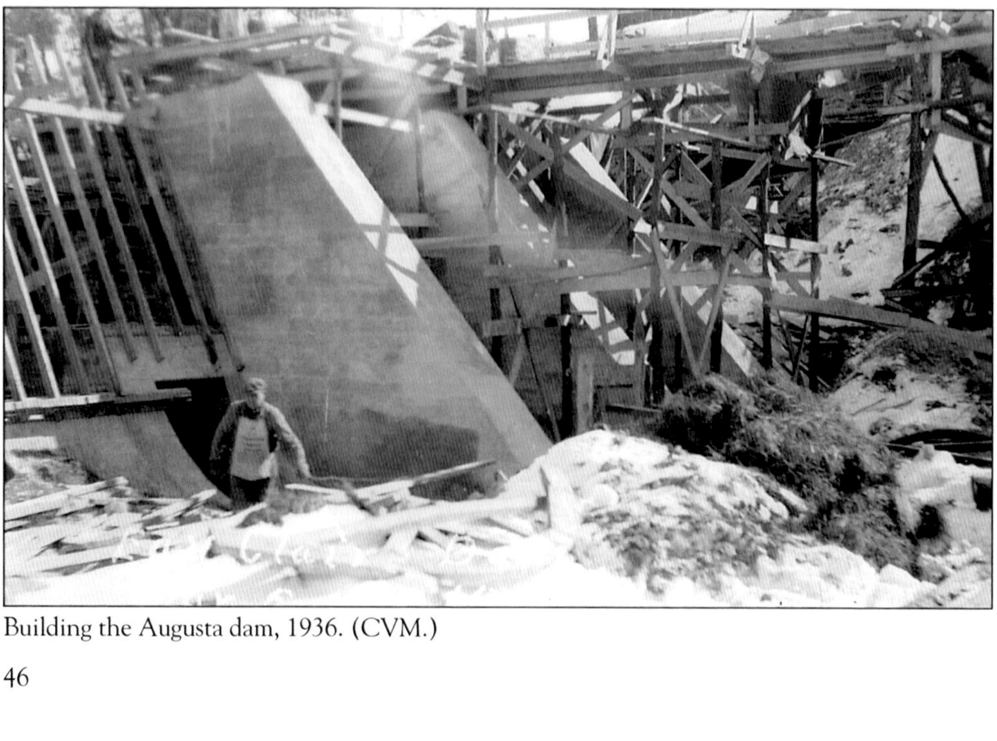

Building the Augusta dam, 1936. (CVM.)

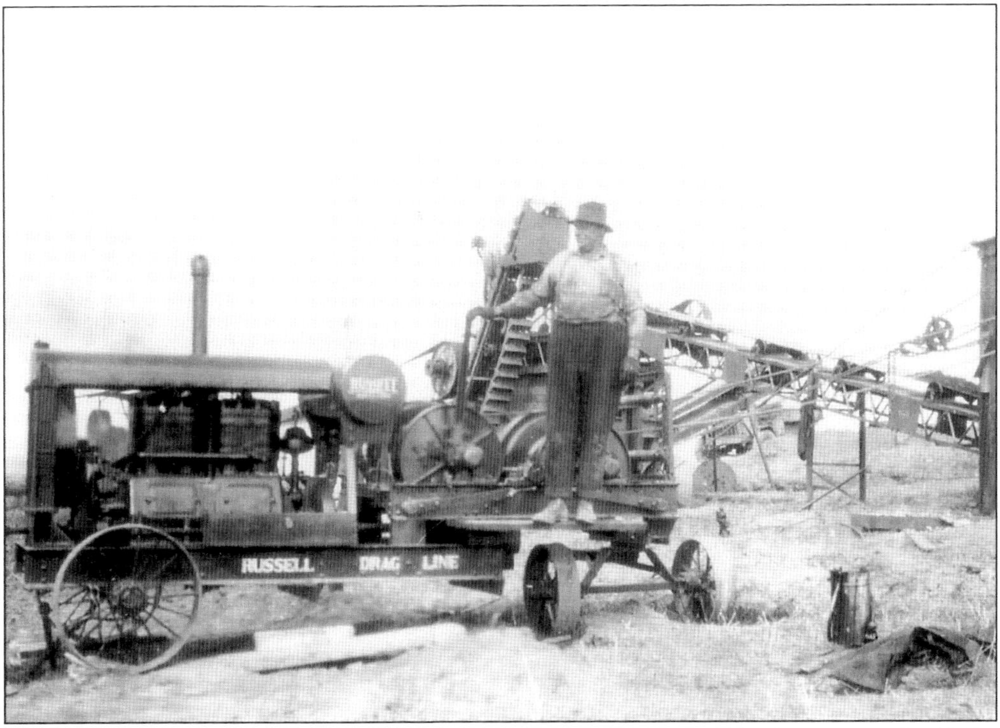

Earl "Slim" Kirkham stands on road construction equipment outside Augusta, early 1940s. (Courtesy of Jane Justesen.)

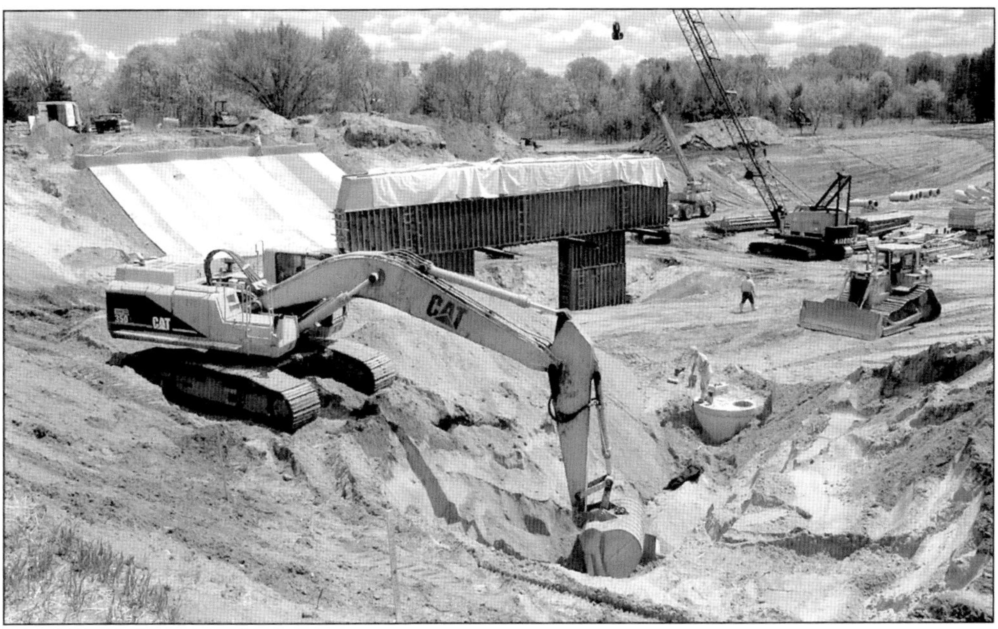

Construction crews work on the Spooner Avenue Bridge for the Highway 53 bypass in Altoona, May 2003. (Photograph by Dan Reiland. Courtesy of the Eau Claire *Leader-Telegram*.)

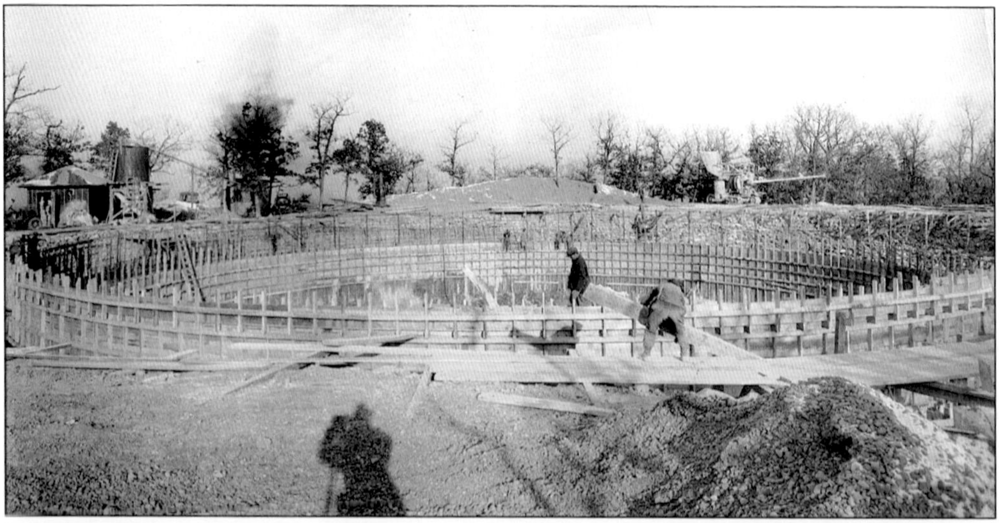

L.G. Arnold, Inc., buildt the water reservoir on Mount Tom in Eau Claire, *c.* 1924. (CVM.)

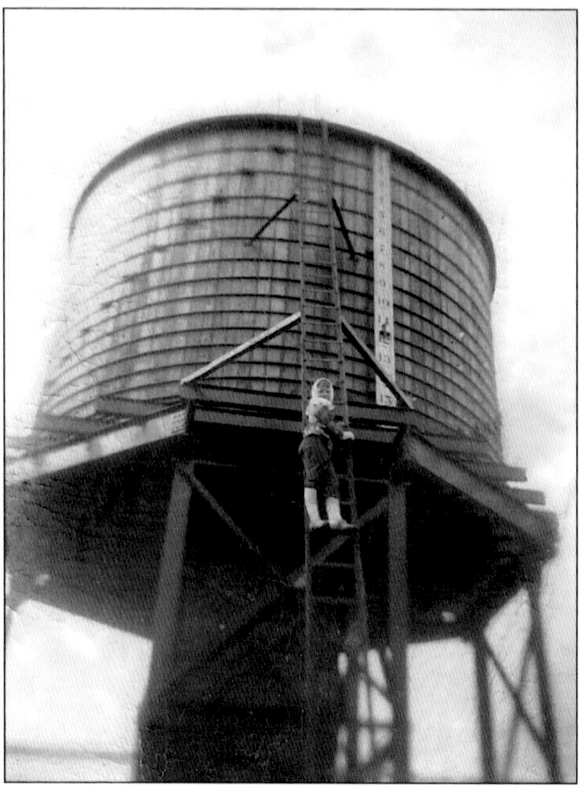

Alice Larson climbs up the ladder of the Fairchild water tower. (Courtesy of Alice (nee Larson) Pingel.)

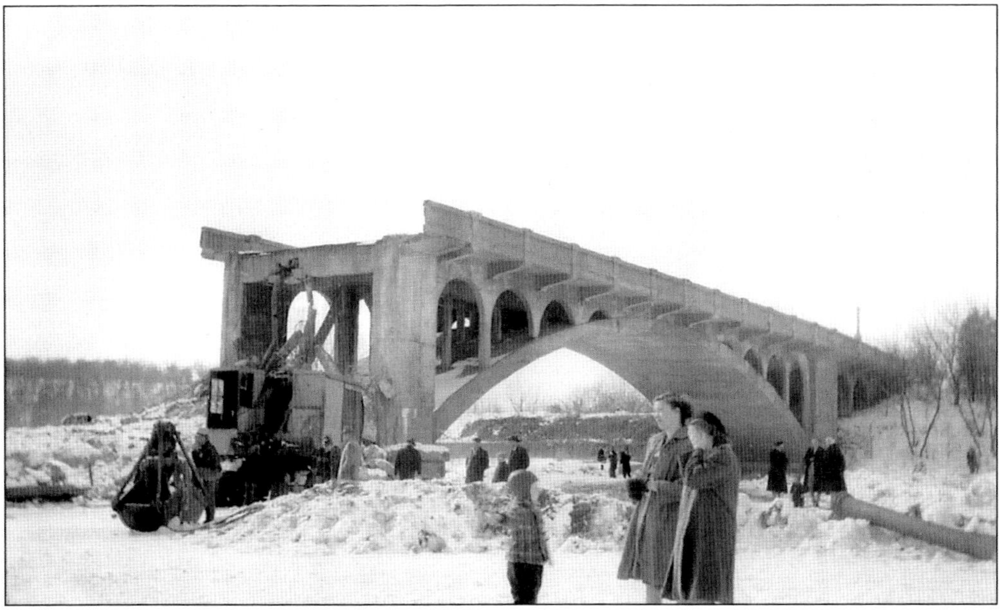

What remains of the collapsed Water Street Bridge in Eau Claire is seen here in February 1945. The photo was taken while standing on in the middle of the river on the ice. (Photograph by Adrian Schute. Courtesy of Carol Benning.)

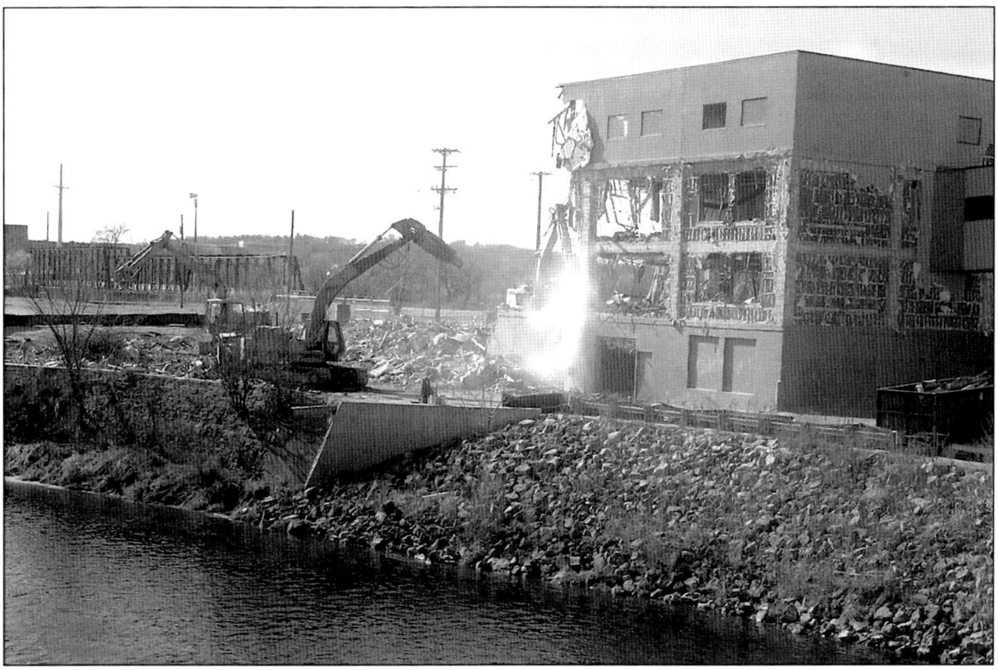

A Northern States Power building was razed to make way for the city's new Phoenix Park and Royal Credit Union facility. The site is at the confluence of the Eau Claire and Chippewa Rivers, as viewed from Barstow Street Bridge, Eau Claire, March 2003. (Photograph by Andi Stempniak. Courtesy of the Eau Claire *Leader-Telegram*.)

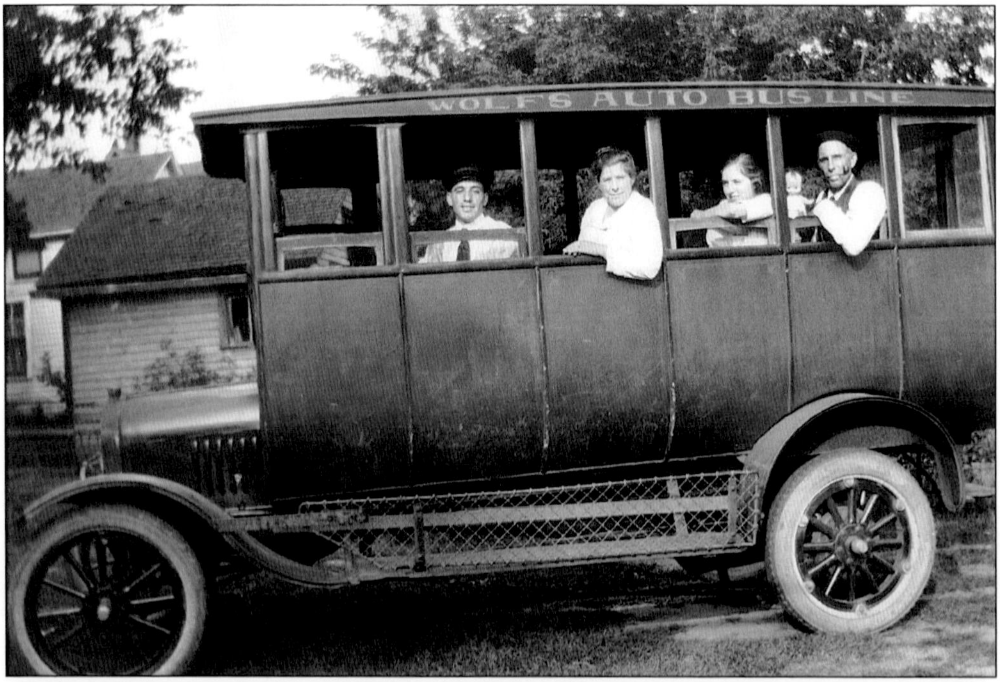

Wolf's Auto Bus Line was a combination bus and taxi service in Eau Claire, and is pictured here c. 1920. From left to right are Andrew Garton, Margaret Garton, Esther Garton, and Edwin Garton. The bus met all trains and stopped at all Eau Claire hotels. (CVM.)

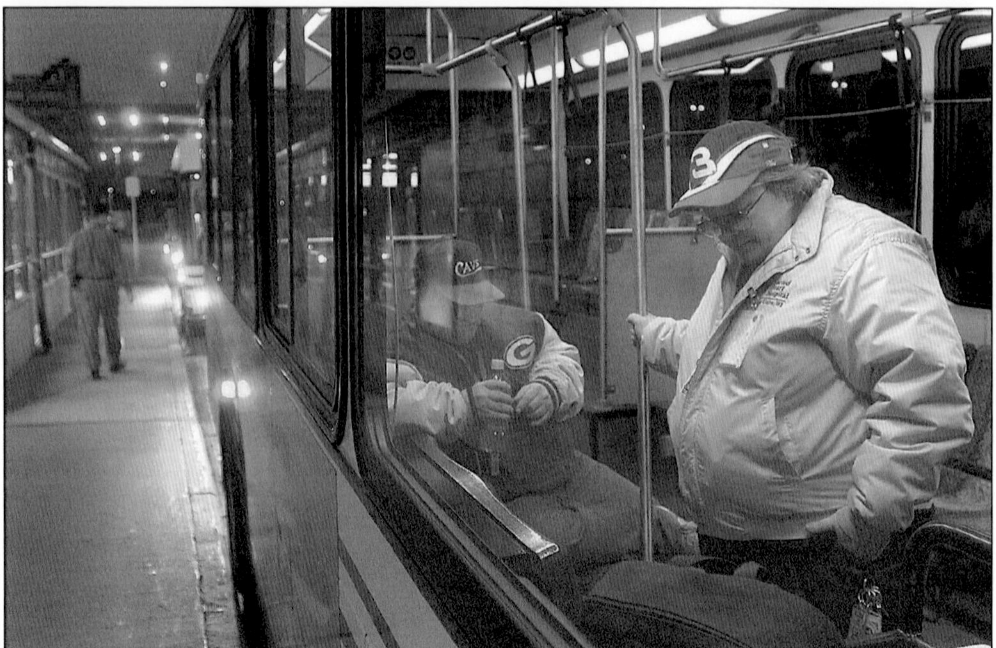

Eileen Phelps, right, of Altoona, and Peter Hayden, of Eau Claire, wait for an Eau Claire Transit Company (ETC) South Loop bus to leave the transfer station, downtown Eau Claire, October 2003. (Photograph by Shane Opatz. Courtesy of the Eau Claire *Leader-Telegram*.)

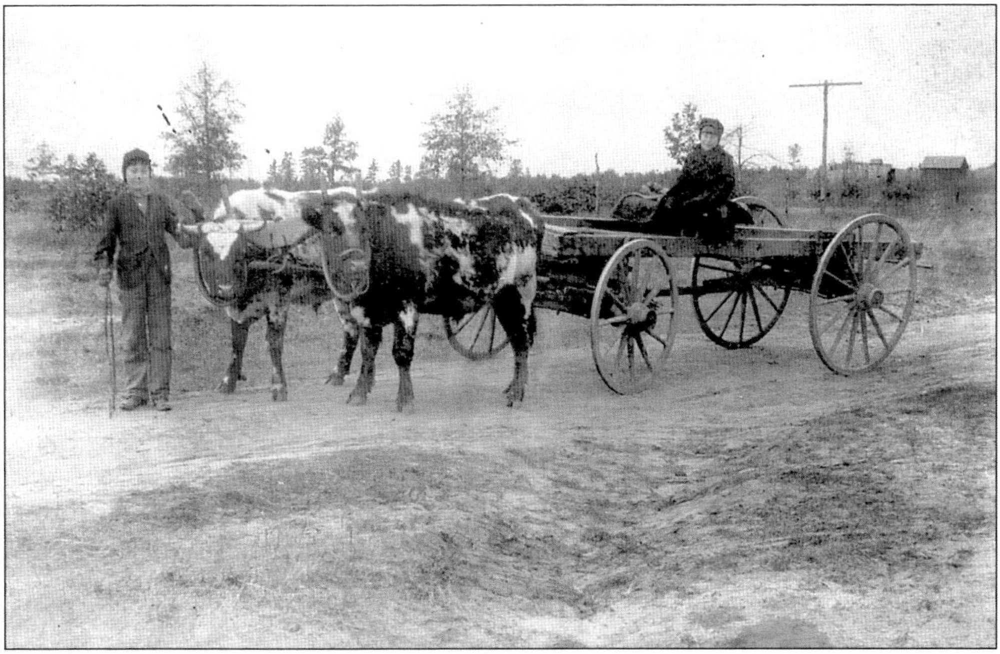

Chester L. Smith, 13, and Arby F. Smith, 9, were photographed with an ox team and wagon, north of Fairchild in 1908. (CVM.)

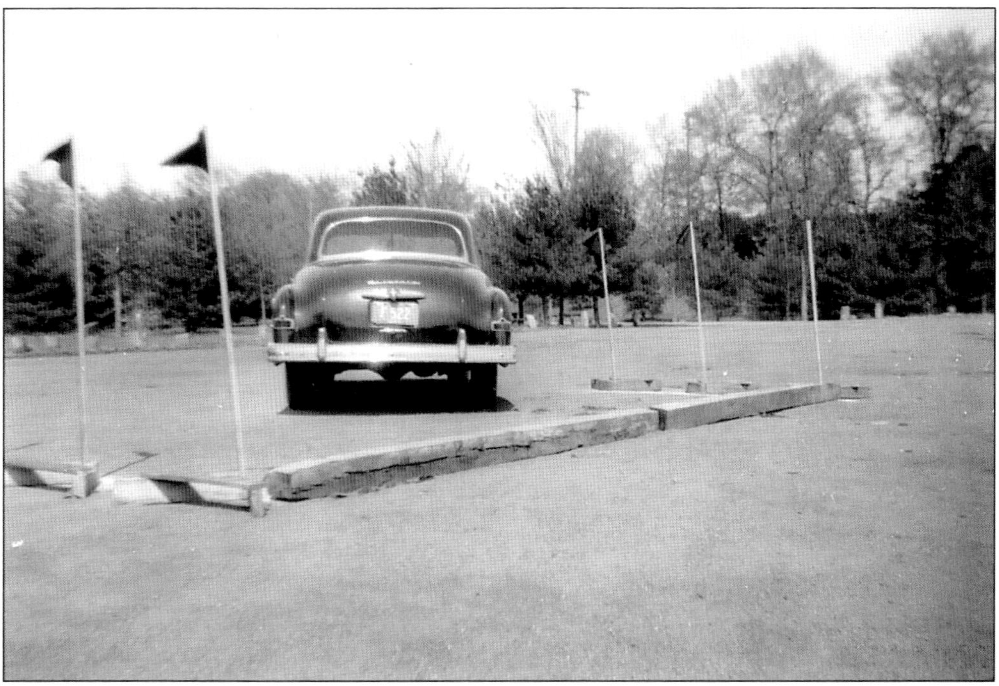

Parallel parking is being practiced at the Teenage Driving Road-e-o, sponsored by the Eau Claire Jaycees, May 1954. (CVM.)

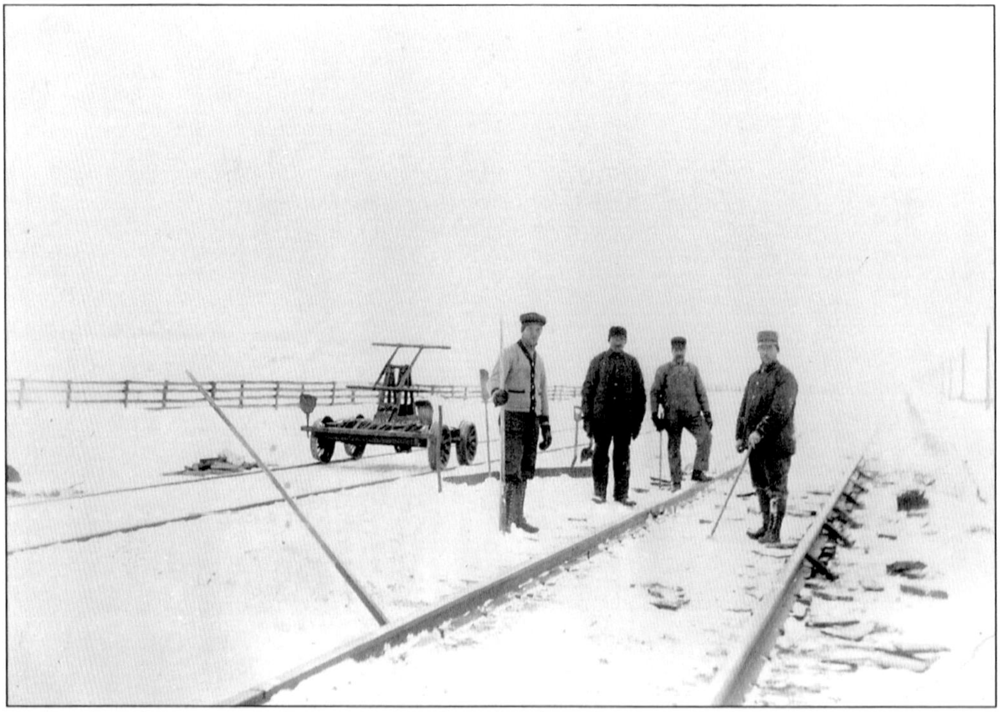

Railroad workers in Eau Claire County take a break to have their picture taken. Bill Heuer is on the left. (FCHS.)

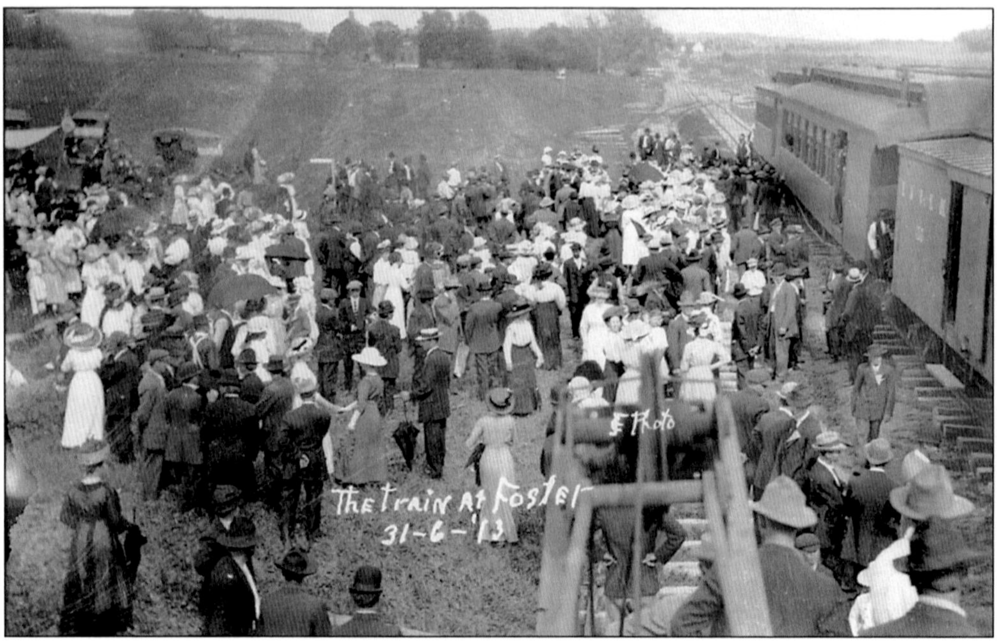

Residents celebrate the arrival of rail service at Foster, June 1913. (CVM.)

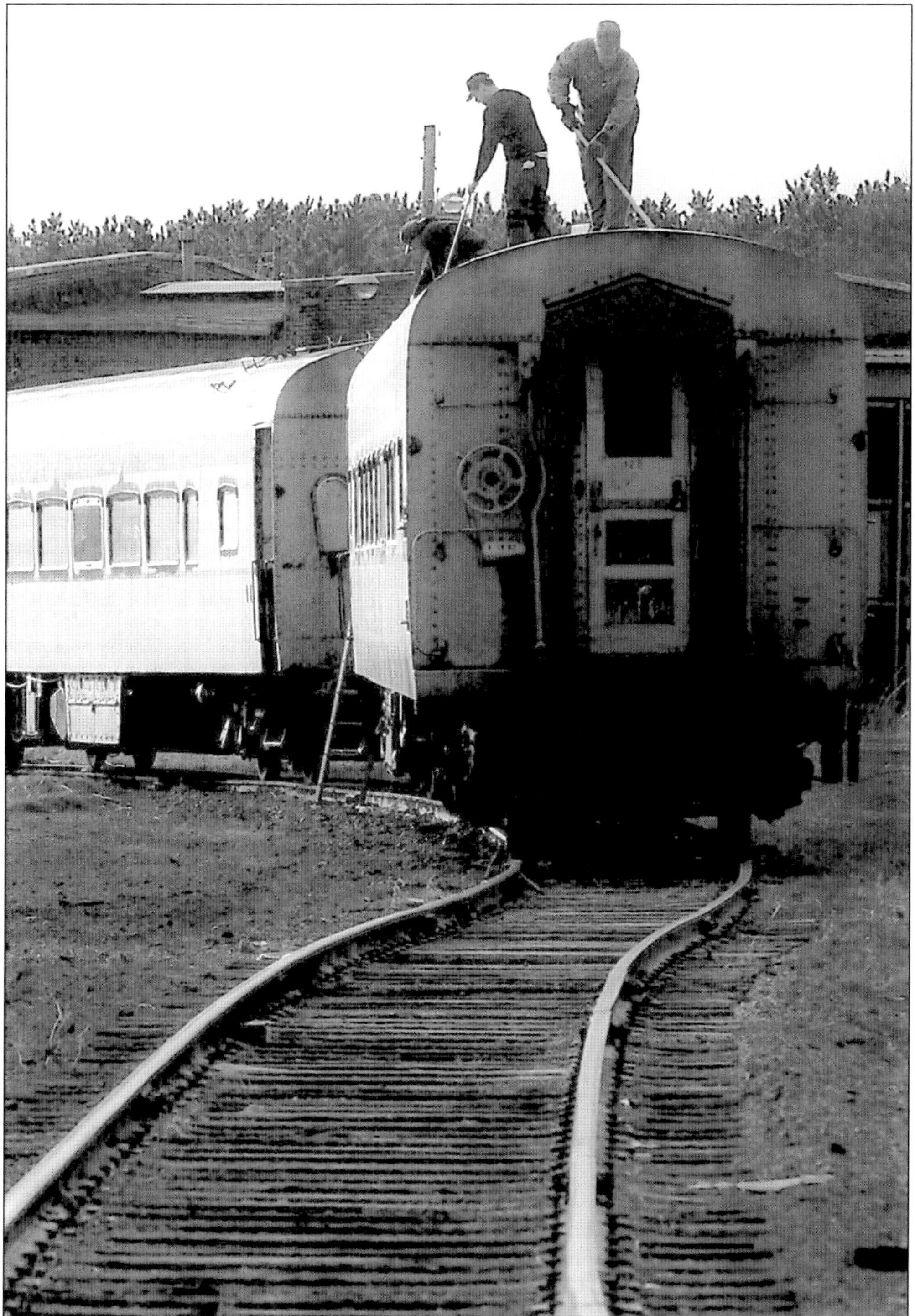

Randy Lambertus and Paul Miller, both of Eau Claire, paint the roof of a passenger car in the Altoona rail yards, April 2004. (Photograph by Shane Opatz. Courtesy of the Eau Claire *Leader-Telegram*.)

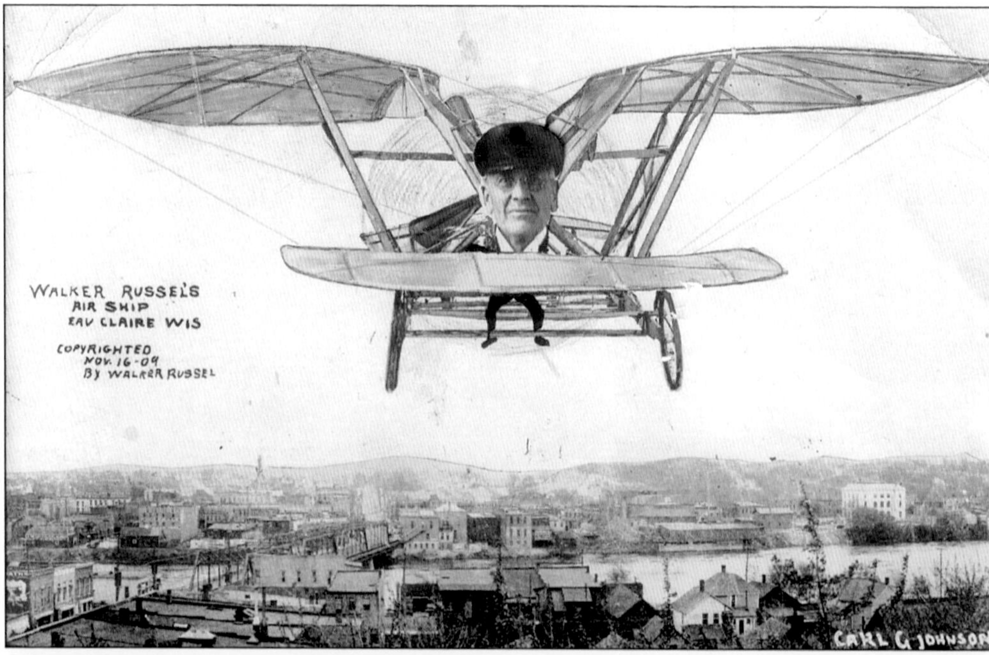

Chair-maker and inventor Walker Russel is here superimposed over a drawing of his airship "The Prairie Chicken," which is superimposed over a bird's eye 1919 photograph of downtown Eau Claire. This bit of photographic fakery, printed on postcards, was produced by the Carl G. Johnson Company, Photo Engravers and Commercial Photographers of Eau Claire. Russel used the image to advertise the maiden voyage of his flying machine, which would "be trumpeted the world over." To which the Eau Claire *Leader* added, "And Eau Claire both sides of the river will be boomed, no doubt." Unfortunately for Russel and Eau Claire, his Prairie Chicken never took flight. Russel died just four years later in 1913. (CVM.)

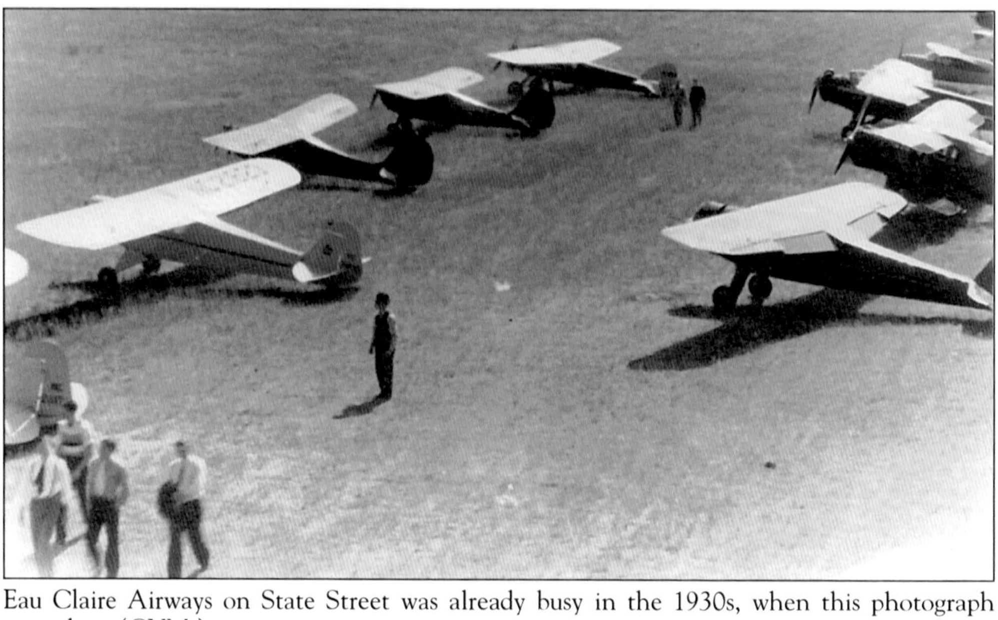

Eau Claire Airways on State Street was already busy in the 1930s, when this photograph was taken. (CVM.)

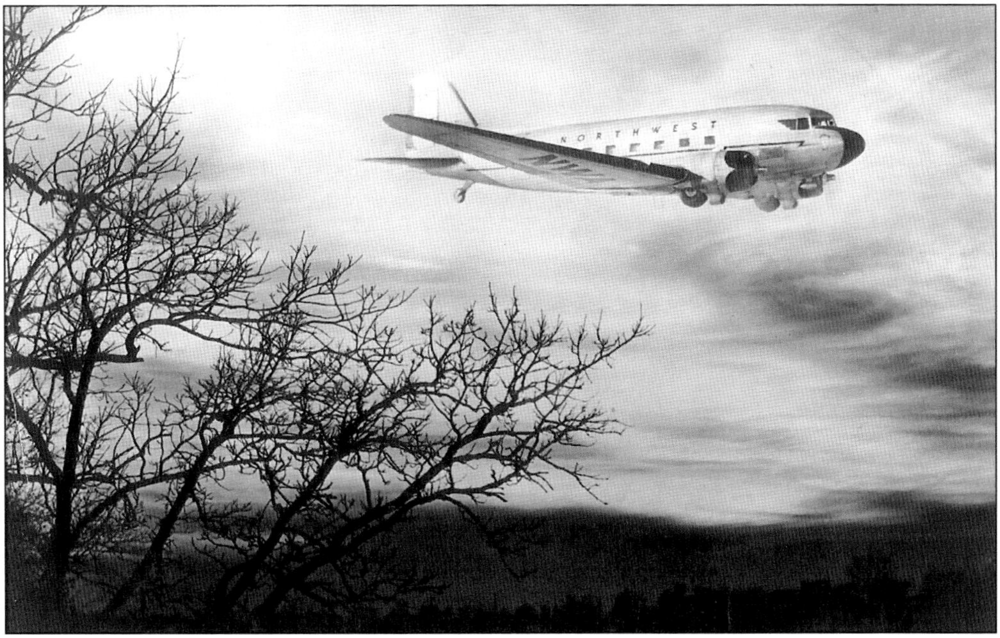

A Northwest Airlines (NWA) Douglas DC-3 is photographed in flight over the Chippewa River, Eau Claire County, perhaps during the late 1940s. The Eau Claire Municipal Airport announced its formal opening in 1945, while the runways were still under construction. The airport was officially dedicated in 1947, with a ceremony featuring a Northwest Airlines DC-3 aircraft. (CVM.)

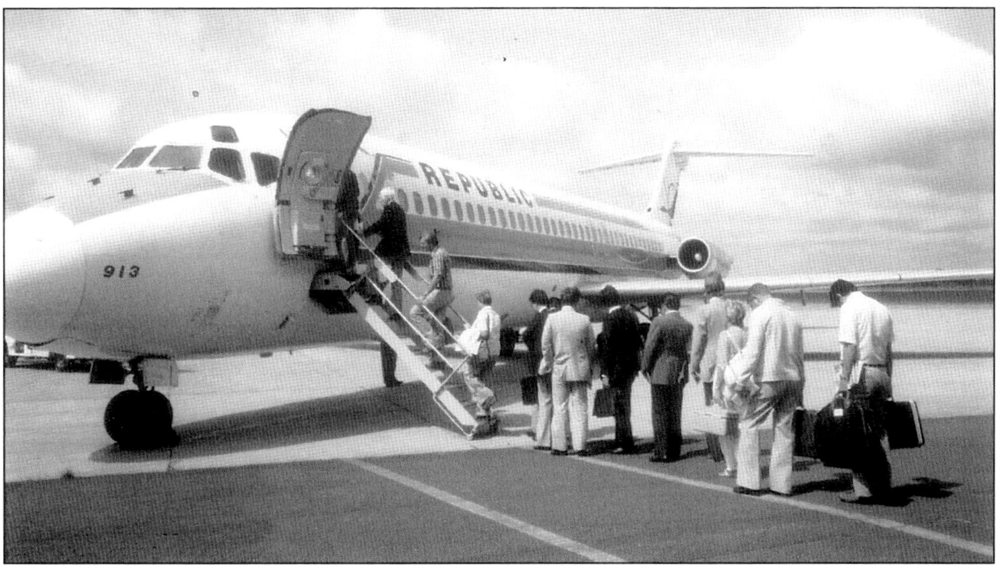

Passengers wait to board a Republic Airlines flight at Eau Claire Regional Airport in August 1982. Eau Claire County took over ownership of the airport from the City of Eau Claire in 1979. To complicate matters, the airport actually sits in Chippewa County but within the incorporated limits of the City of Eau Claire. In 1992, it was renamed the Chippewa Valley Regional Airport and in 1999, an Ownership and Operation Agreement was entered into and executed by County Board Chairs of Chippewa, Dunn, and Eau Claire Counties. (Courtesy of Eleanor Jones.)

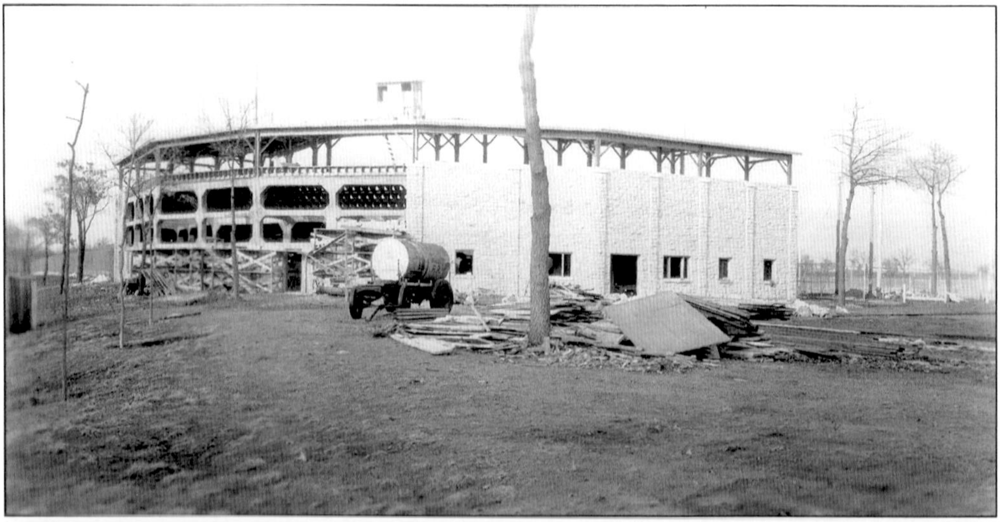

Construction is underway on the baseball stadium at Carson Park, Eau Claire, c. 1933. The stadium has been home to the Eau Claire Bears, Braves, and Cavaliers. The inaugural game of the new Eau Claire Express of the Northwoods League is scheduled for June 1, 2005, at Carson Park against the St. Cloud River Bats. The Northwoods League is sanctioned by the Summer Collegiate Baseball Association (SCBA). The federal government's Works Progress Administration (WPA) built the original baseball stadium. At the opening game, in June 1937, the Minneapolis Millers beat the Eau Claire Bears 6-2 in front of a crowd of 5,000. (CVM.)

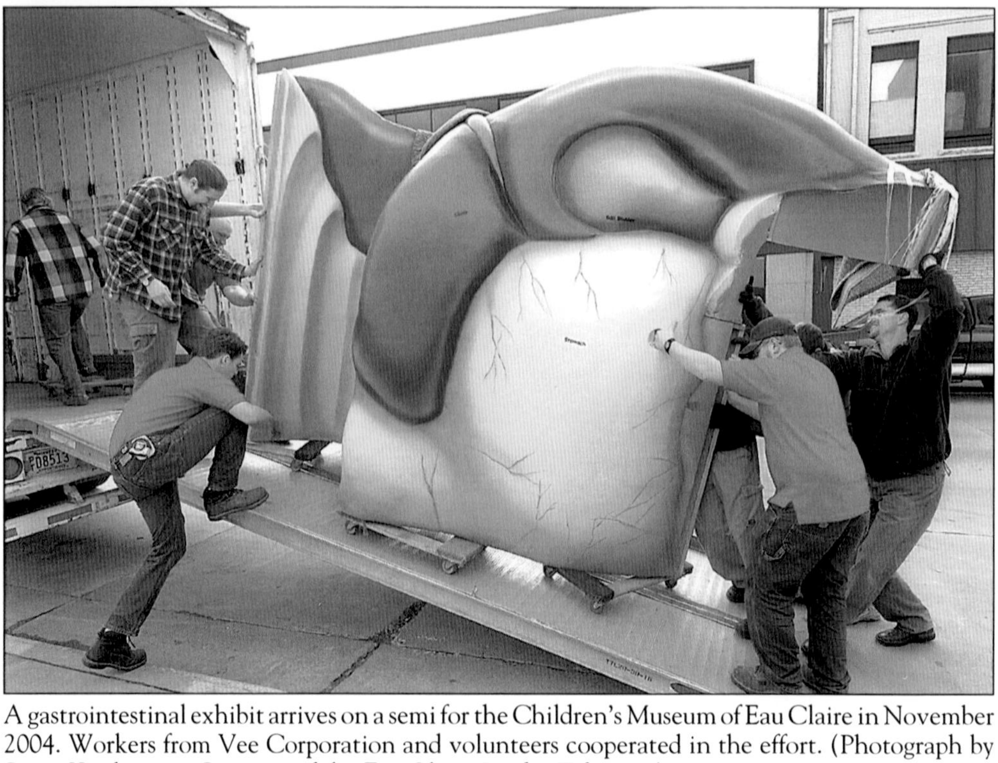

A gastrointestinal exhibit arrives on a semi for the Children's Museum of Eau Claire in November 2004. Workers from Vee Corporation and volunteers cooperated in the effort. (Photograph by Steve Kinderman. Courtesy of the Eau Claire *Leader-Telegram*.)

Five

Services, Public and Private

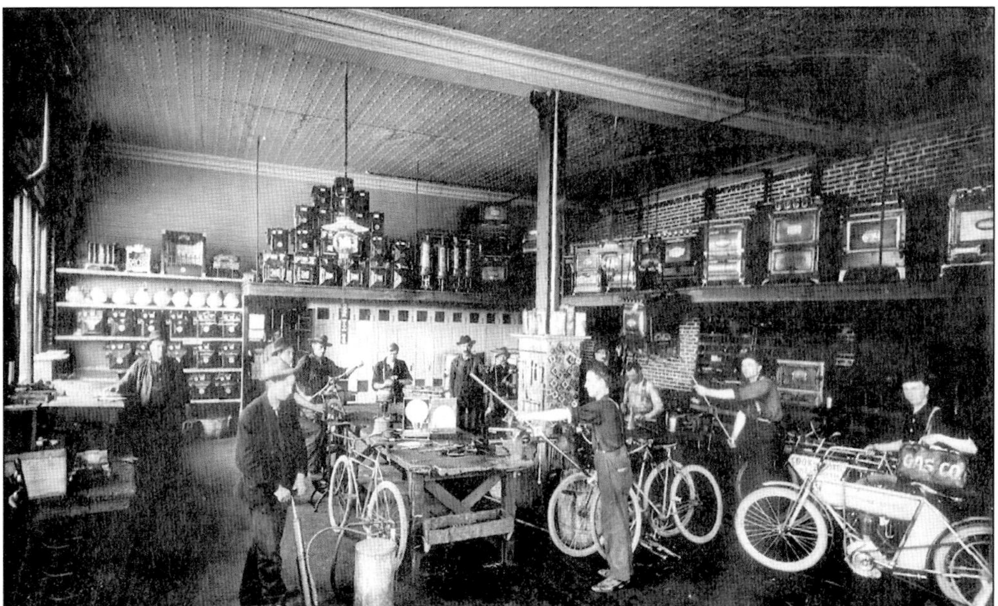

The Eau Claire Gas Works is pictured here before 1912. The man pumping his bicycle tire is Albert Erickson. Other men with bicycles are August Voss, Mick Schekel, and Mr. Sneen. They rode bikes on the job carrying pipes over their shoulders, with tool bags strapped to their bike frames. (CVM.)

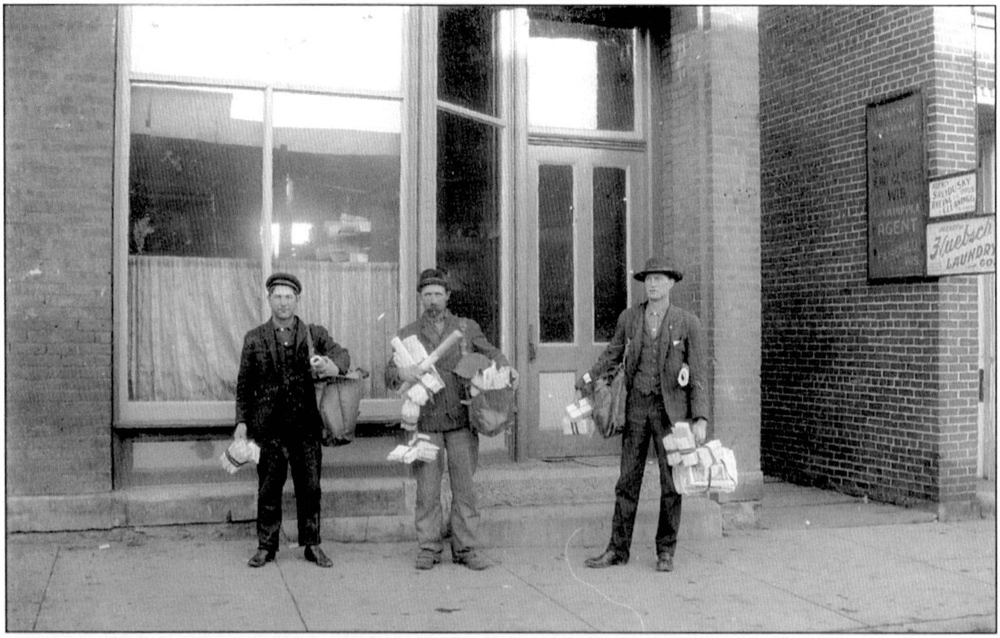

Fairchild mail carriers Francis Lightfoot, Julius Roepke, and Henry Schultz pose for this photograph in the 1920s. (CVM.)

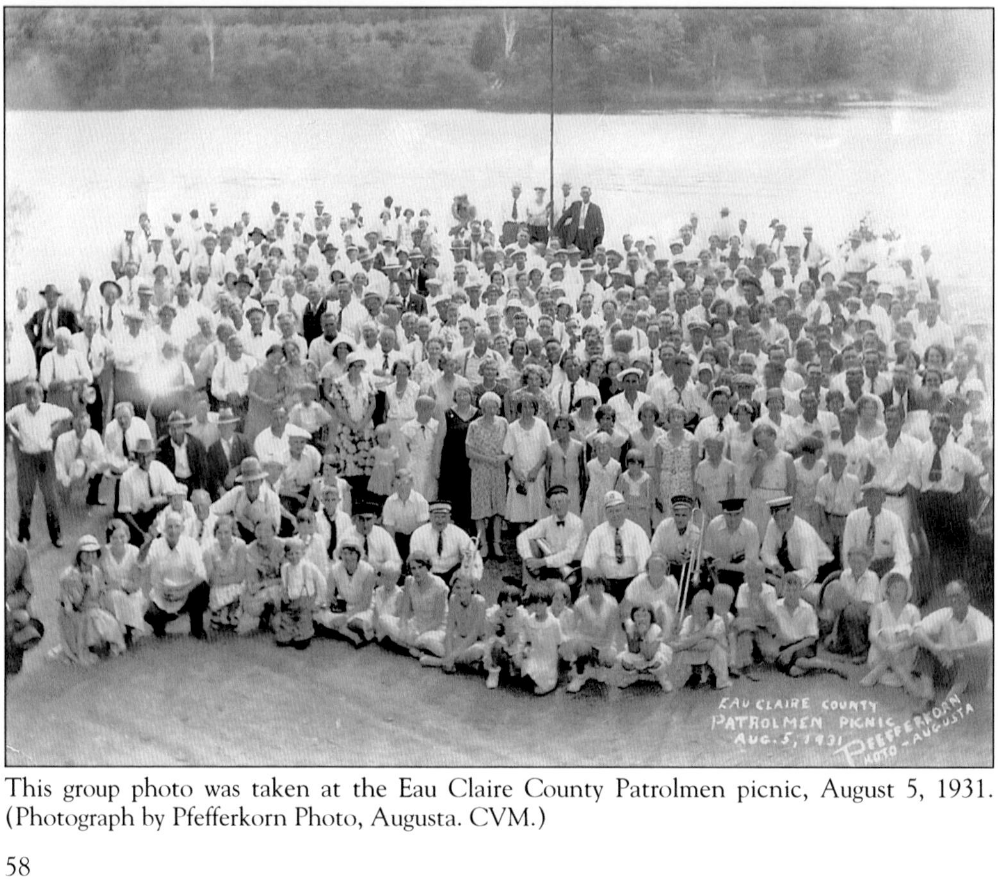

This group photo was taken at the Eau Claire County Patrolmen picnic, August 5, 1931. (Photograph by Pfefferkorn Photo, Augusta. CVM.)

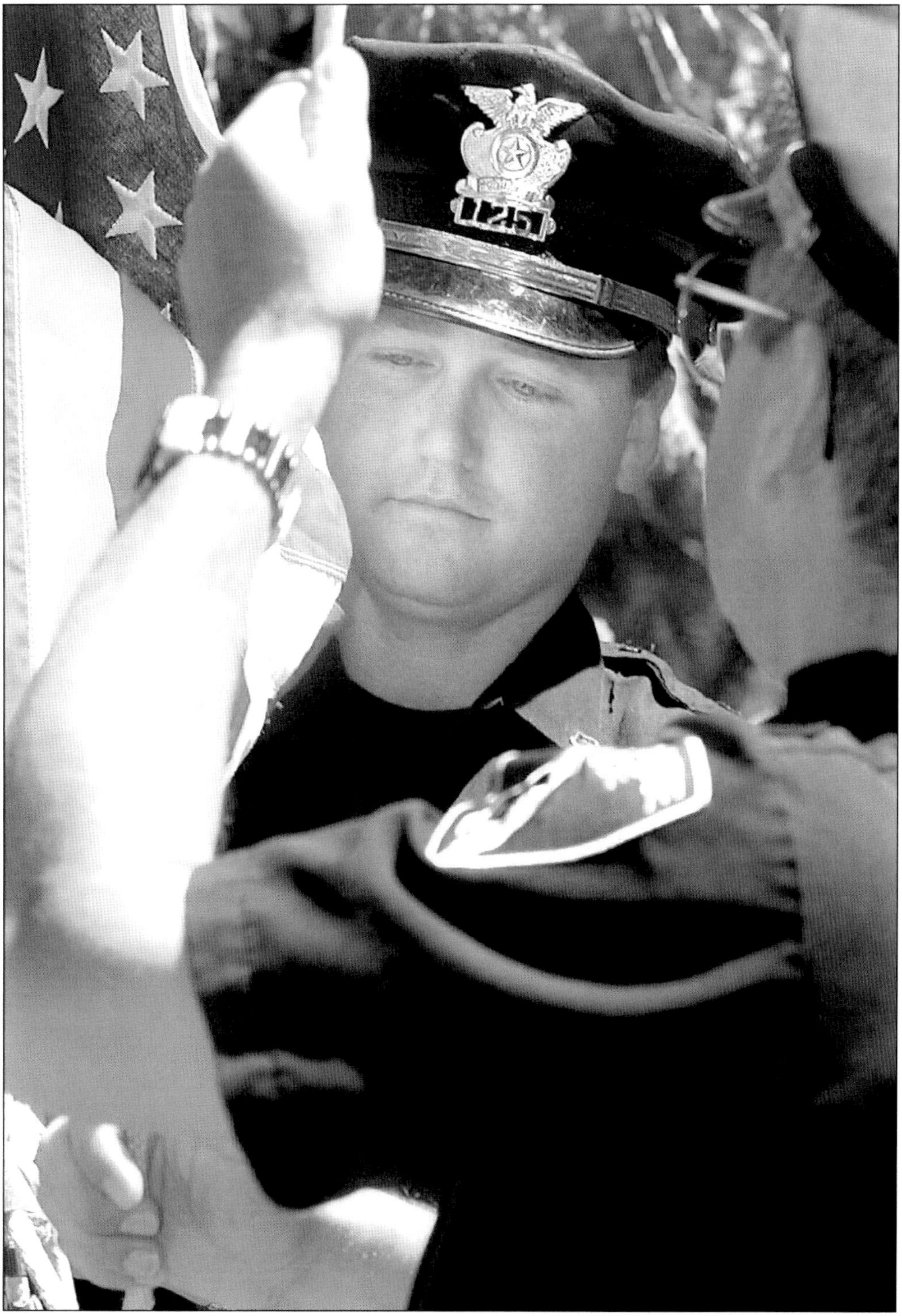

Greg Ziets and Ken Rasmussen, both of the Eau Claire Police Department, raise the American flag during a ceremony at the Chippewa Valley Museum, Carson Park, Eau Claire, July 4, 2002. (Photograph by Matthew Resenhoeft. Courtesy of the Eau Claire *Leader-Telegram*.)

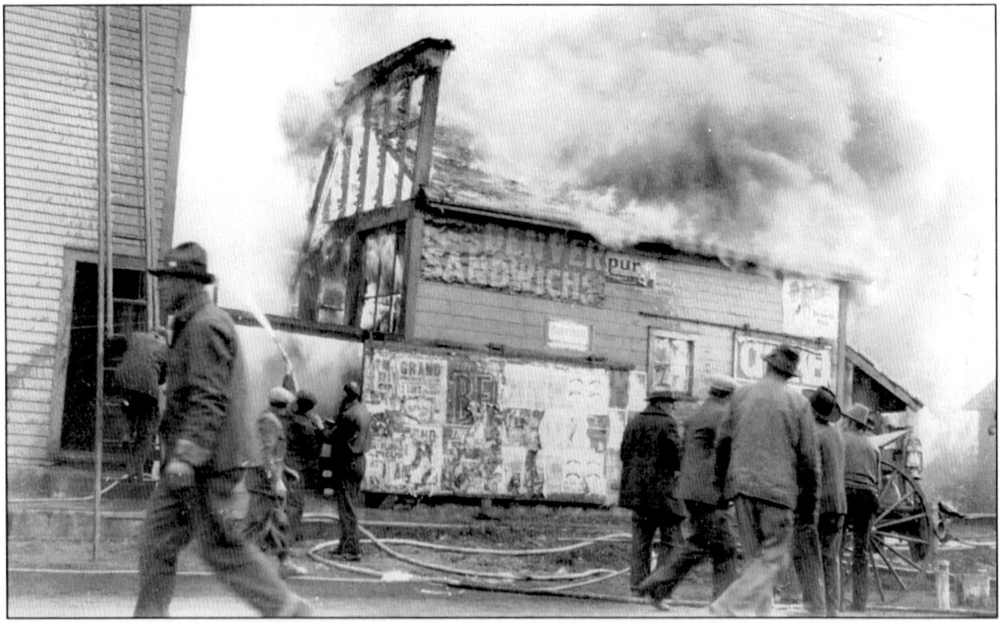

Firemen work to combat the Piesner fire in Fall Creek, 1929. (FCHS.)

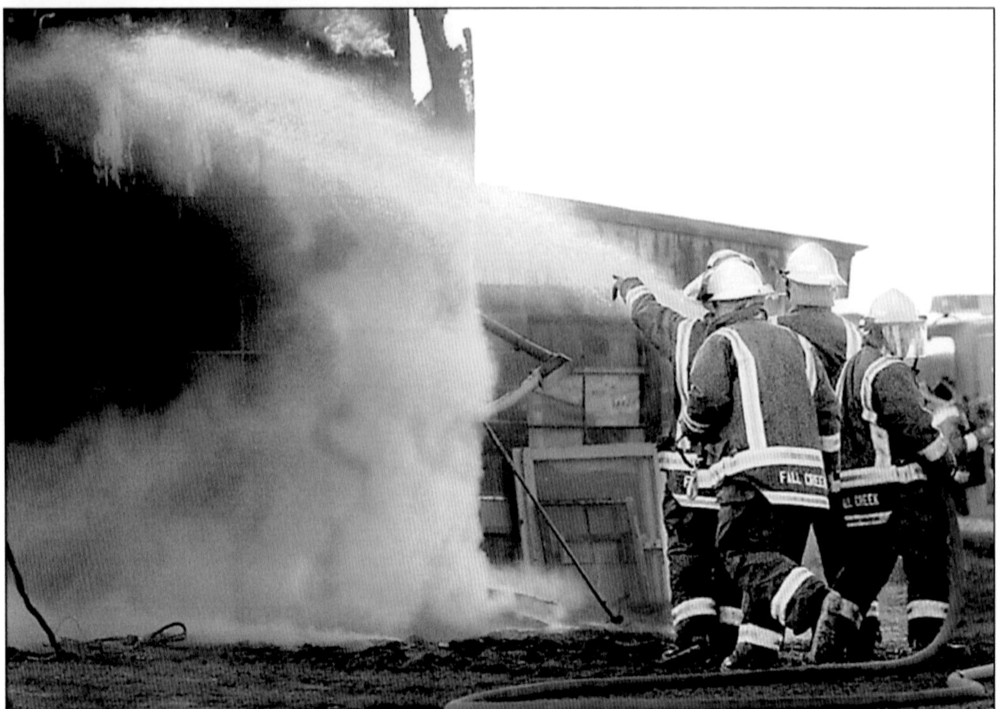

Fall Creek firefighters attack a fire that destroyed a barn on County Highway J, Town of Lincoln, April 2004. (Photograph by Steve Kinderman. Courtesy of the Eau Claire *Leader-Telegram*.)

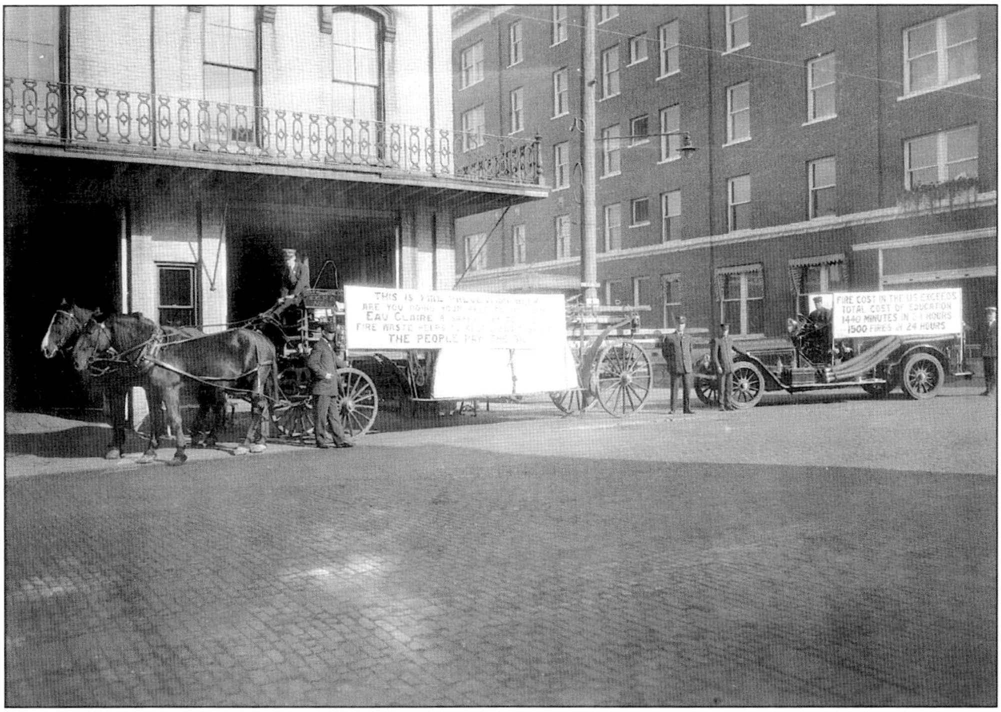

The Eau Claire Fire Department is pictured here in 1916. Shown from left to right are Charles Fraker, Fred Welsh, Nels Giroux, Heck Mayhew, Alvin Books, and J.P. Welsh. (CVM.)

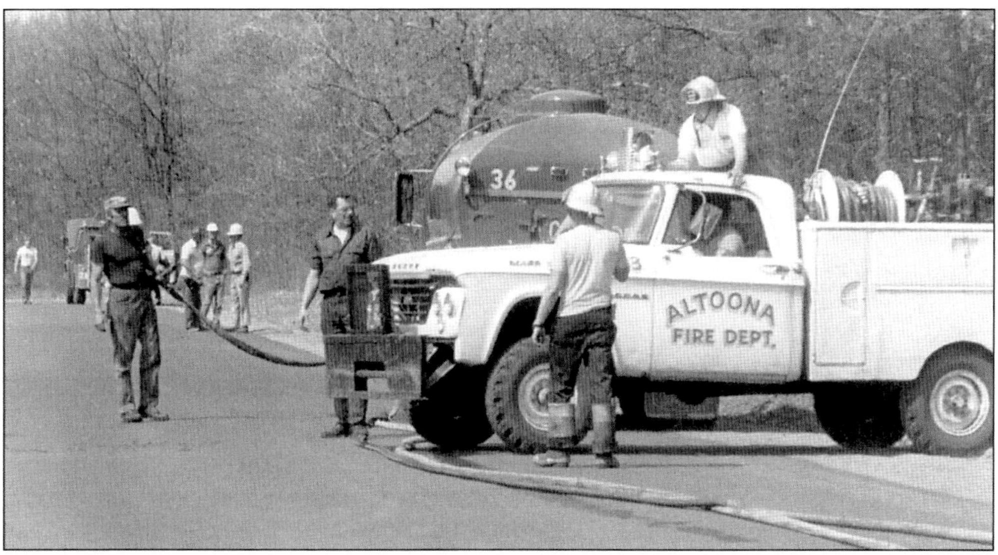

Pictured here is a training exercise for the Altoona Fire Department, mid-1970s. (CVM.)

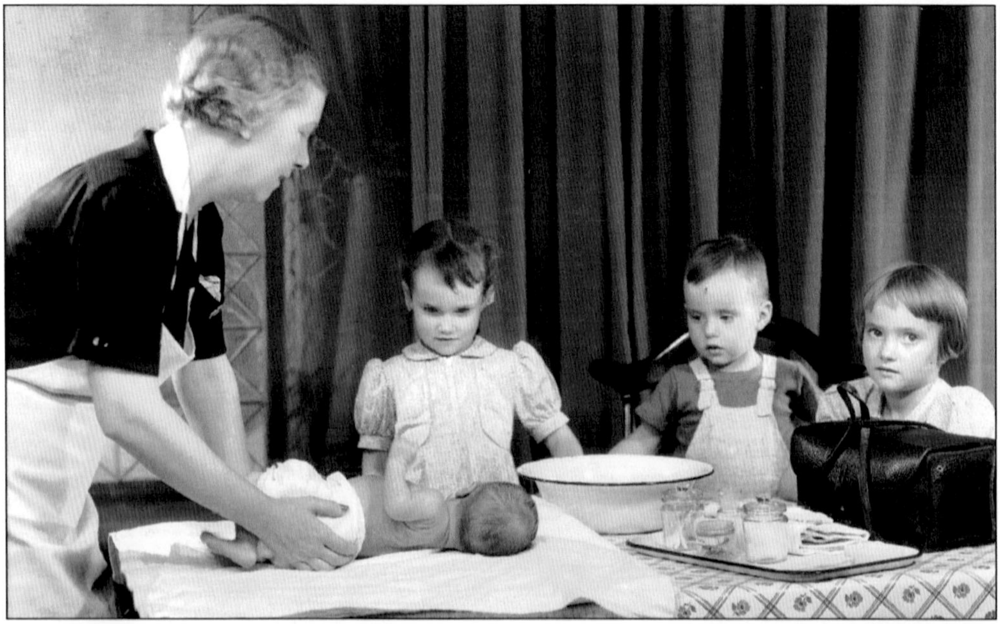

Doris Peterson, R.N., with the Visiting Nurse Association, instructs children of the Kenneth Loew family about the family's new baby, 1942. The Eau Claire chapter of the Visiting Nurse Association was the first in the state. In earlier years, it ran a tent clinic for tuberculosis patients and raised money to maintain a free hospital bed in Eau Claire. (CVM.)

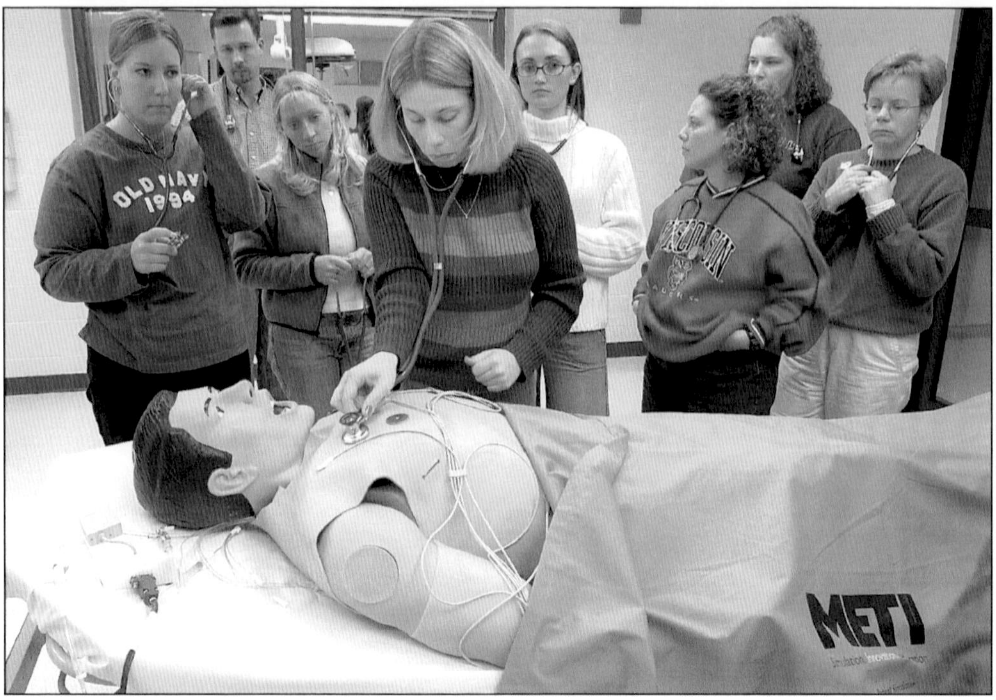

Charity Hoff, of Altoona, listens to the lungs of "Stan" during her Nursing Basic Assessment class at the Chippewa Valley Technical College, Eau Claire, September 2001. (Photograph by Andi Stempniak. Courtesy of the Eau Claire *Leader-Telegram*.)

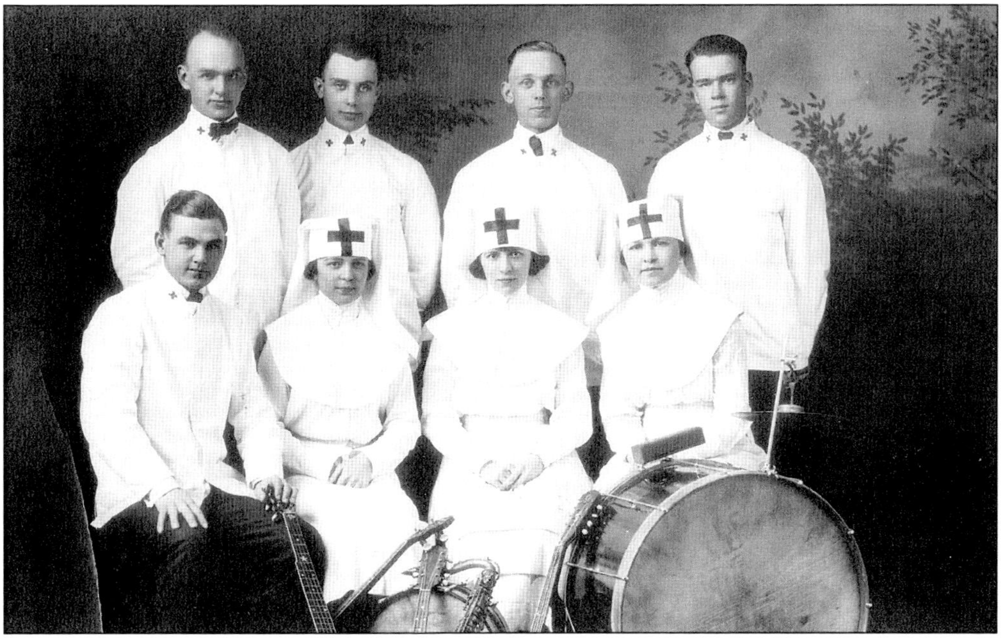

The Red Cross band of Eau Claire is pictured here in 1917. They played in the area to raise money for the Red Cross. Pictured from left to right are: (front) Homer Brodie, Frodie Lockwood, and Margaret Blum; (back row) Marvin T. Slagsvol, Carl Mason, Duane Lang, and Leo Johnson. (CVM.)

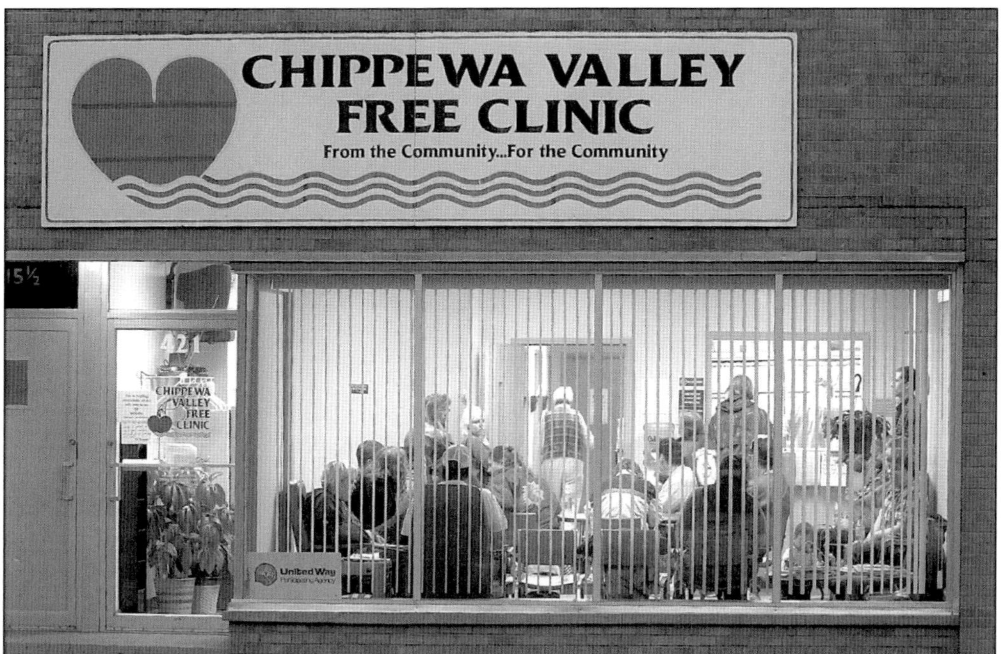

The waiting room is packed at the Chippewa Valley Free Clinic, Eau Claire, October 2001. (Photograph by Shane Opatz. Courtesy of the Eau Claire *Leader-Telegram*.)

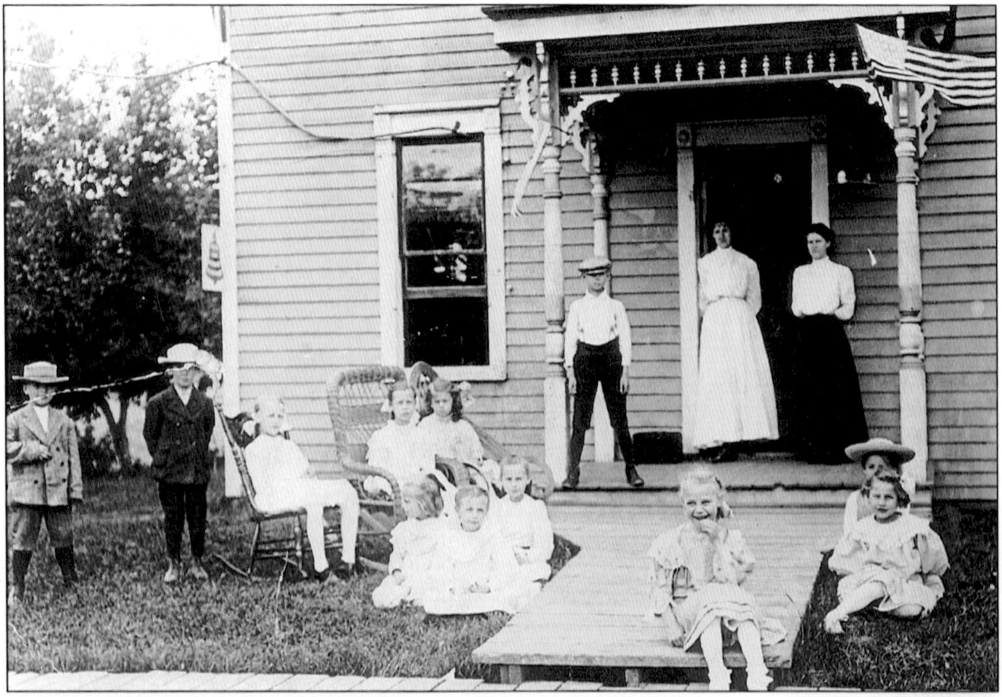

This is the Fall Creek Telephone Office in 1907. Louise Roesler (in white dress on porch) was the first switchboard operator. Girls in chairs, from left to right, are Grace Roesler, Lydia Kunz, and Alma Hoehn. George Roesler is the boy on the porch. (FCHS.)

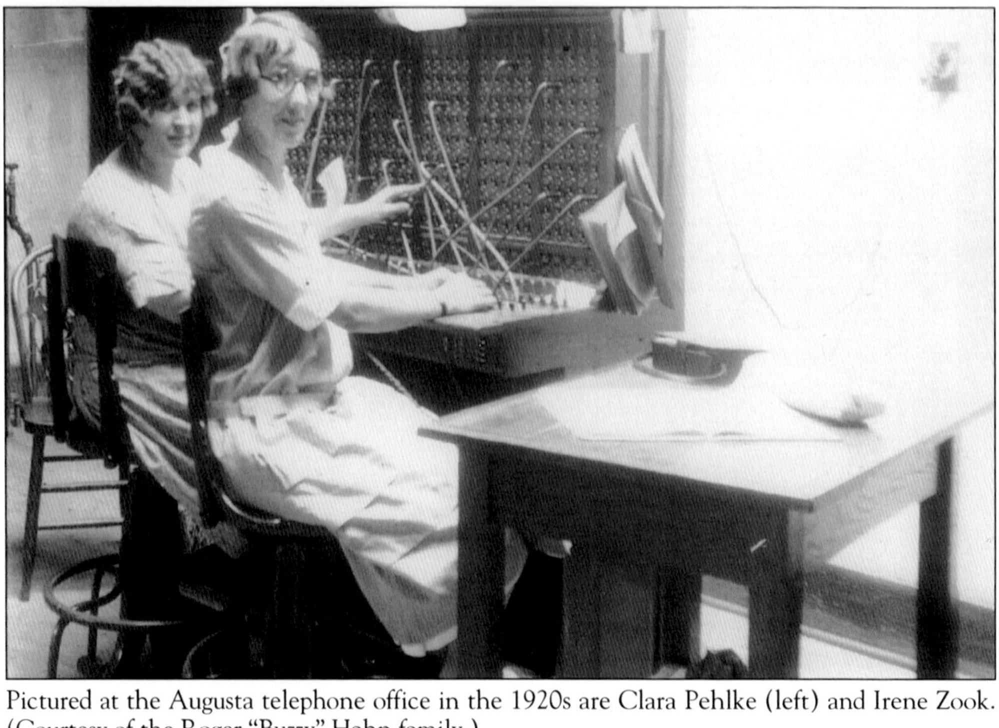

Pictured at the Augusta telephone office in the 1920s are Clara Pehlke (left) and Irene Zook. (Courtesy of the Roger "Buzzy" Hahn family.)

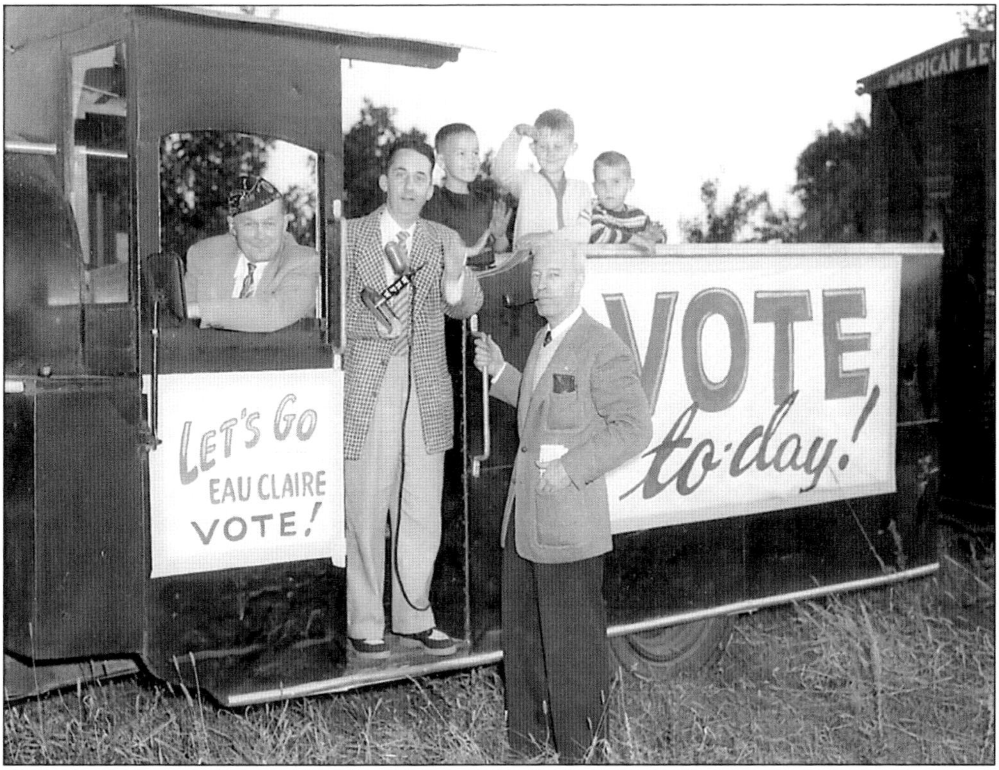

American Legion Service Officer Jack Kelly sits in the driver's seat of this 1932 parade float on Lincoln chassis, while A. Owen Ayres (with pipe) stands below. (CVM.)

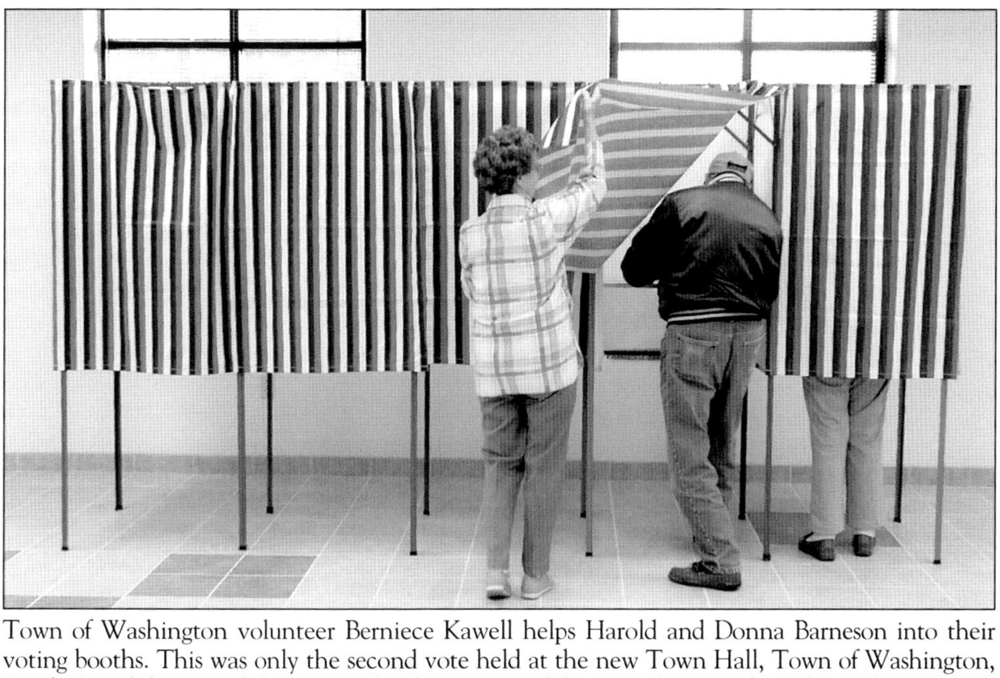
Town of Washington volunteer Berniece Kawell helps Harold and Donna Barneson into their voting booths. This was only the second vote held at the new Town Hall, Town of Washington, April 2004. (Photograph by Dan Reiland. Courtesy of the Eau Claire *Leader-Telegram*.)

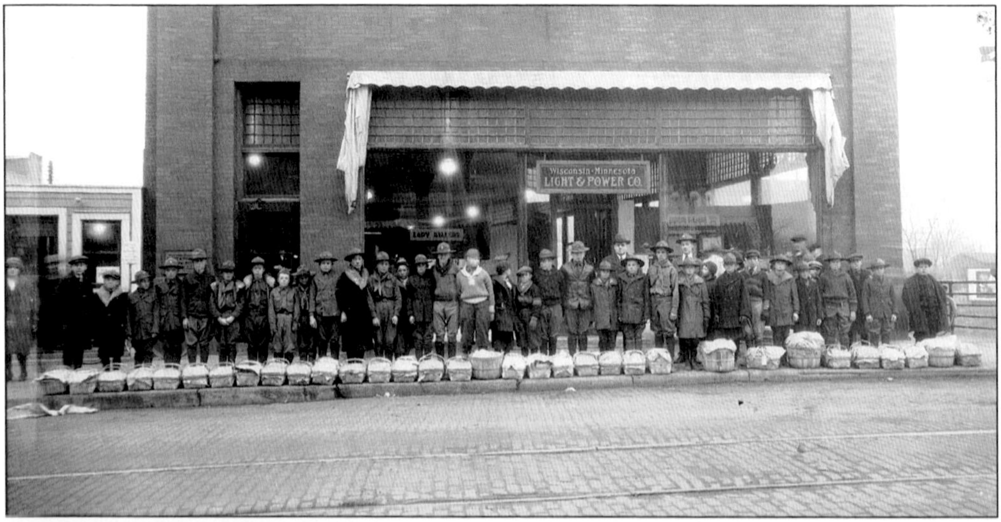

Boy Scouts with holiday gift baskets stand in front of the Wisconsin-Minnesota Power & Light Company, downtown Eau Claire, probably between 1918 and 1922. The "doughboy" hat became popular after World War I. By 1922, all Boy Scouts were required to wear standard uniforms. (CVM.)

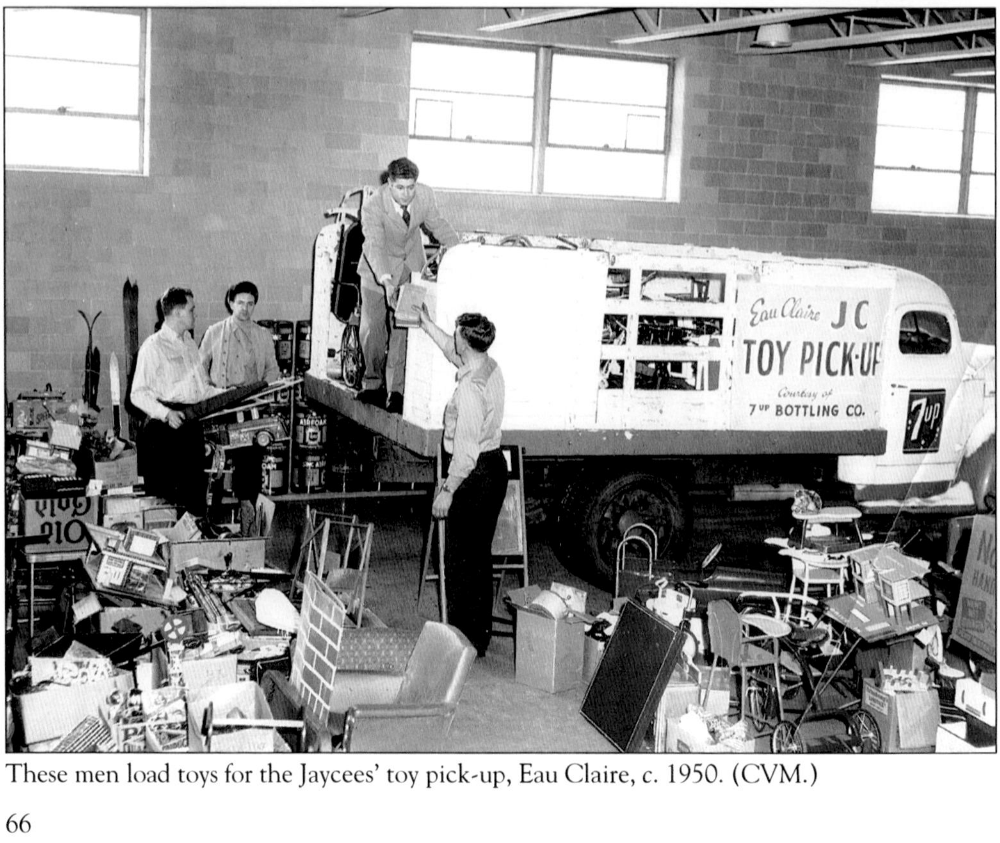

These men load toys for the Jaycees' toy pick-up, Eau Claire, c. 1950. (CVM.)

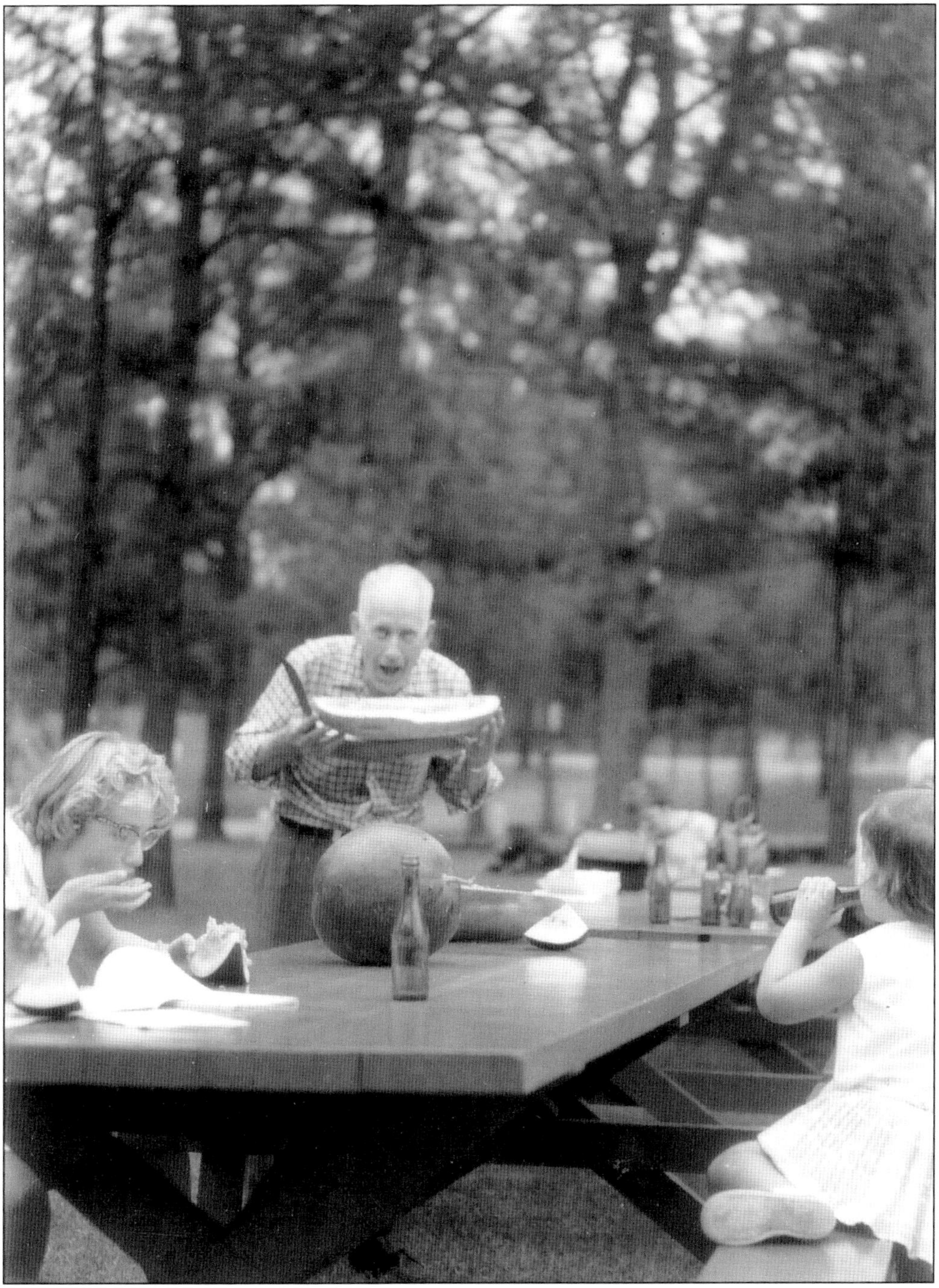

Clarence Bolles clowns around with a hunk of watermelon at a Telephone Pioneers picnic, Lake Eau Claire Park, Augusta, September 1962. In 2004, Telecom Pioneers (as the organization is now known) had more than 750,000 active and retired telecommunications workers from the U.S., Canada, and Mexico, and held claim to being the world's largest industry-related community service organization. (CVM.)

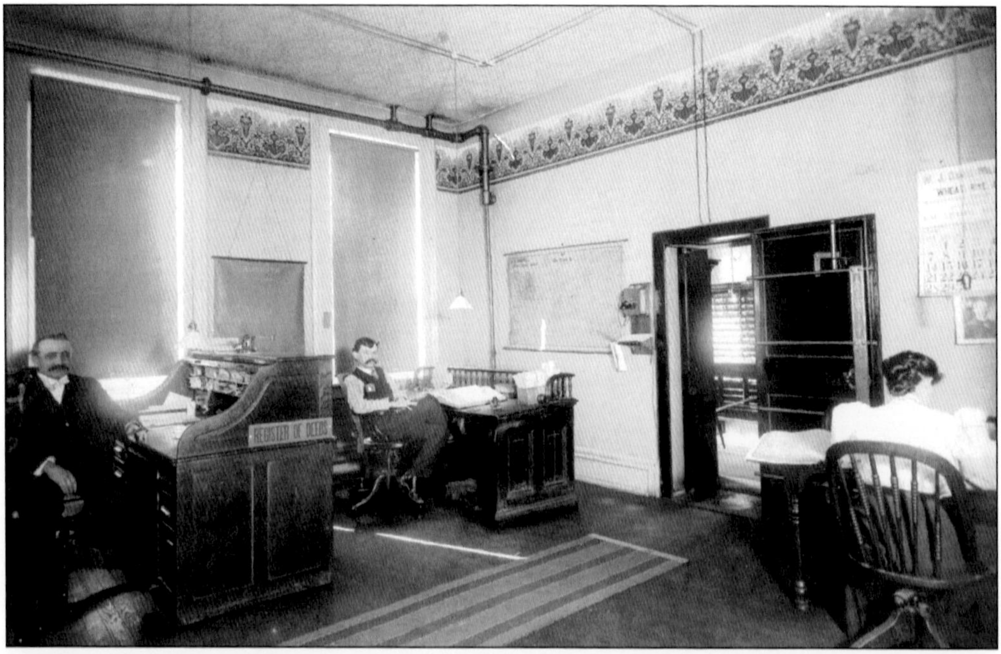

The Eau Claire County Register of Deeds office in Eau Claire is seen here, c. 1900. Pictured from left to right are Anton Anderson, Arthur Rilette, and Grace Barnes. (CVM.)

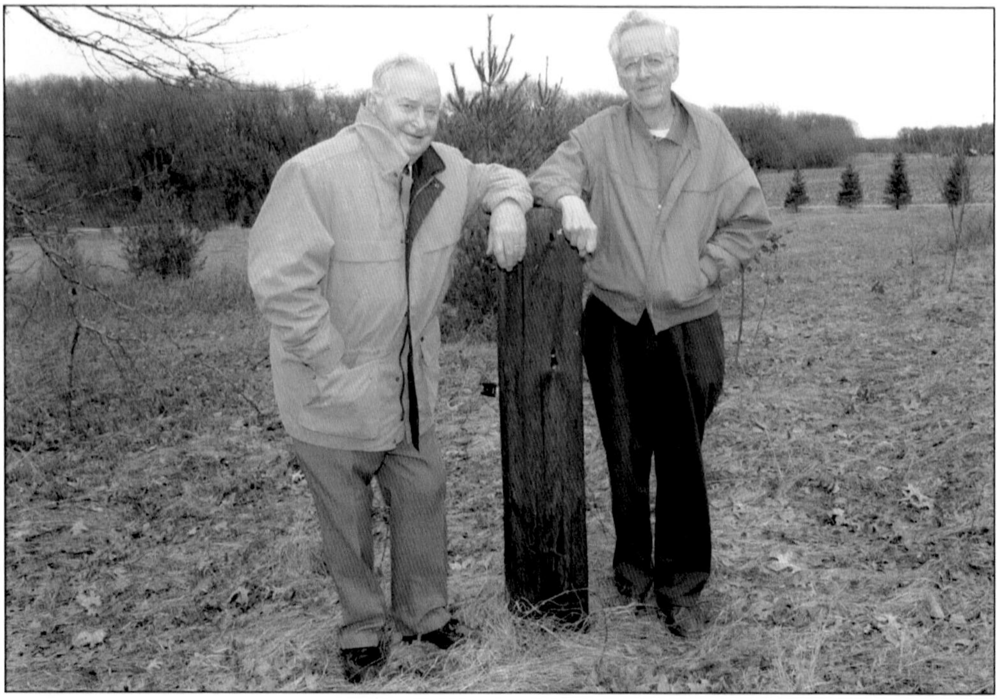

Ralph Guettinger and Garth Ryder stand in their respective Townships of Brunswick and Pleasant Valley along Maple Road, near County Highway F, April 2001. Both men retired from their town boards that year. (Photograph by Dan Reiland. Courtesy of the Eau Claire *Leader-Telegram*.)

Six

A Place for Work and Commerce

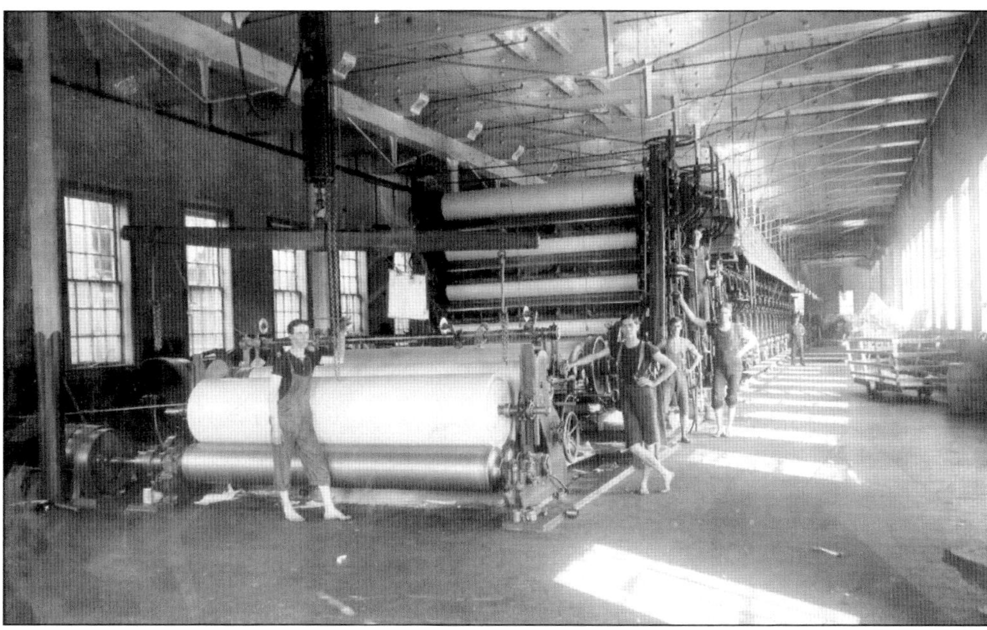

Workers pose for this picture at the Eau Claire Paper Mill in 1910. In 1881, W.B. Beach asked the city for enough water rights to run a 200-horsepower wheel, 10 acres of land, and $5,500 cash. He was going to build a paper mill. Beach brought in a milling machine 110 feet long on six rail cars. By 1884, the Dells Paper and Pulp Company was producing 2 million pounds of paper and paying a local payroll of $27,000 (well over a half-million in year 2000 dollars). (CVM.)

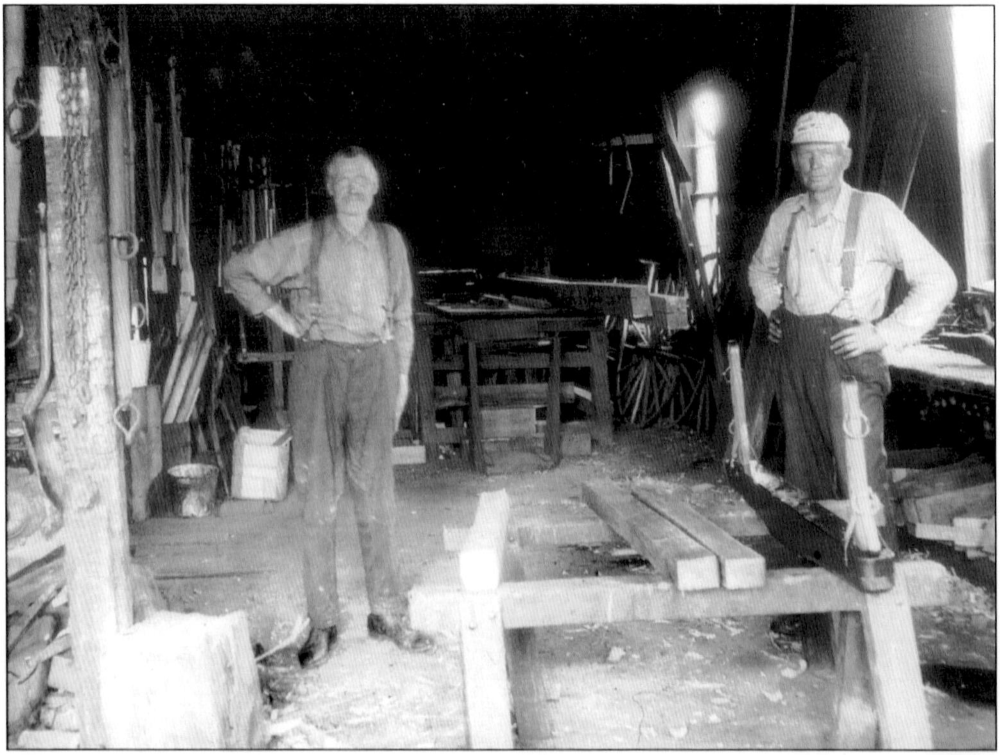

This is the Brown Blacksmith Shop in Augusta, 1920s. (Courtesy of the Roger "Buzzy" Hahn family.)

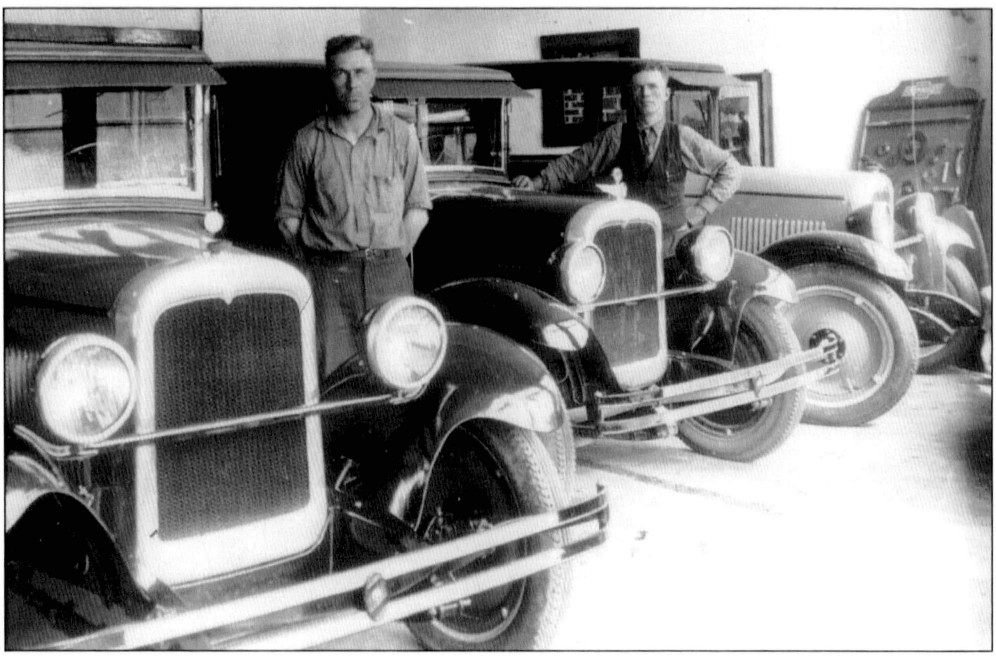

The Augusta Auto Company is pictured here in the 1920s. (Courtesy of the Roger "Buzzy" Hahn family.)

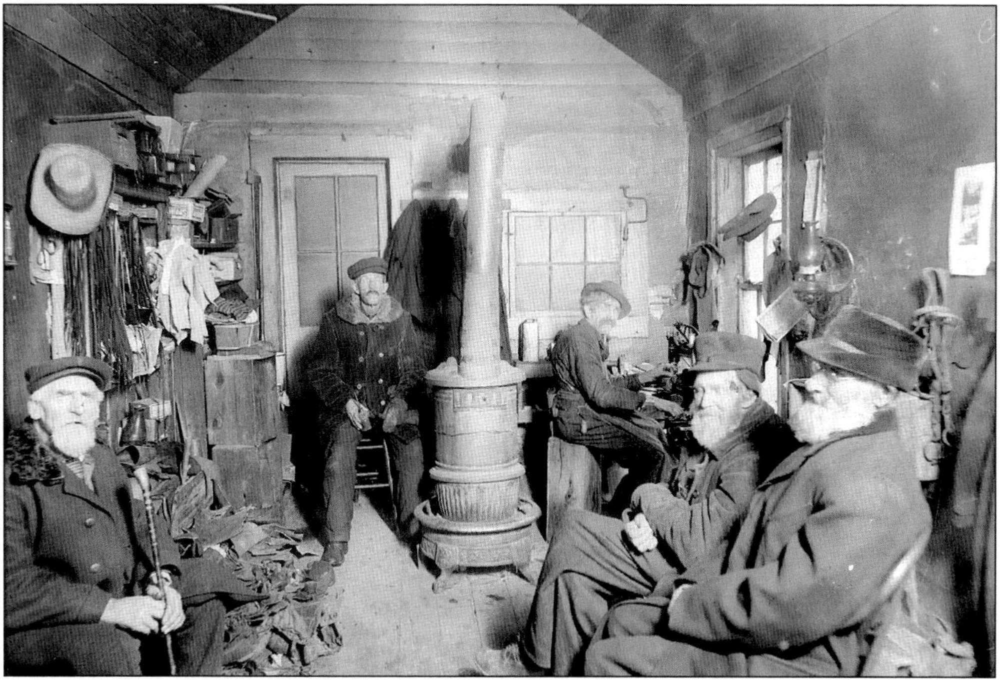

Gathered at a shoe shop in Augusta in 1910 are, from left to right, Mr. Tebo, Mr. Searle, Kelsey Dennison, Edwin West, and Mr. Sheppard. (CVM.)

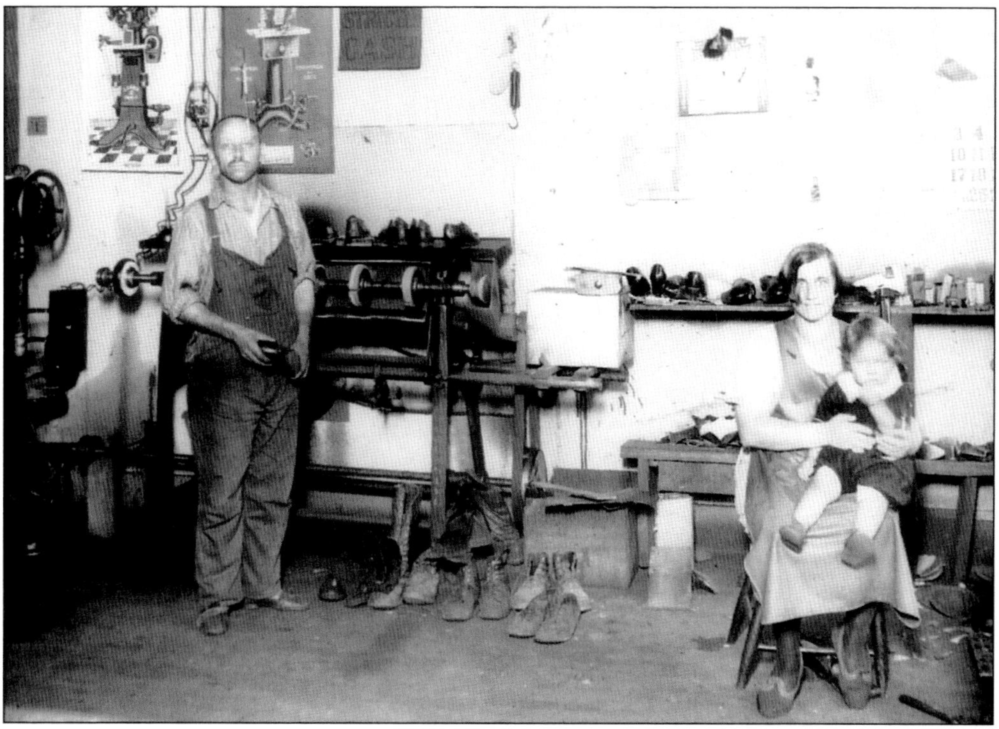

Mr. and Mrs. Frank Lowry are photographed at the Lowry Shoe Shop, Augusta, 1920s. (Courtesy of the Roger "Buzzy" Hahn family.)

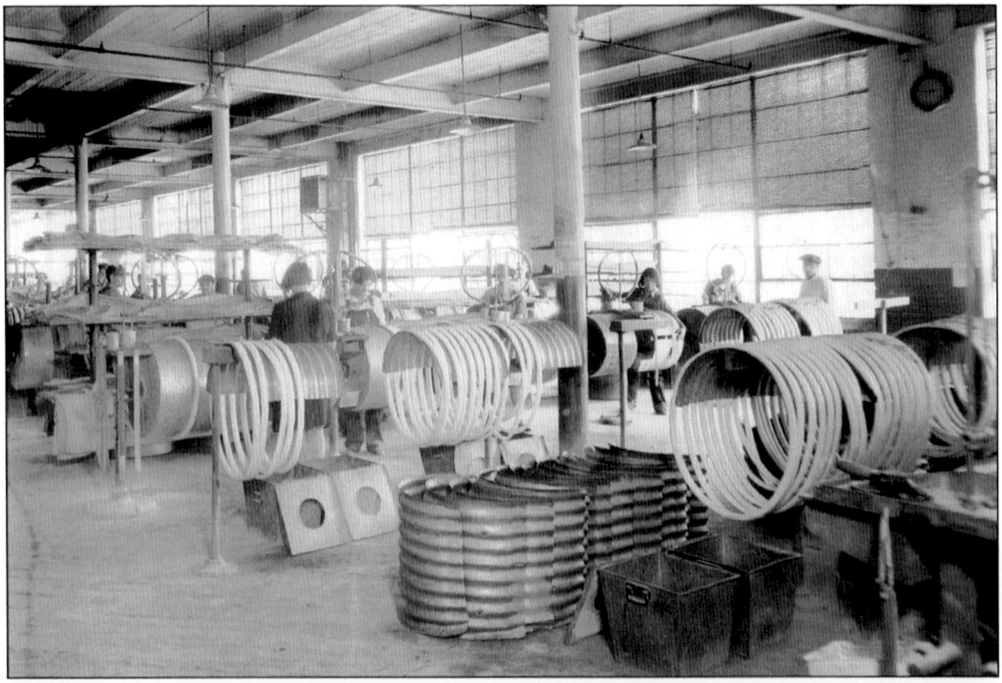

Men and women work in the bicycle tire building department at the Gillette Rubber Company, Eau Claire, probably in the 1920s. Gillette became Uniroyal-Goodrich. (CVM.)

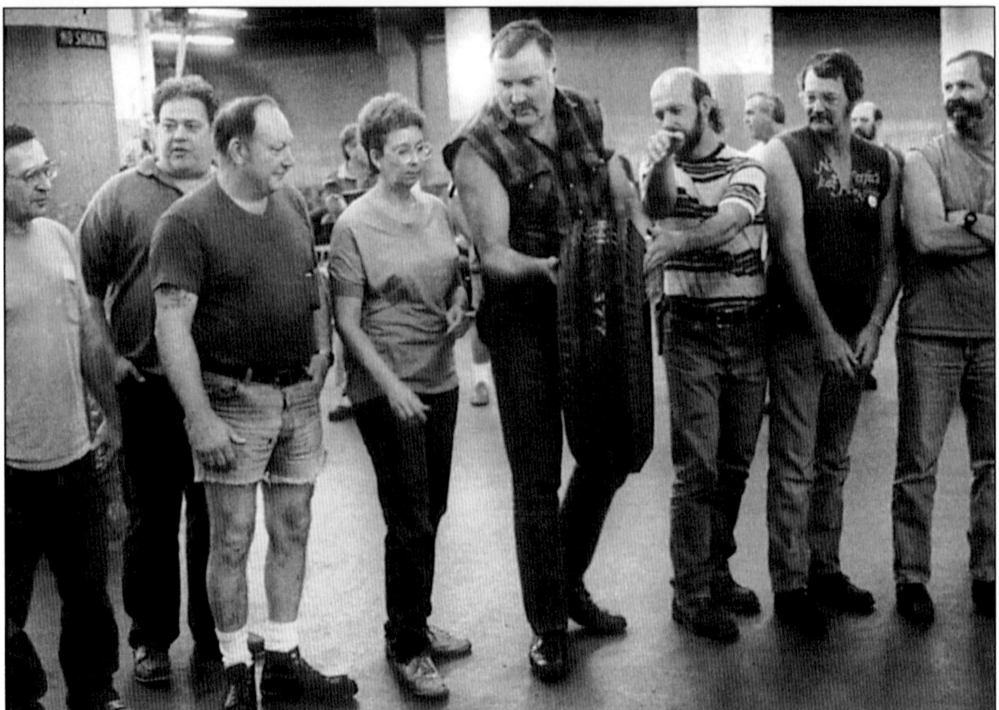

Uniroyal-Goodrich worker John Kinville takes his turn passing the last tire shipped from the plant after 75 years in operation, Eau Claire, June 1992. (CVM.)

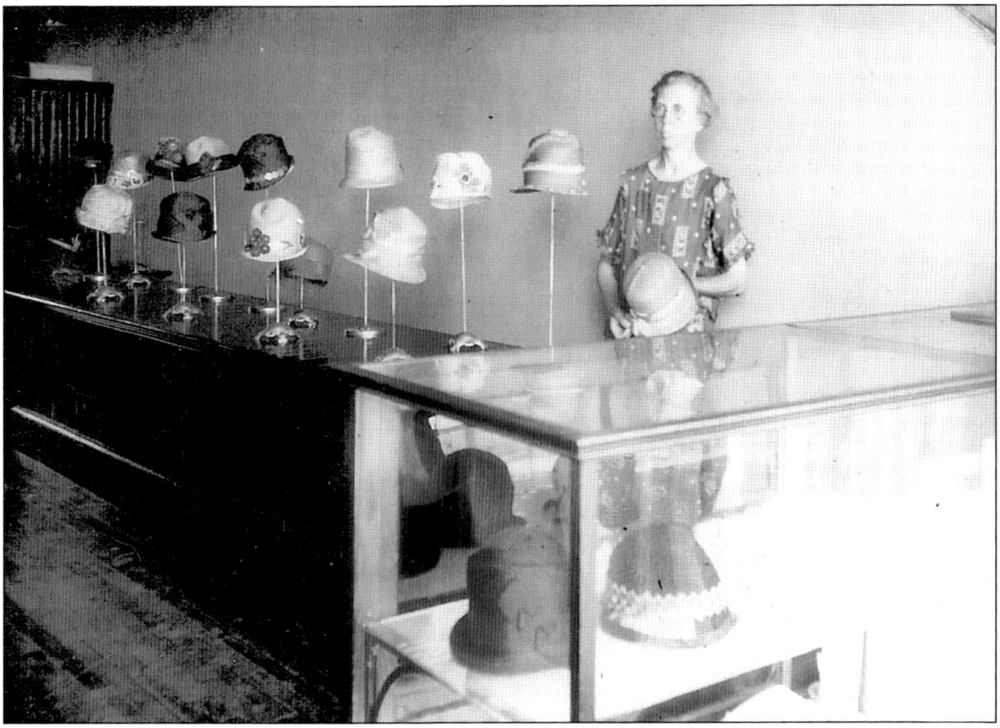

Mattie Justesen in seen here in her millinery shop, Augusta, 1920s. (Courtesy of the Roger "Buzzy" Hahn family.)

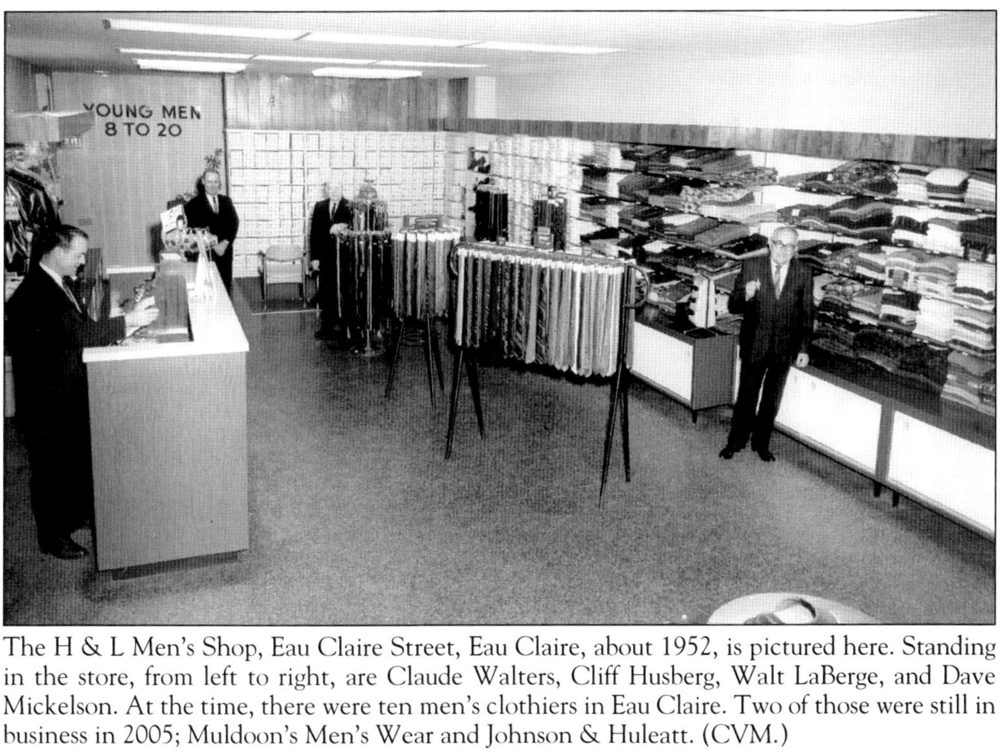

The H & L Men's Shop, Eau Claire Street, Eau Claire, about 1952, is pictured here. Standing in the store, from left to right, are Claude Walters, Cliff Husberg, Walt LaBerge, and Dave Mickelson. At the time, there were ten men's clothiers in Eau Claire. Two of those were still in business in 2005; Muldoon's Men's Wear and Johnson & Huleatt. (CVM.)

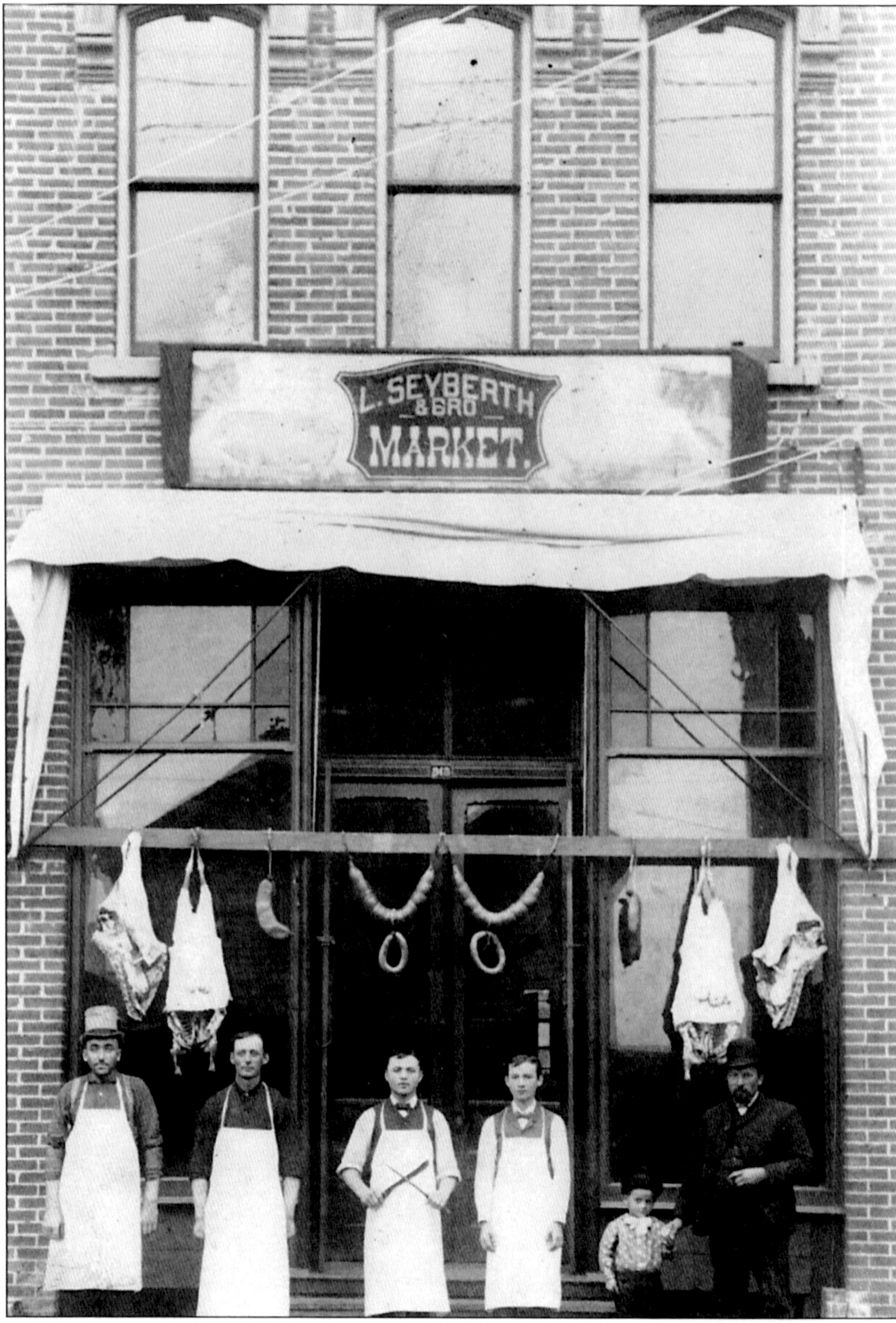

Pictured here in the 1880s is the L. Seyberth & Brother Meat Market, Bellinger Street, Eau Claire. Leonard Seyberth, far left, was the owner, shown here with his sons William, John, and George. The two standing at right are unidentified. (CVM.)

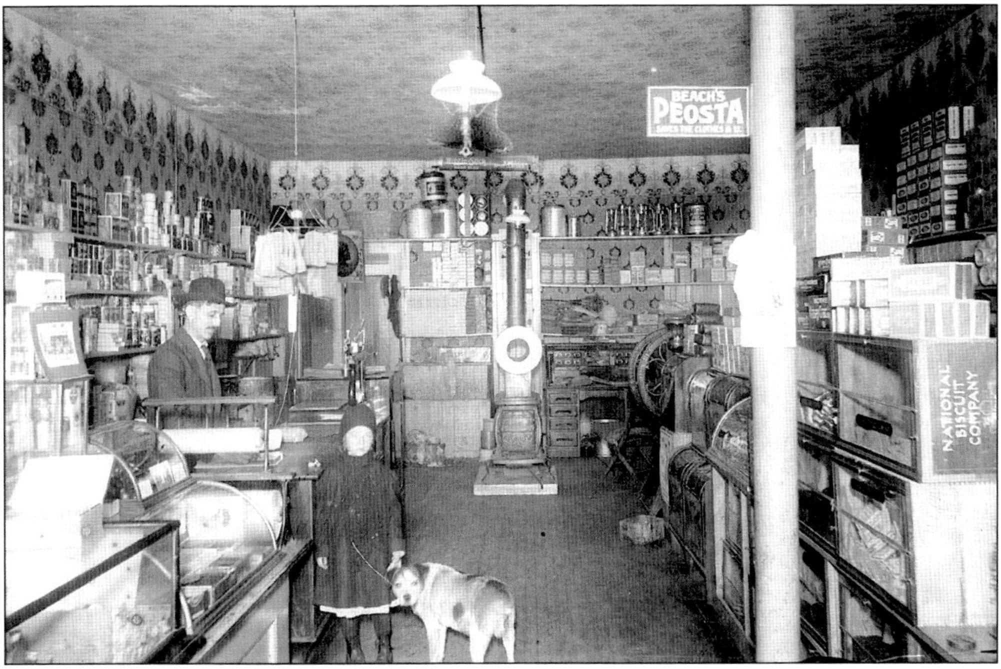

Felix Deroin stands behind the counter of his grocery store, and Onastasia Neary and her dog stand in front. The store was at 834 Water Street, Eau Claire, 1905-1914. Deroin came to Eau Claire from Canada in 1889 and opened his grocery store in 1892. He retired in 1915. His brother Joseph ran a tavern at 858 Water Street. In 1890, 70 percent of the people living in the Chippewa Valley had either been born outside the U.S., or had foreign-born parents. (CVM.)

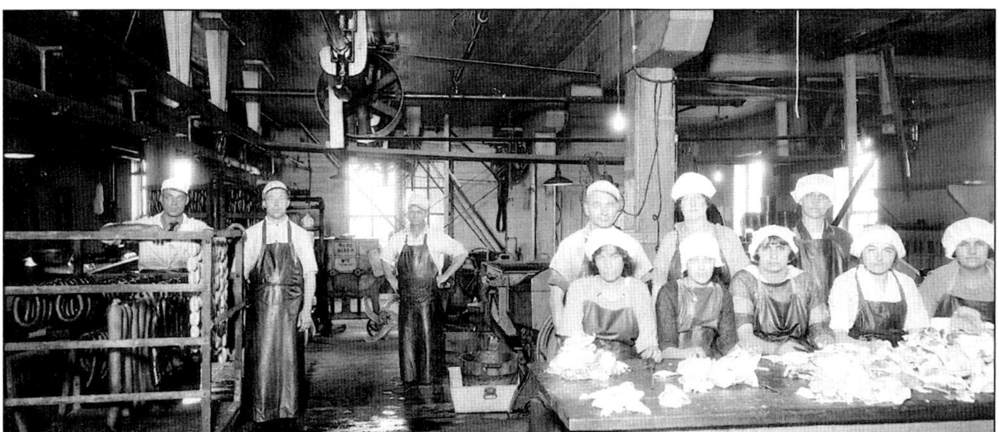

The Drummond Meat Packing Plant in Eau Claire is seen here after World War I. In 1895, after 25 years in business, David, Duncan, and John Drummond built a new facility, which took up an entire block of Barstow Street. By 1900, it had expanded again, moving its main office and cold storage to Galloway Street. At that date, Drummond could butcher 500 hogs a day, and shipped meat throughout the U.S. and Canada, as well as to Europe. During World War II, the company opened a canning line; it produced 4 million pounds of meat for the government. After the war, the plant was sold to a division of Safeway Stores, which shut it down. Armour Food Company reopened the plant, producing frozen beef for shipment out of state. (CVM.)

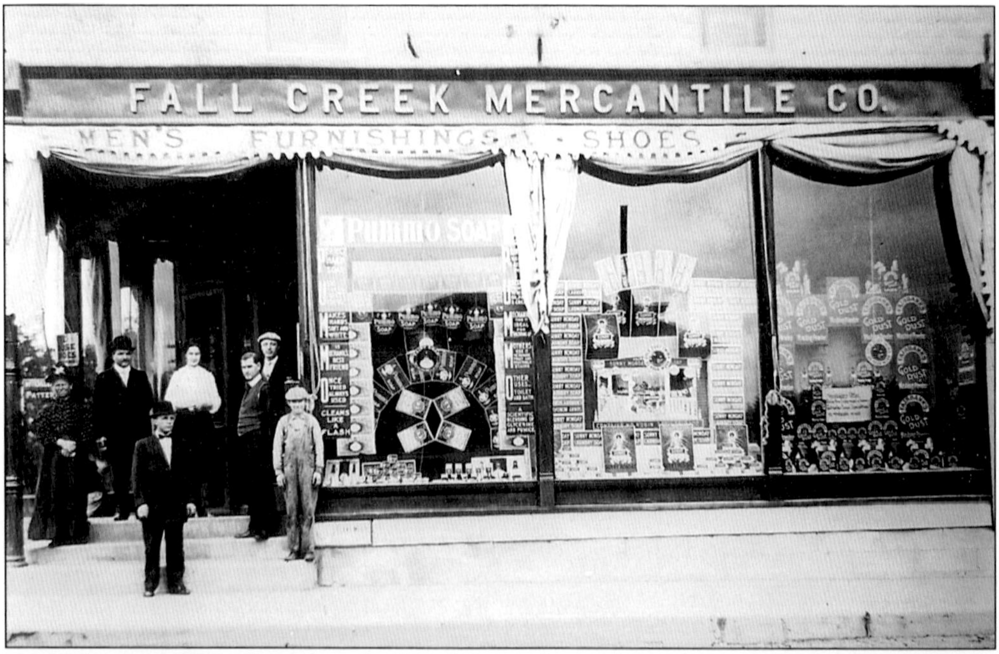

Pictured at the Fall Creek Mercantile, from left to right on the steps, are Mrs. Lane, J.E. Zetzman, George Zetzman, Lydia Plath, Fred Perso, Ed Zetzman, and Sigmund (Zich) Heuer. (FCHS.)

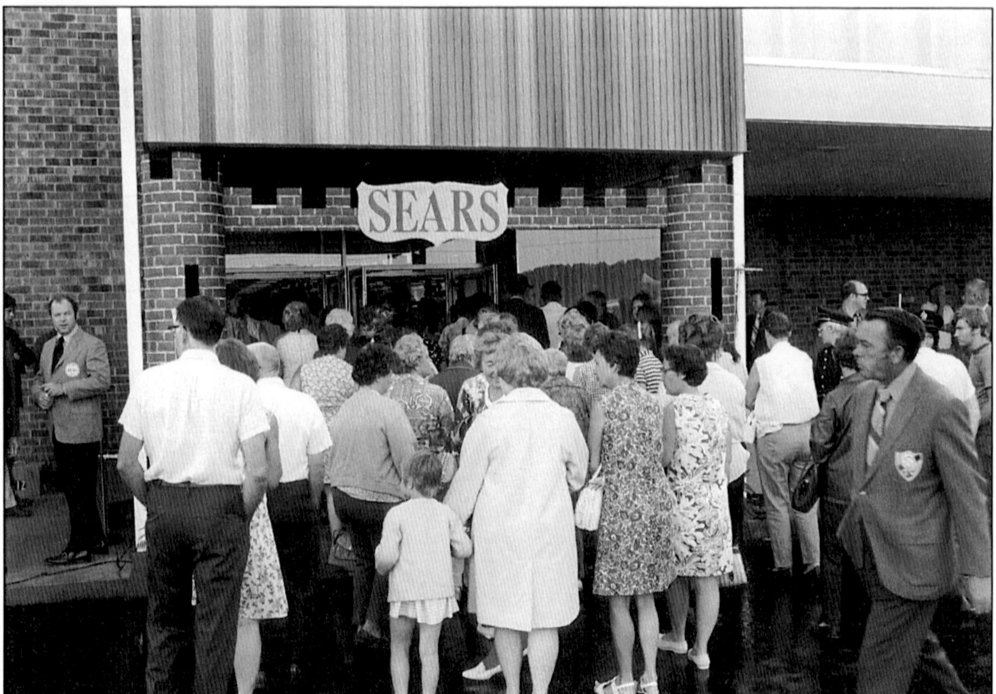

Shoppers line up in anticipation of the new Sears store at London Square Mall, Eau Claire, September 1971. (CVM.)

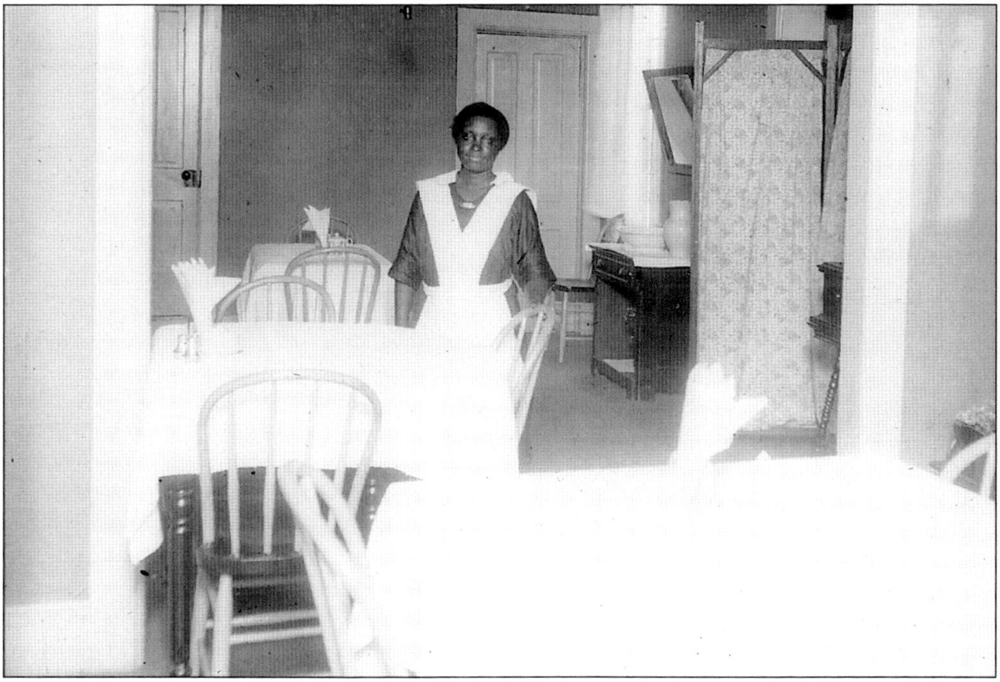

Mary Christopher poses for a photograph in her Augusta restaurant, 1920s. (Courtesy of Roger "Buzzy" Hahn family.)

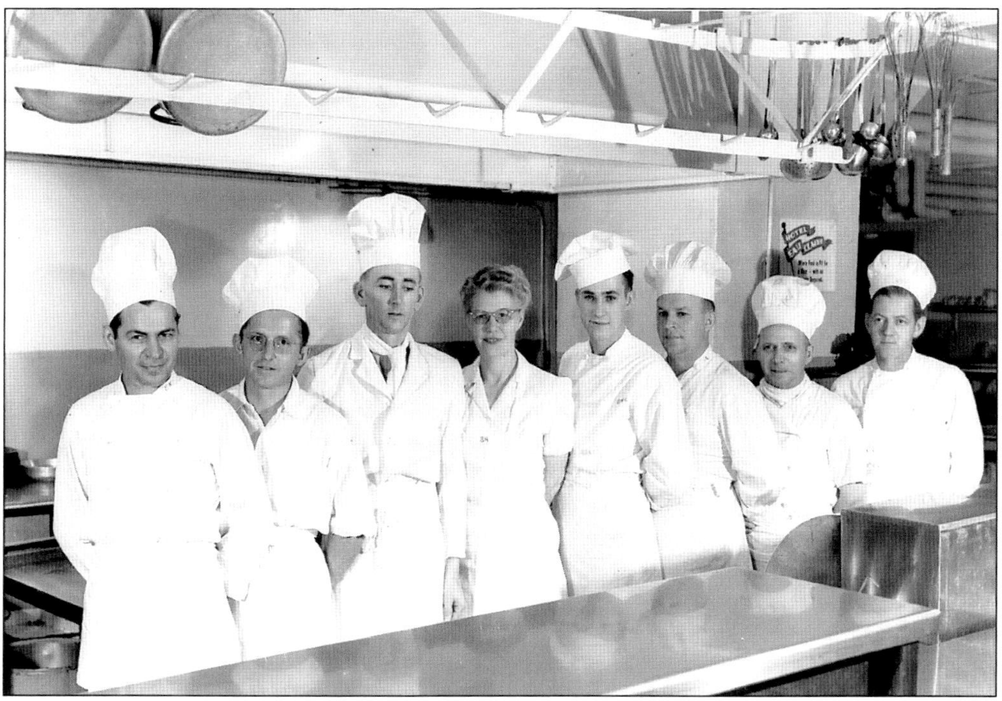

Cooks at the Hotel Eau Claire, June 1949, are, from left to right, Bob Kenne, Bob Shock, Mauria Perry, Bernice Hanke Baker, butcher Gene Chinnock, and head chefs Albert Sobel, Bill Ross, and Jim Fitch. (CVM.)

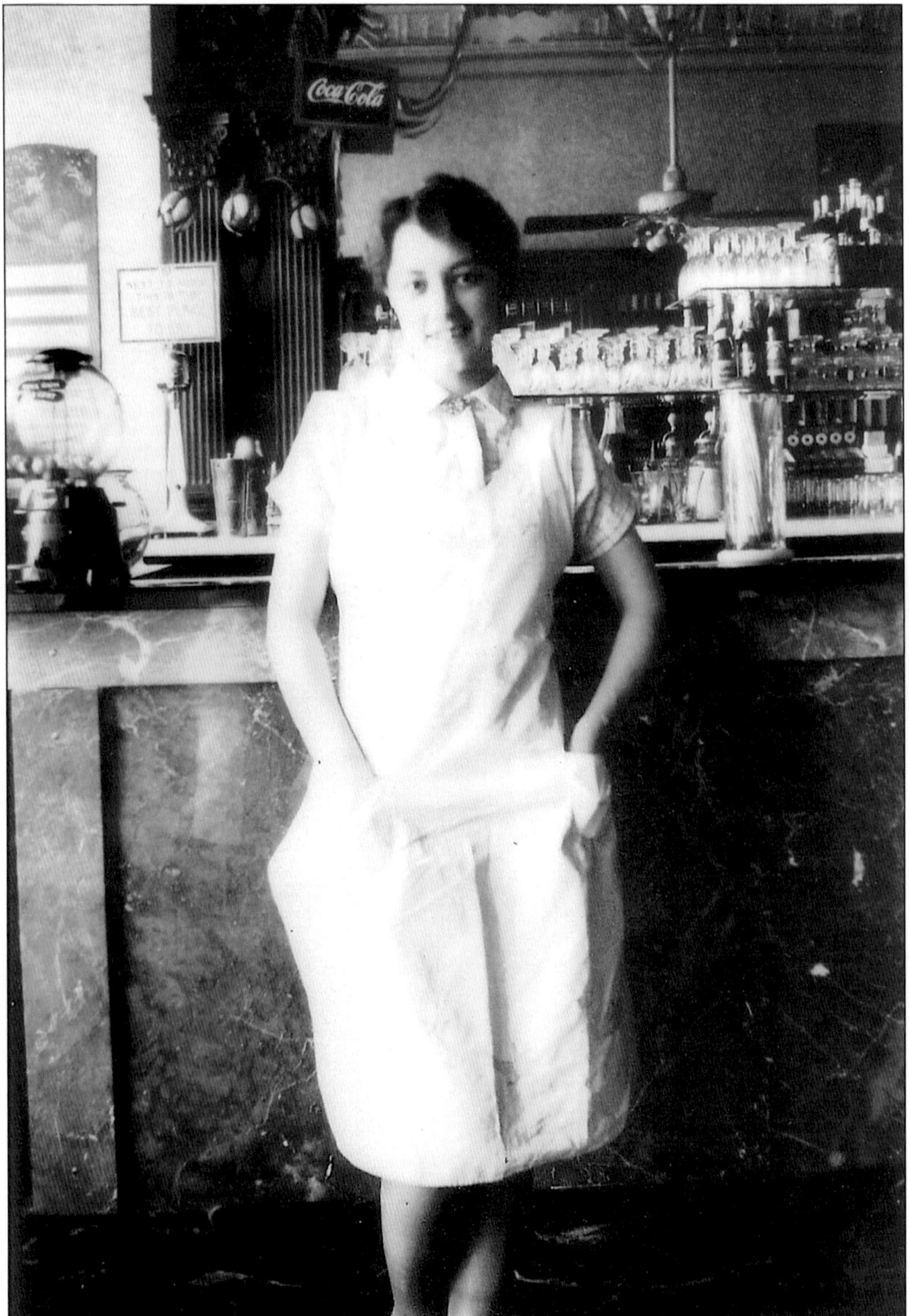

Lucille Hoesly is pictured here at Dor Smith's, Eau Claire, *c.* 1927. Dor Smith's was an ice cream parlor and tobacco shop. (CVM.)

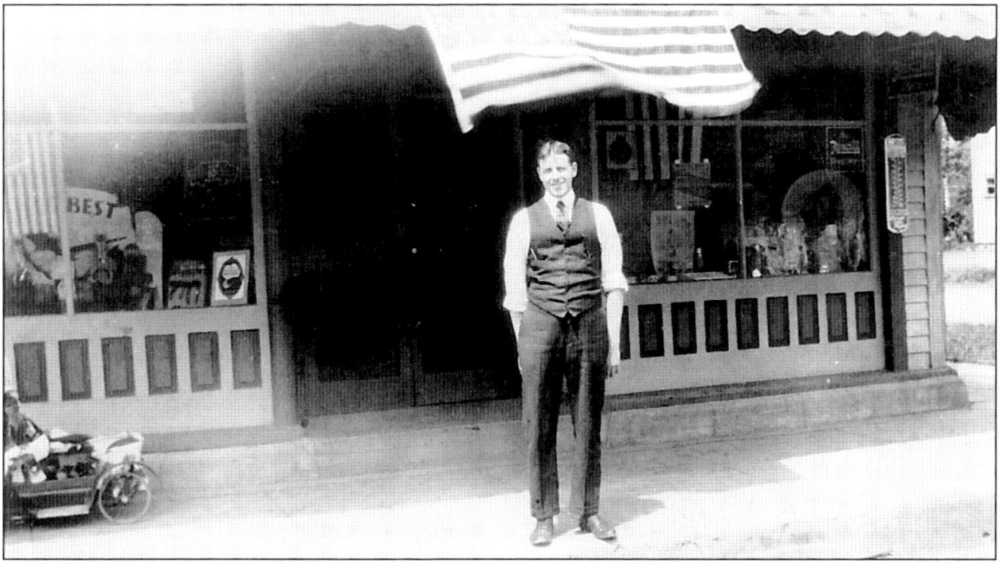

Alfred Bjerke, a registered pharmacist, bought Hoehn's Pharmacy in Fall Creek in 1922, when this photograph was taken. For the next 37 years, he worked with his wife Elsie and his two brothers, Orville and Jul. After Alfred's death in 1959, Elsie ran the store herself. The Bjerke's son Paul continued to manage the store until 1977, when it closed. As of 2004, the countertop and equipment were still in use at the ice cream parlor inside the Chippewa Valley Museum in Eau Claire. (CVM.)

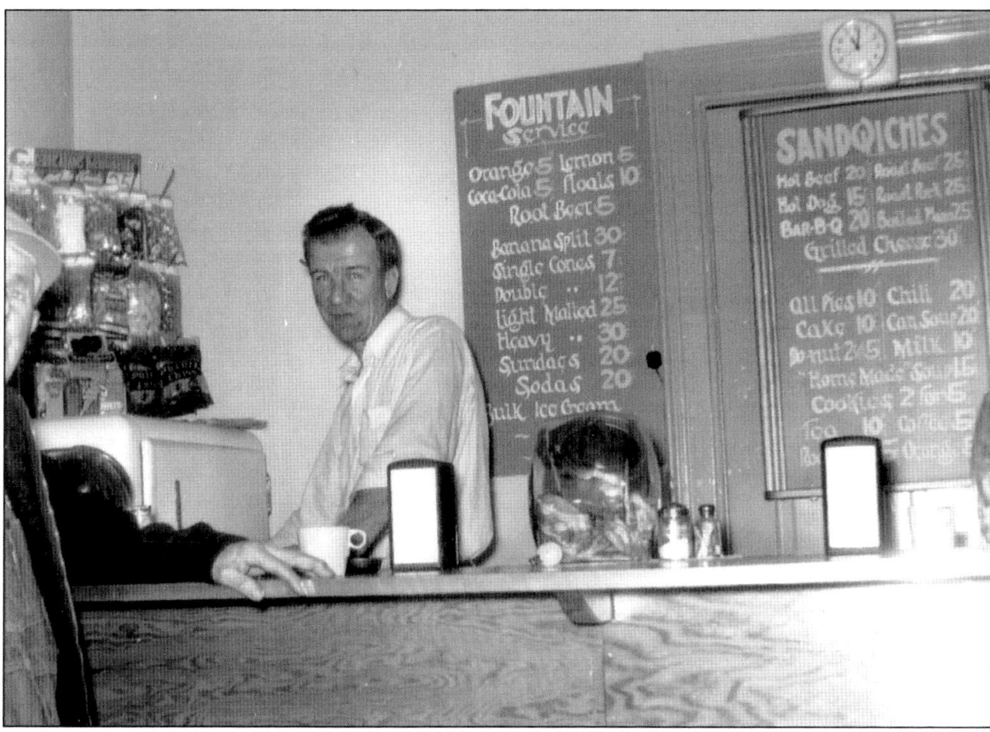

Herbert Neuman stands behind the counter at the drug store and restaurant in Fairchild, 1950. (Courtesy of Alice (nee Larson) Pingel.)

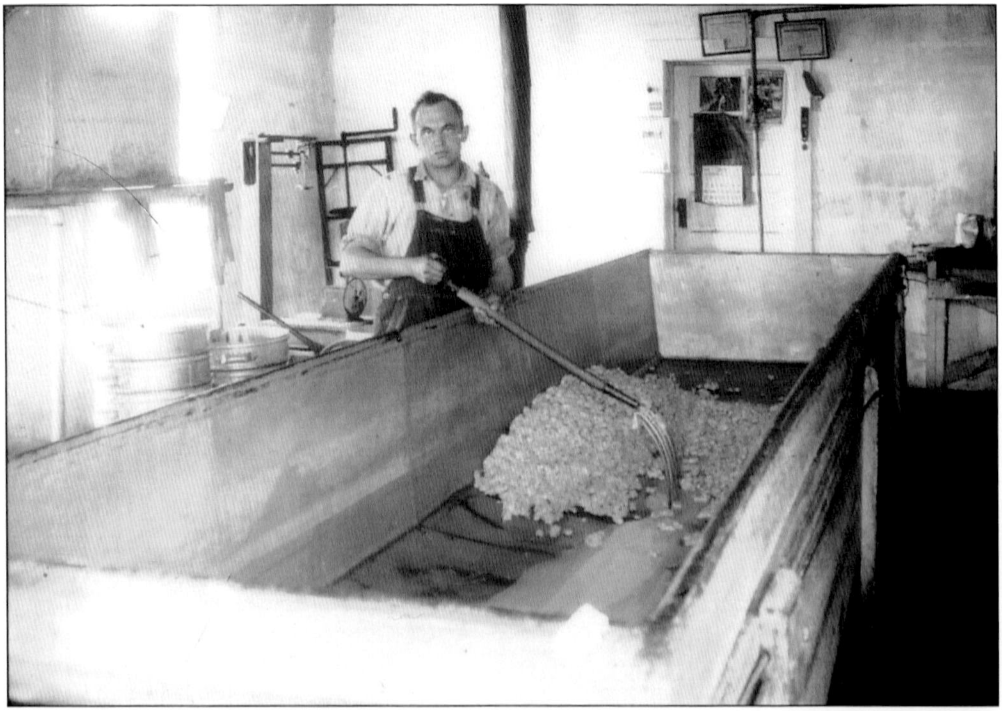

Carlson's Cheese Factory, Augusta, is seen here in the 1920s. (Courtesy of the Roger "Buzzy" Hahn family.)

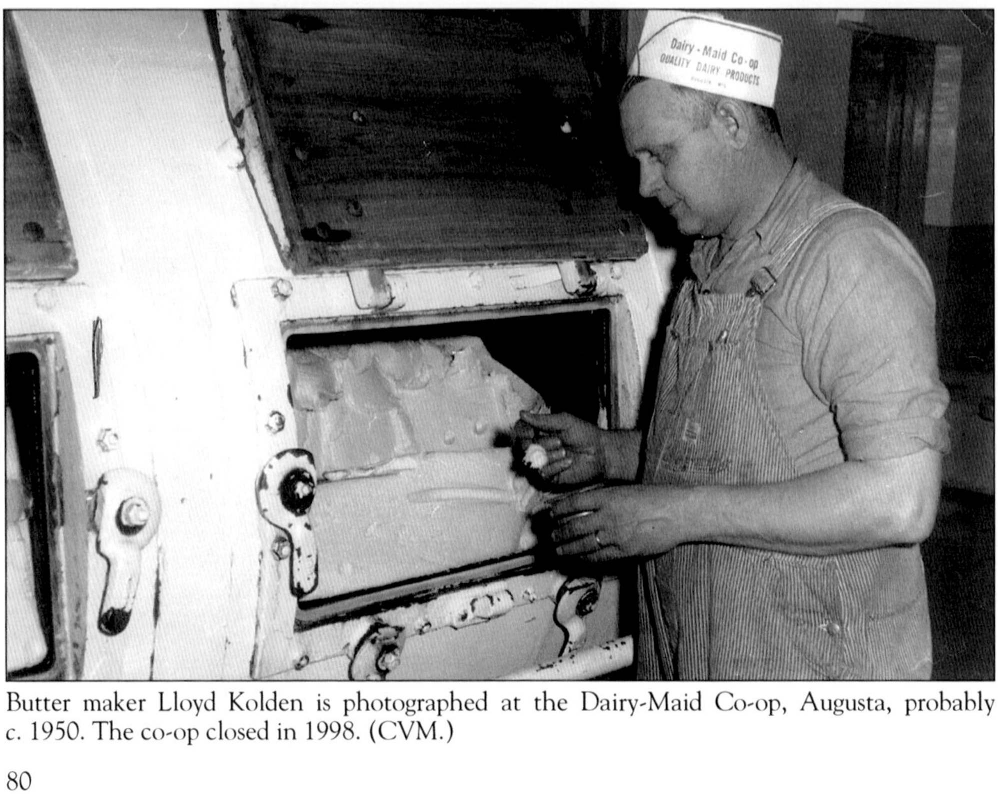

Butter maker Lloyd Kolden is photographed at the Dairy-Maid Co-op, Augusta, probably c. 1950. The co-op closed in 1998. (CVM.)

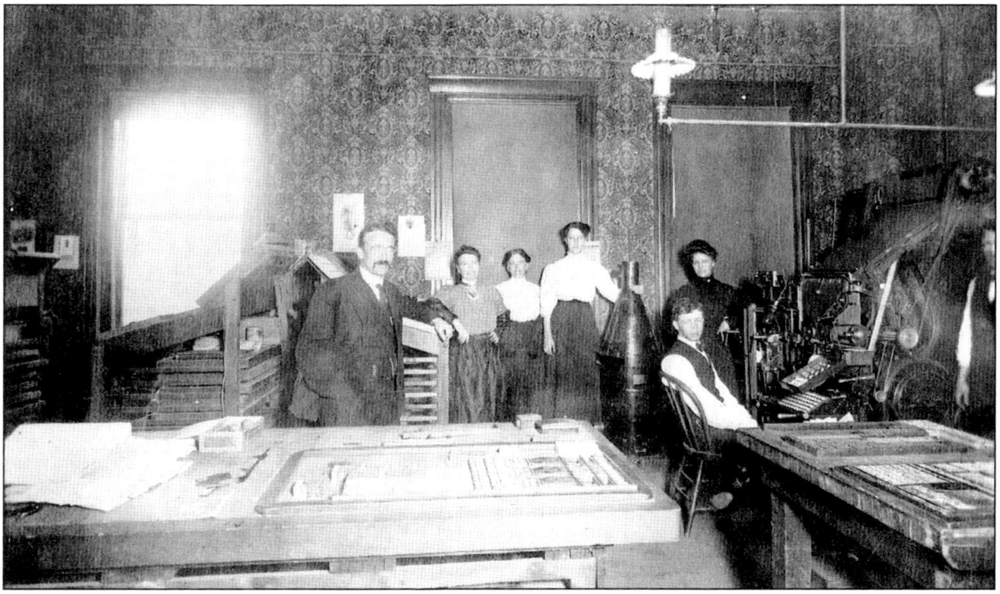

Waldemar Ager (left) poses with print shop workers at Fremad Publishing, South Barstow Street, Eau Claire, 1907-8. Ager (1869-1941) was an author, lecturer, Norwegian-American advocate, and temperance proponent. In the late 1990s, Ager's home was moved to 514 West Madison Street, where volunteers have restored the porch and trim to its original appearance and opened it for programs and exhibitions. The Ager Association was formed to preserve his literary heritage. (Courtesy of the Eivind Ager collection. CVM.)

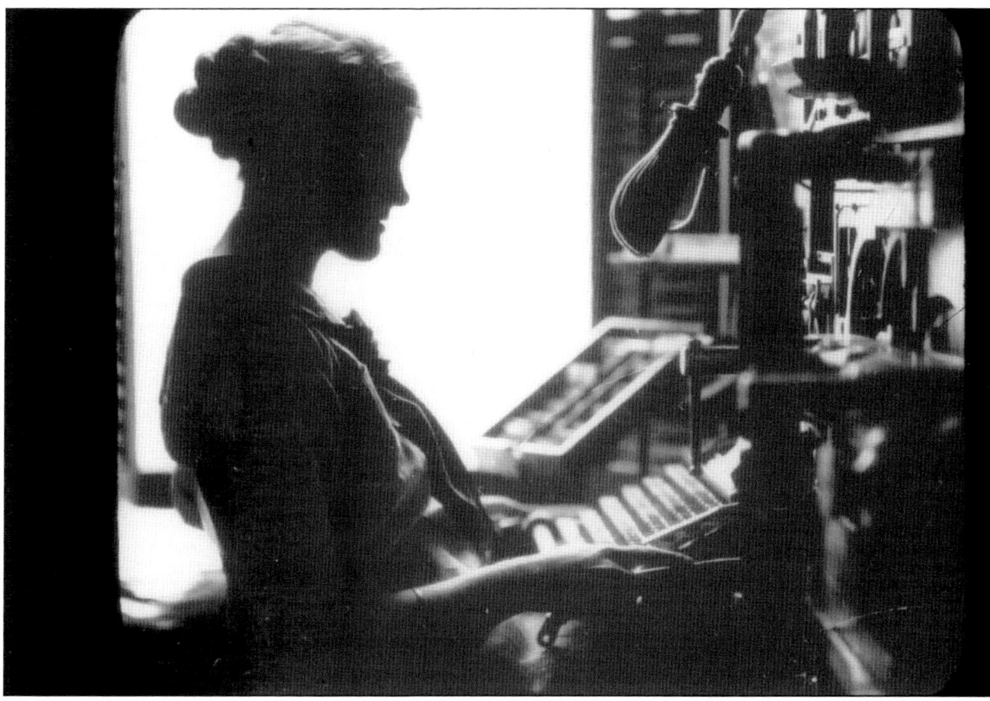

Mrs. Krenz sets type at the Augusta Area *Times* in the 1920s. (Courtesy of the Roger "Buzzy" Hahn family.)

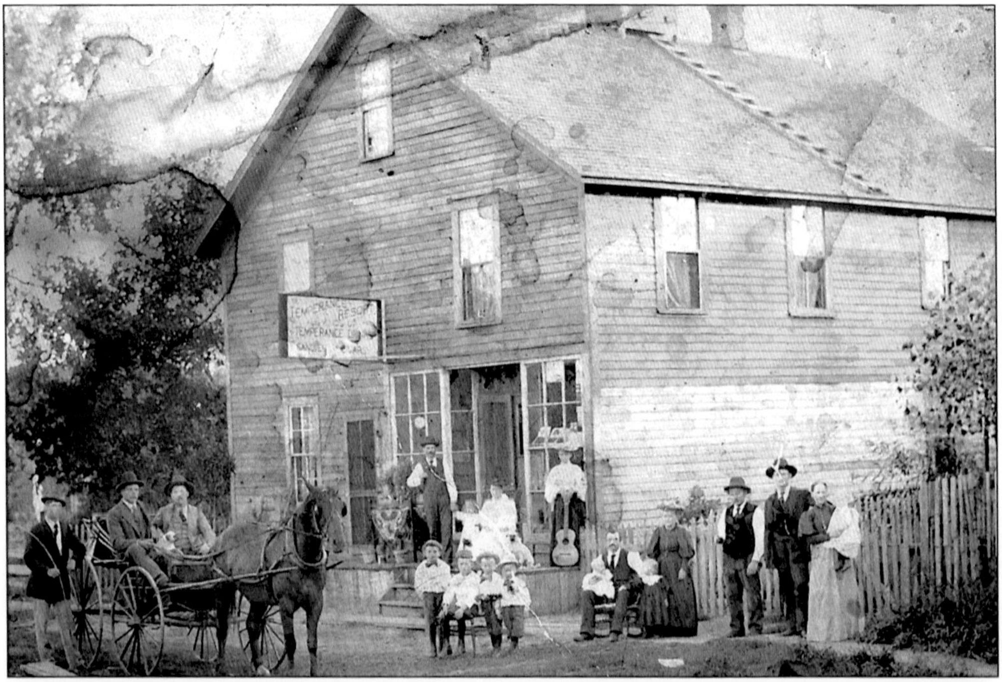

Carl Hanson is pictured with his family at Porter's Mills, Town of Brunswick, about 1895. The building behind them was a general store, "Temperance Resort," and the Hanson family home. (CVM.)

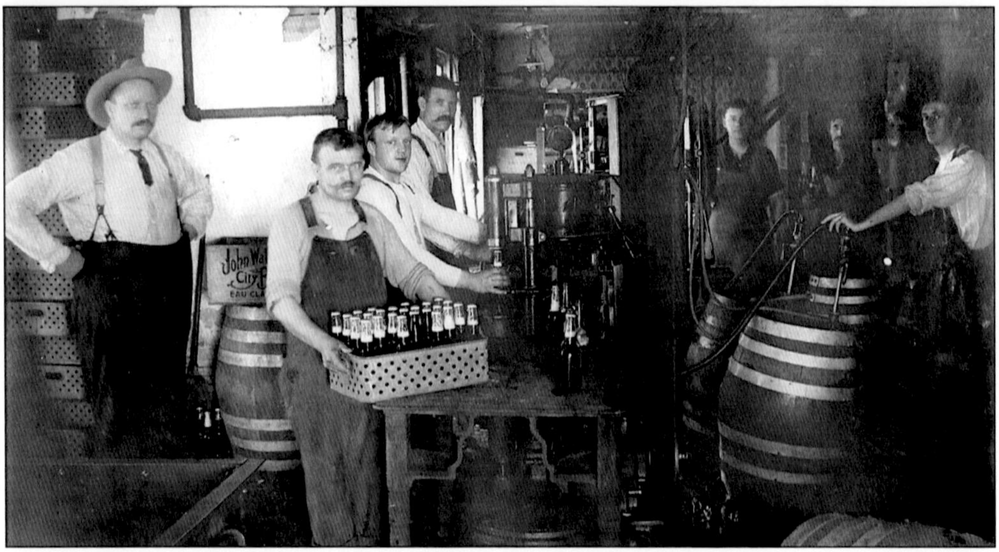

Pictured here is the bottling room at the John Walter Brewing Company, Eau Claire, 1916. Johannes (John) Walter started his brewery in Spencer, Wis., in 1874. He moved the business to Eau Claire in 1893. After his first Eau Claire site was destroyed by a fire in 1909, he relocated to 318 Elm Street, where the buildings still stand in 2005. In 1913, he built a new bottle house, one of the first in the industry to have tiled floors for sanitation purposes. By the mid-1980s, the company, still family-owned, was struggling. Michael Healy, a Chicago financier, bought and reorganized it as Hibernia Brewing Company. It closed in 1990 after 97 years. (CVM.)

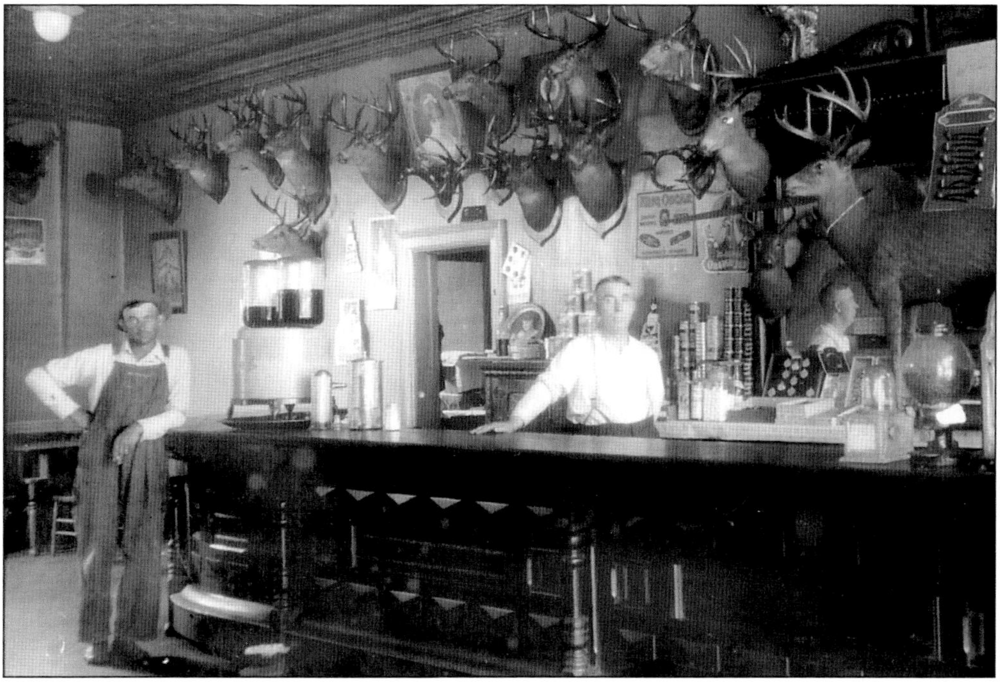

These two men were photographed at the Badger Saloon, Fairchild, *c.* 1920. (Courtesy of the Roger "Buzzy" Hahn family.)

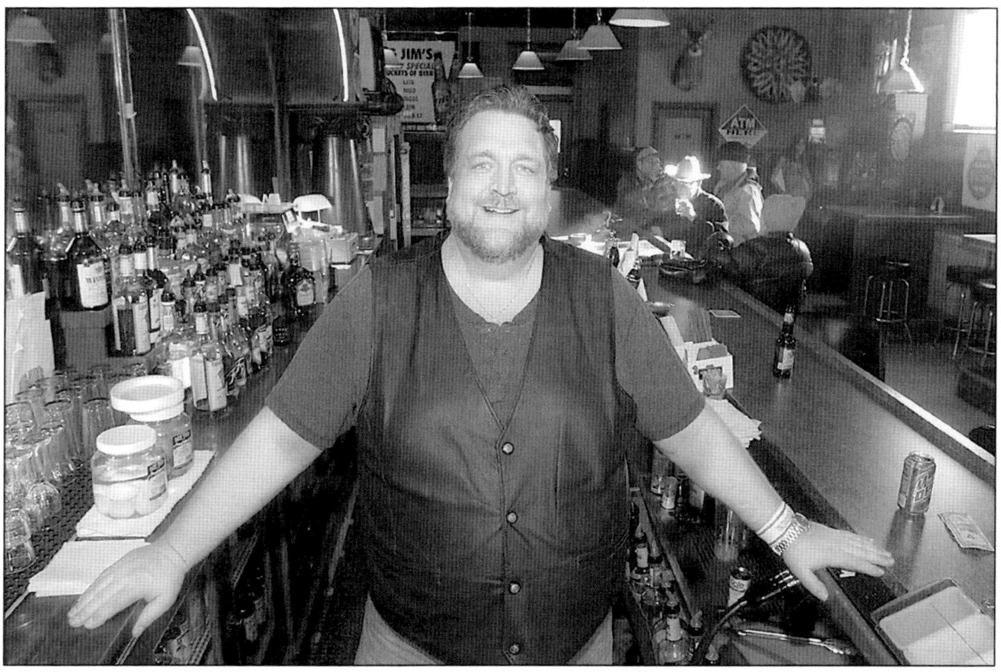

Jim Gagnon stands behind the bar at Big Jim's Sports Bar in Fall Creek, March 2003. Gagnon had been a professional wrester and promoter with All-American Wrestling; the motto for its training program was "Enter a Humanoid, Exit a Wrestler." (Photograph by Shane Opatz. Courtesy of the Eau Claire *Leader-Telegram*.)

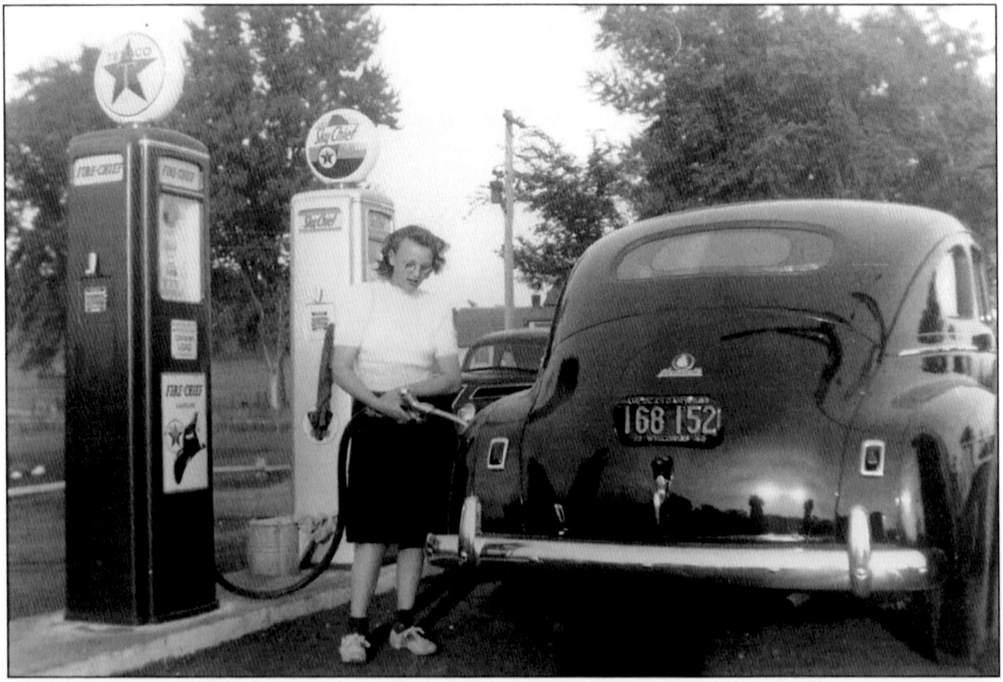

Olga Ventzke worked at a Texaco filling station during World War II, Highway 12, Altoona, probably 1942. The station was across from the Hillcrest Golf Course. (CVM.)

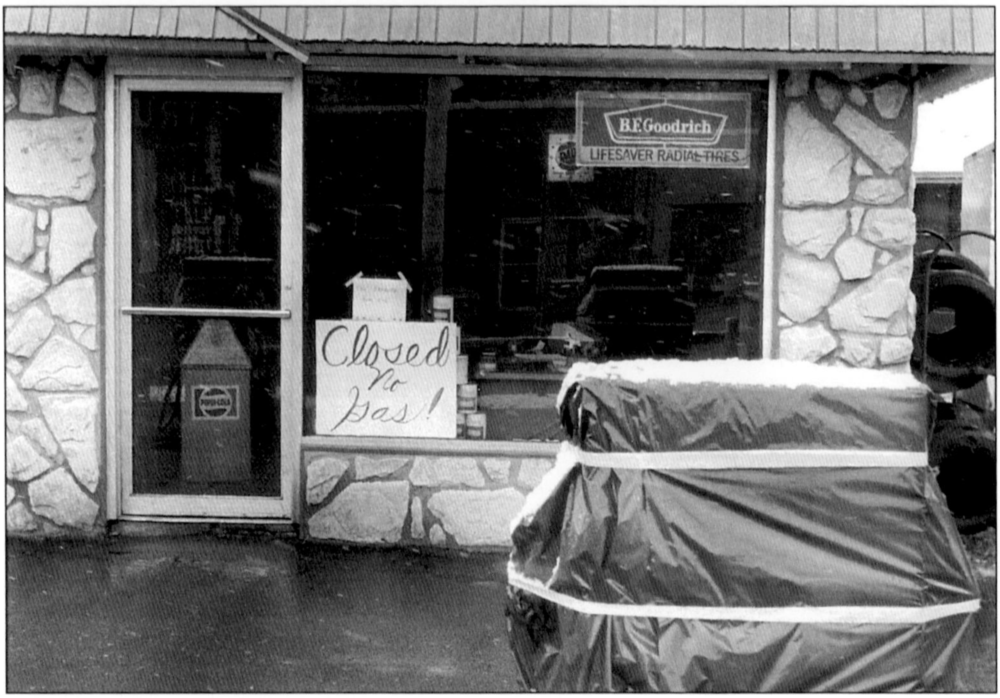

Evidence of the gas shortage in Eau Claire is seen here in April 1979. The shortage was caused by the Iranian revolution, which took Iran out of the oil market, leading to a worldwide shortage in the first quarter of 1979 of about two million barrels per day. (CVM.)

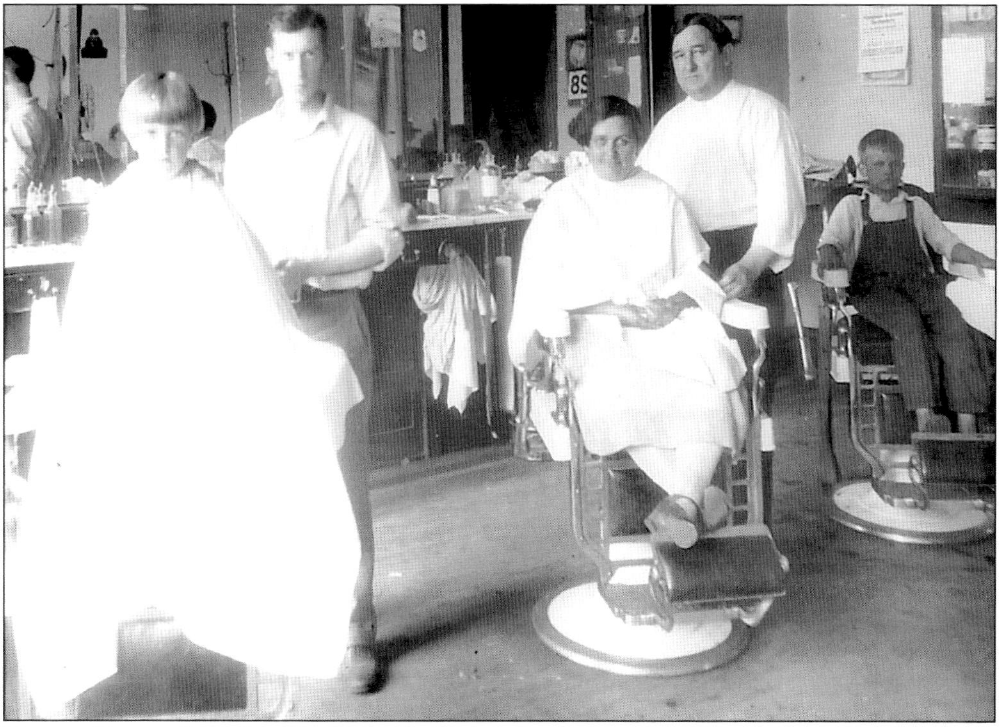

Herman Emanuel's Barber Shop in Fall Creek is pictured here in the 1920s. Laverne Creviston is the barber on the left and Herman Emanuel is the barber on the right. (Courtesy of the Roger "Buzzy" Hahn family.)

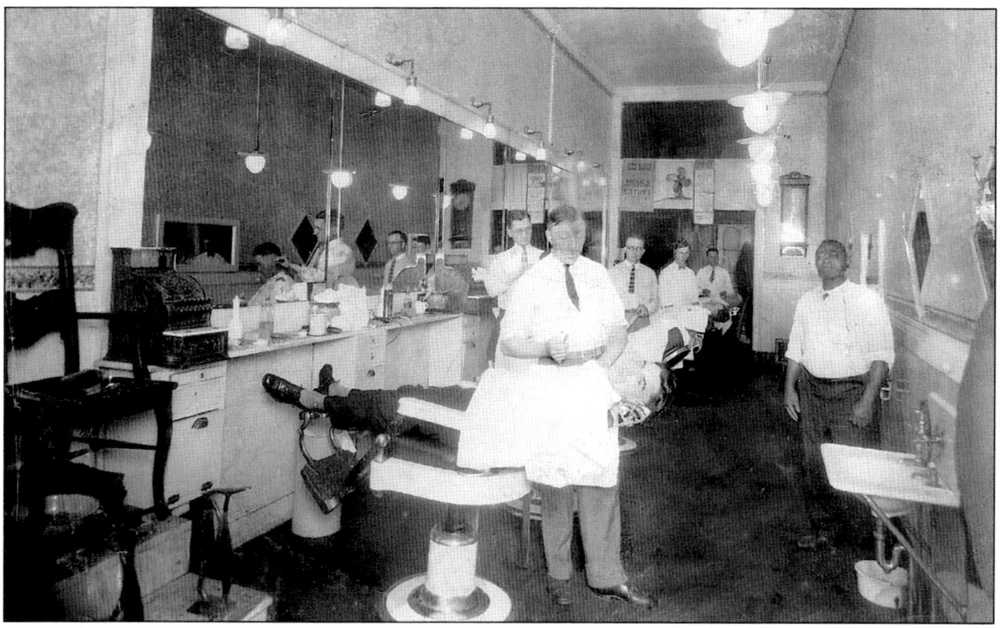

Johnny's Barbershop on Putnam Street in downtown Eau Claire looks busy in this c. 1960 photograph. The two barbers at far left are Walter Lange and Walter Ringer. The barber at far back is Bob Hetner. (CVM.)

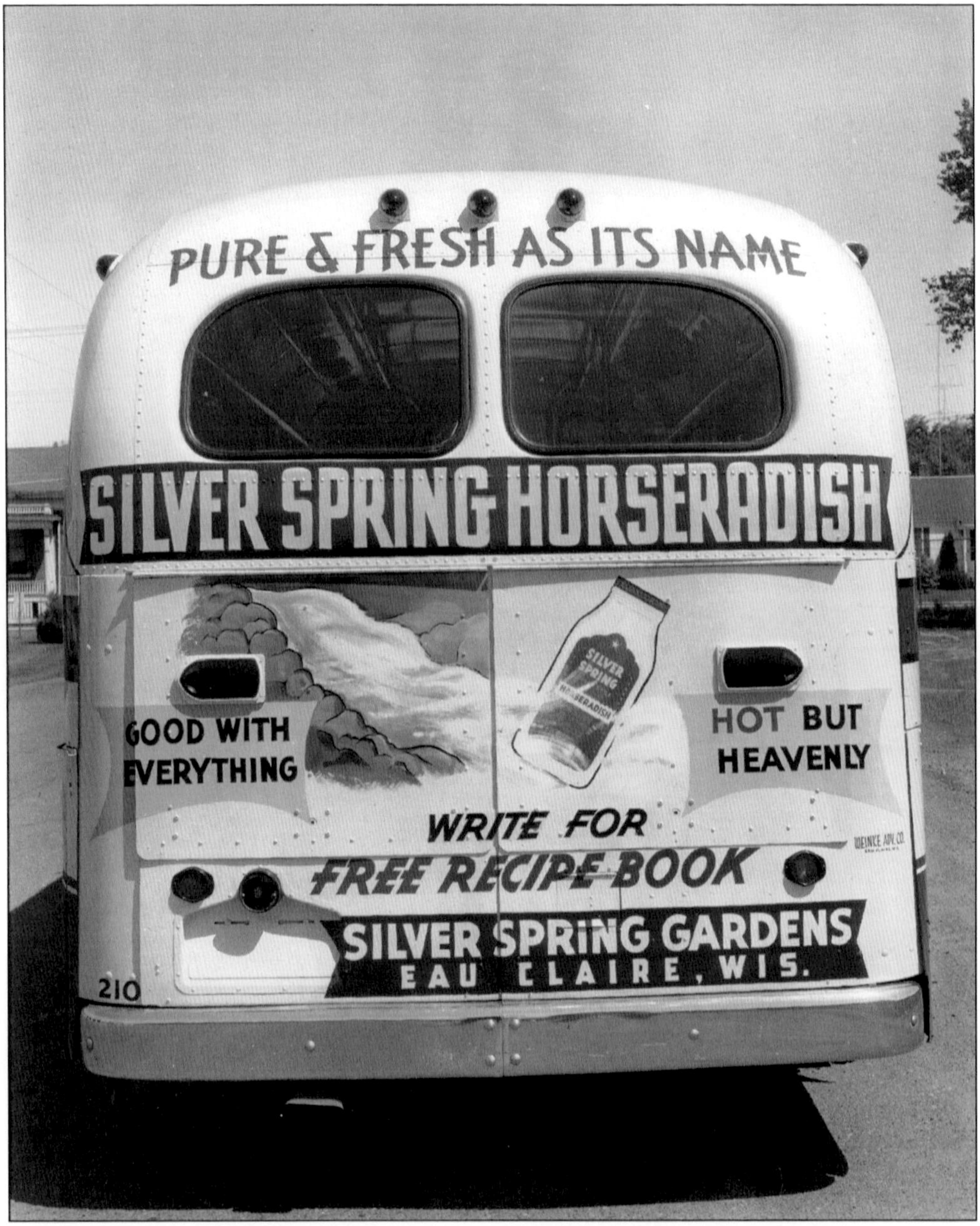

The Eau Claire Transportation Company bus advertised Silver Spring horseradish in the 1950s. This is a tale of three businesses. In 1950, ECTC's 34 buses traveled just under a million miles in the City of Eau Claire. The story of the Town of Brunswick's Silver Spring Gardens and its horseradish began in 1929. Ellis Huntsinger, an out-of-work traveling salesman, planted a half-acre of horseradish in his back yard, grated the roots, bottled the spicy-hot condiment, and sold it door-to-door. By the end of 2004, with the fourth Huntsinger generation on the home farm, the company grew corn, soybeans, horseradish, and forage crops on more than 7,000 acres. They were also the top horseradish producer in the U.S. and exported the condiment to Europe, Asia, and Australia. The advertisement was painted by Weinke Advertising Company of Eau Claire; Weinke started as a sign painter and grew his company into an advertising agency. (CVM.)

Seven

A PLACE TO LEARN

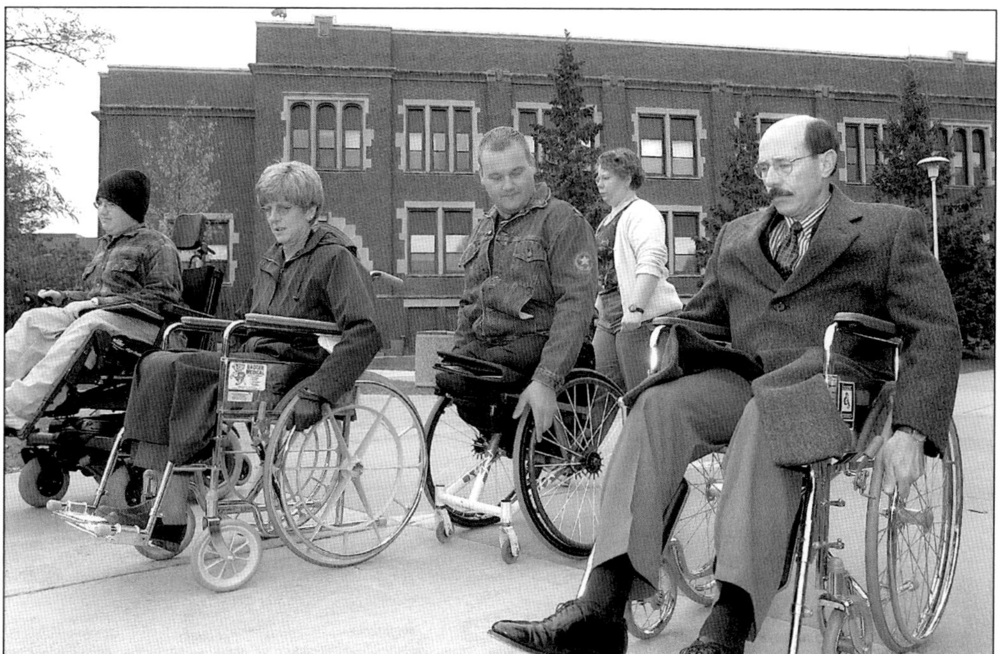

University of Wisconsin-Eau Claire student Joe Gapko, left, leads Beth Hicks, director of services for students with disabilities, Matt Glowacki, and Chancellor Donald Mash on a tour of lower campus as part of Disabilities Awareness Week, October 2002. (Photograph by Andi Stempniak. Courtesy of the Eau Claire *Leader-Telegram*.)

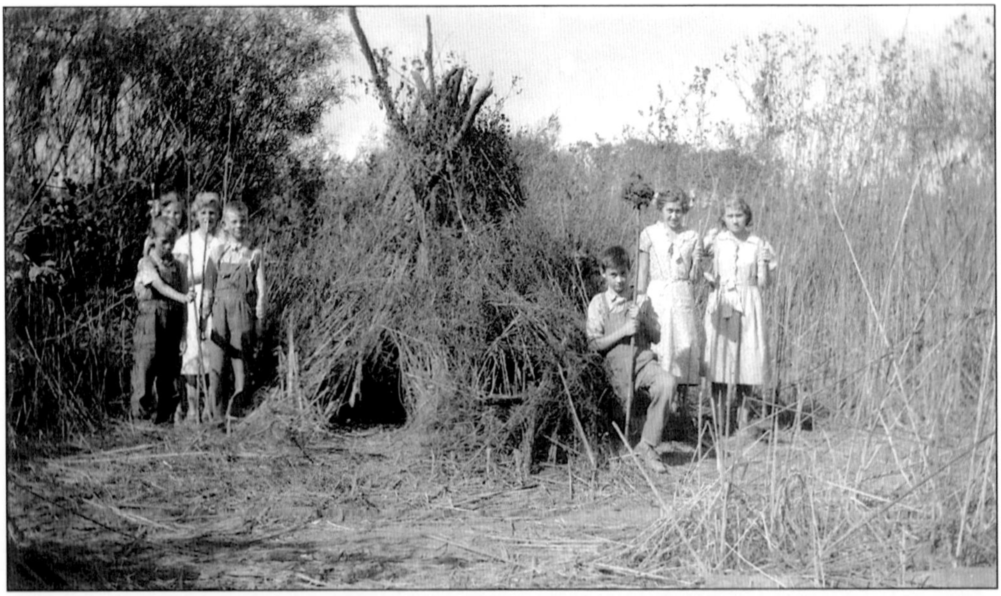

Students at the rural one-room Sunnyview School, Town of Washington, pause to have this picture taken in the 1930s. Sunnyview opened its doors in 1881 and closed in 1961 when Wisconsin school districts consolidated. (CVM.)

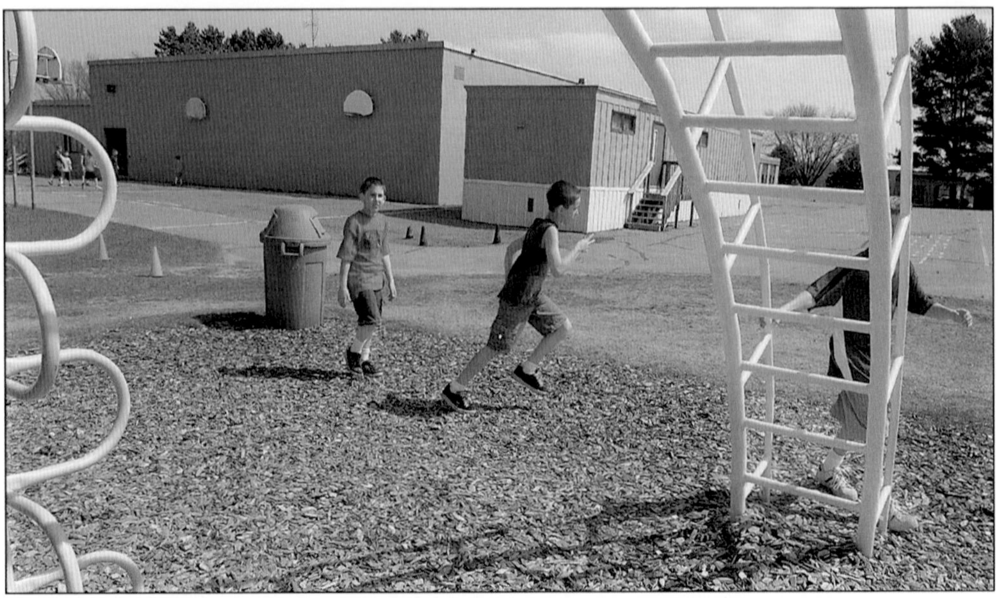

Students play during lunch-hour recess at rural Cleghorn School, Town of Pleasant Valley, April 2002. Cleghorn had recently added two trailers to the school building for additional space, and the computer lab can be seen in the background. While Cleghorn first established a school in 1881, the building pictured was built in 1956. It closed amid great controversy in 2003. (Courtesy of the Eau Claire *Leader-Telegram*.)

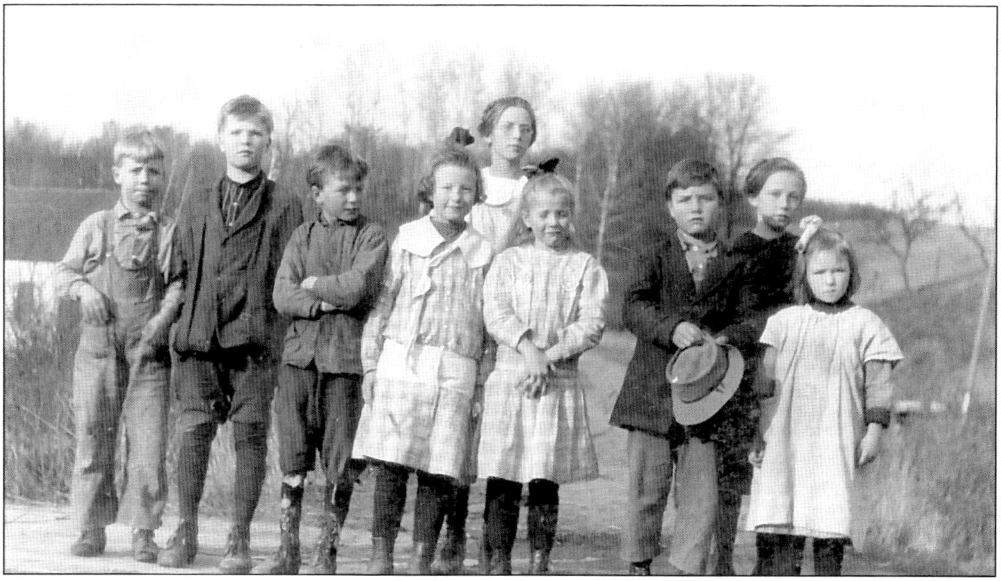

These children attended the Ludington School in the mid-1910s. Otis Larson is far left, Benny Larson is second from left, and Ella Larson is fourth from left. (Courtesy of Alice (nee Larson) Pingel.)

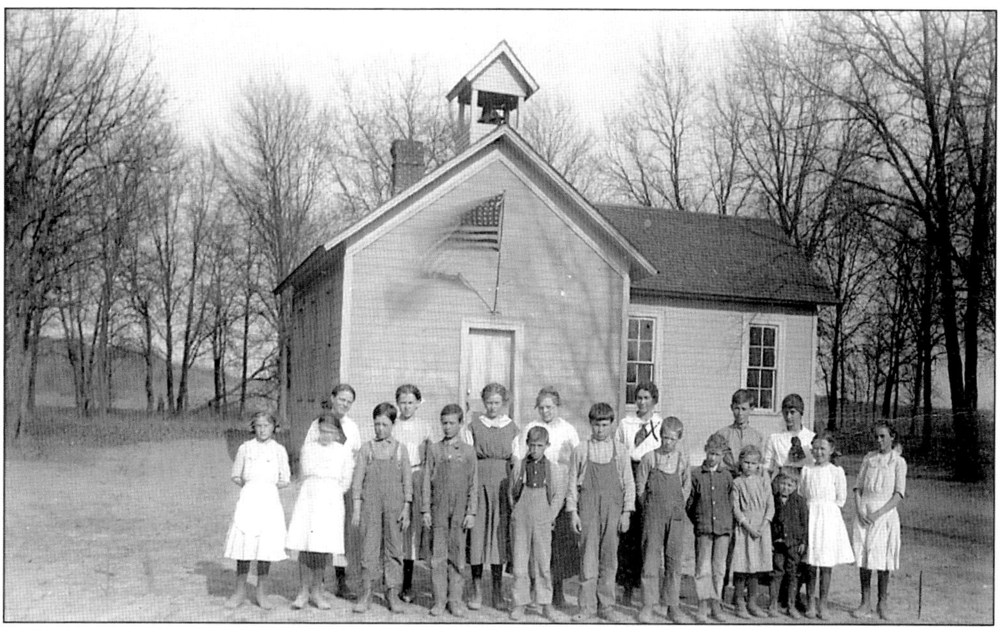

This photograph was taken at the Porter School, Town of Washington, 1915. Teacher Martha Miller, back row, fifth from left, is marked by the X on her blouse. The school dates from about 1877. (CVM.)

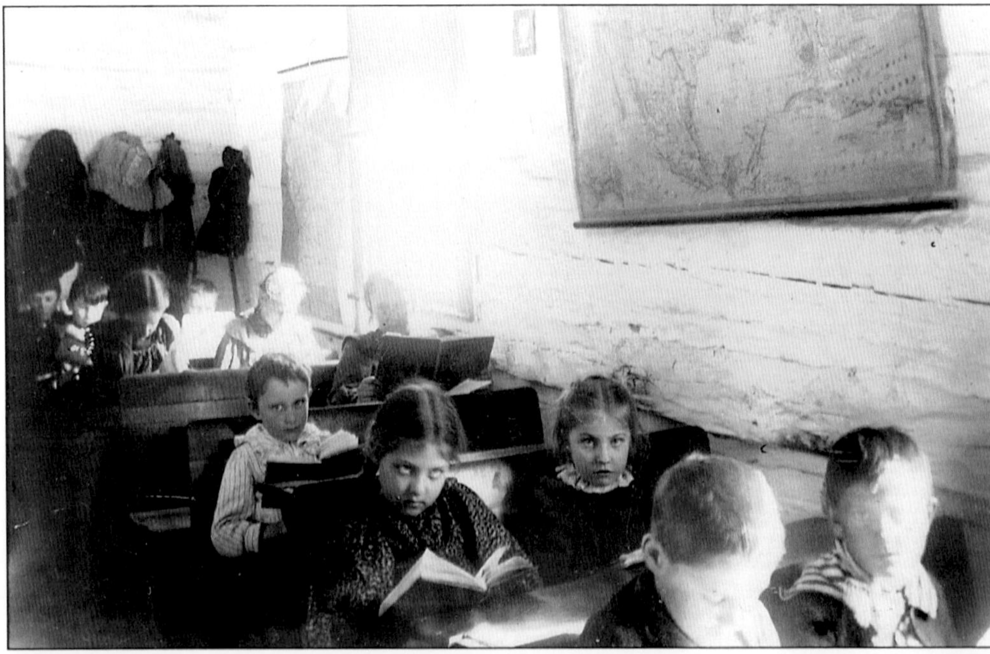

These children are in class at the Oak Knoll School, Town of Seymour, *c.* 1895. Pictured are: (front seat) L. John Meyer, R. Charles Stein; (second seat) L. Fedis Lane, R. Anna Maik; (third seat) Paul Meyer. (FCHS.)

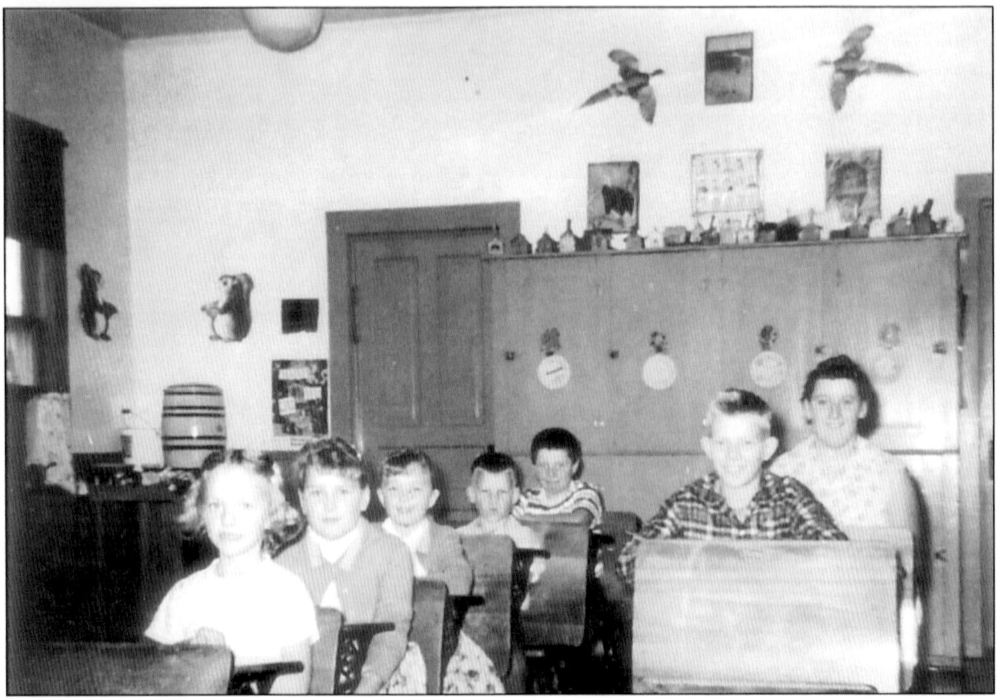

This photo was taken in the last year of the Pineview School, Town of Ludington, 1959-1960. Pictured from front to back are: (left row) Ruth Tumm, Karon Tumm, Sharon Tumm, Jim Tumm, and Don Tumm; (right row) Ronald Knuth, Ruth Knuth. (FCHS.)

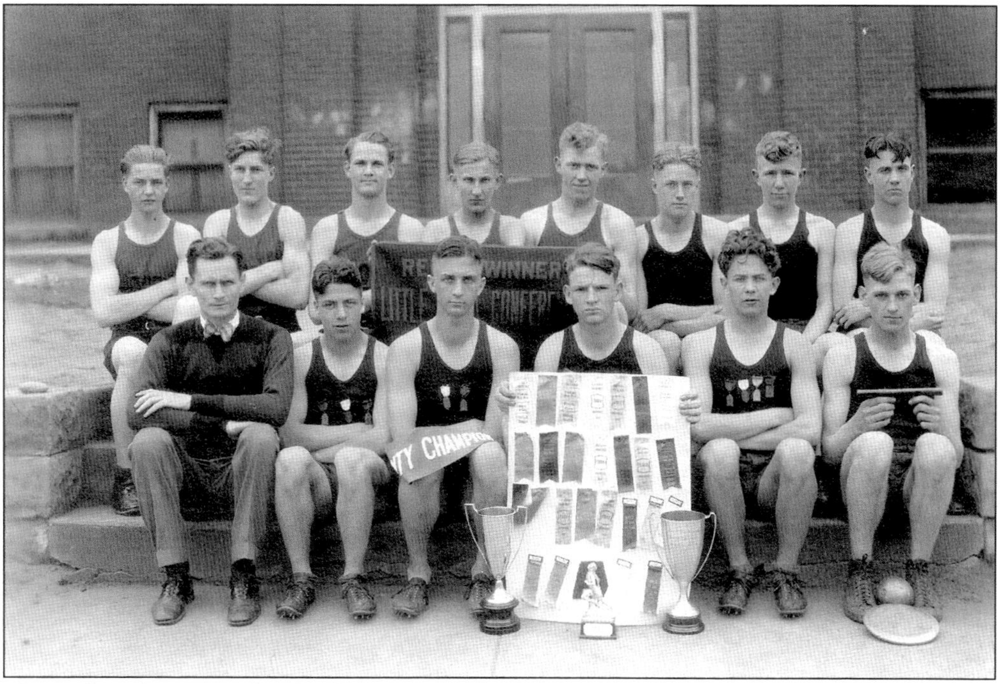

This is the Altoona High School relay winners and basketball team of 1927. All except one boy in the picture were railroad workers' sons. (CVM.)

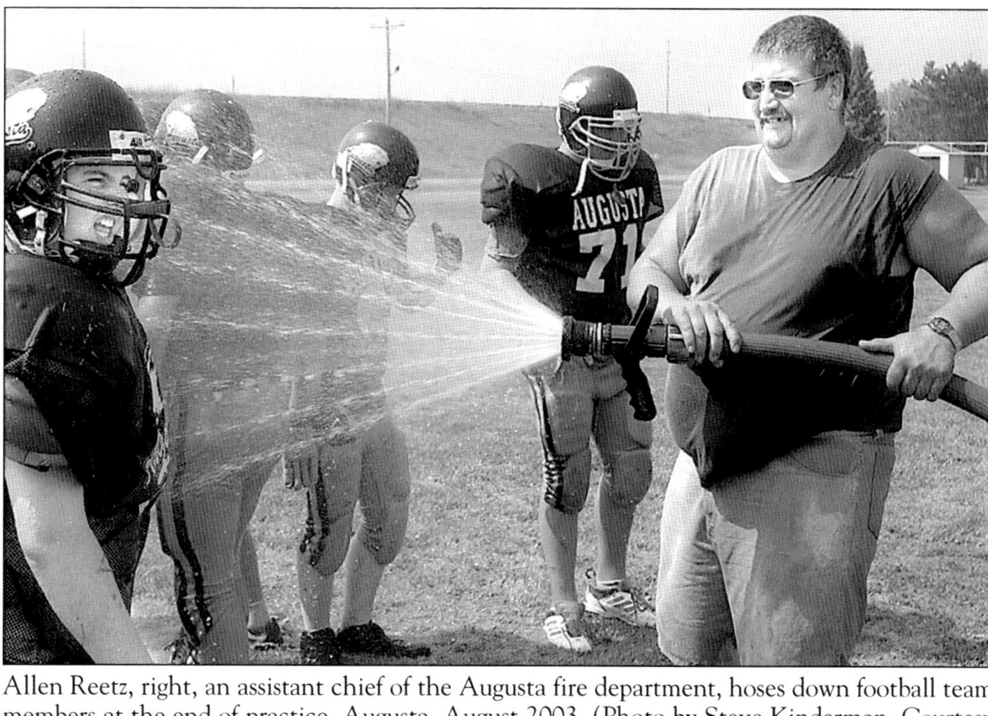

Allen Reetz, right, an assistant chief of the Augusta fire department, hoses down football team members at the end of practice, Augusta, August 2003. (Photo by Steve Kinderman. Courtesy of the Eau Claire *Leader-Telegram*.)

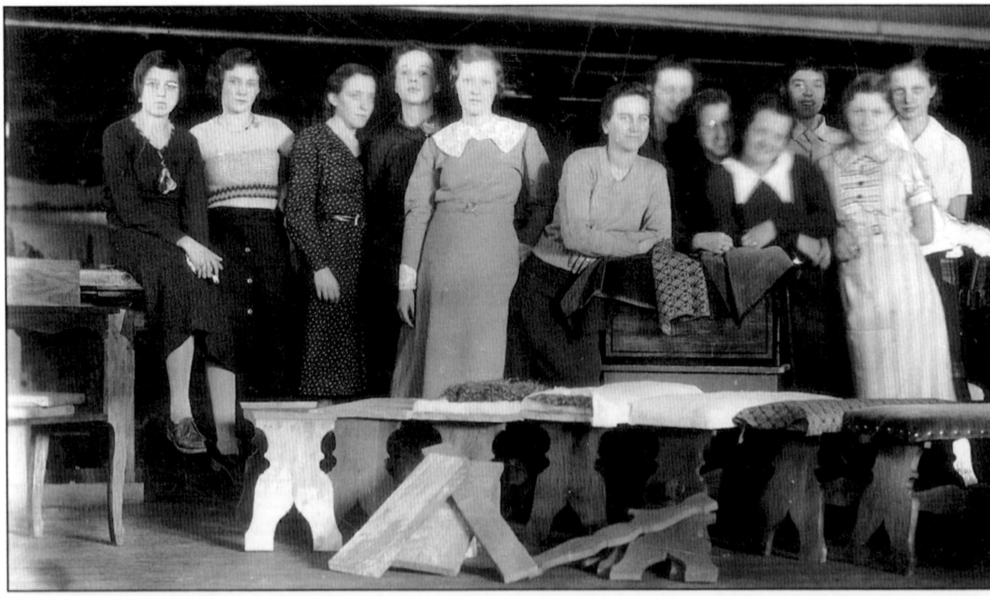

Pictured here is an Augusta High School industrial arts class for girls, 1934 or 1935. Pictured from left to right are Blanche Moody, Doris Peil, Dorothy Hall, Thora Rose, Adeline Krenz Strauch, Margaret Harden, Gertrude Cookley, Edna Acker, Mayone Ida ?, Madeline Wilson, Jane Campbell, and Sylvia ?. The benches in the foreground were made by members of the class. (Courtesy of Jane Justesen.)

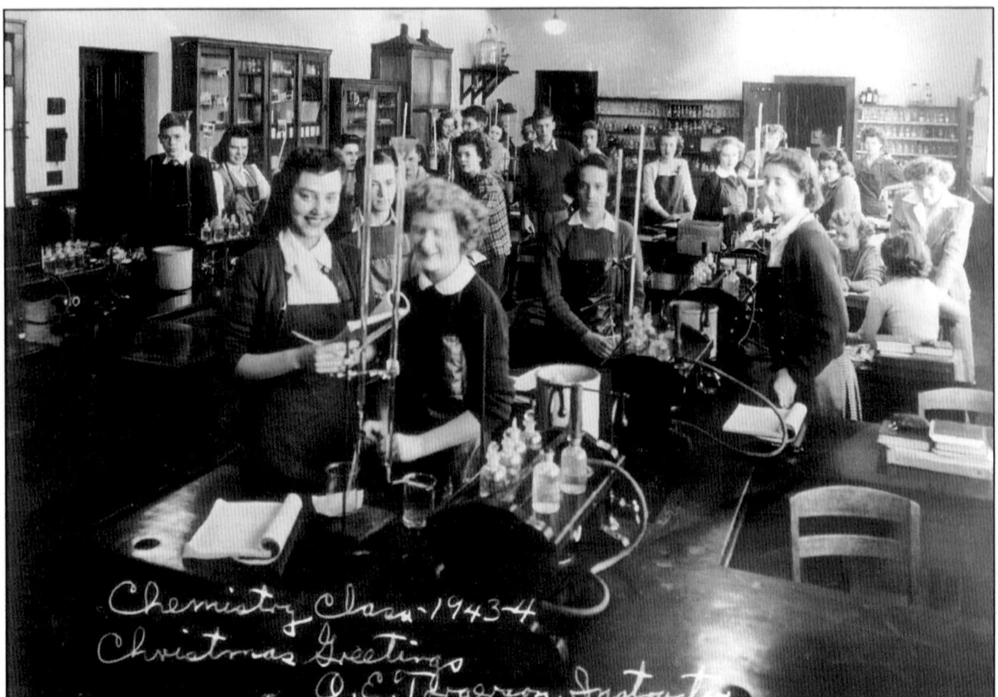

This photograph shows a chemistry class at Eau Claire Senior High School, 1943-44. (Courtesy of Bev Peterson.)

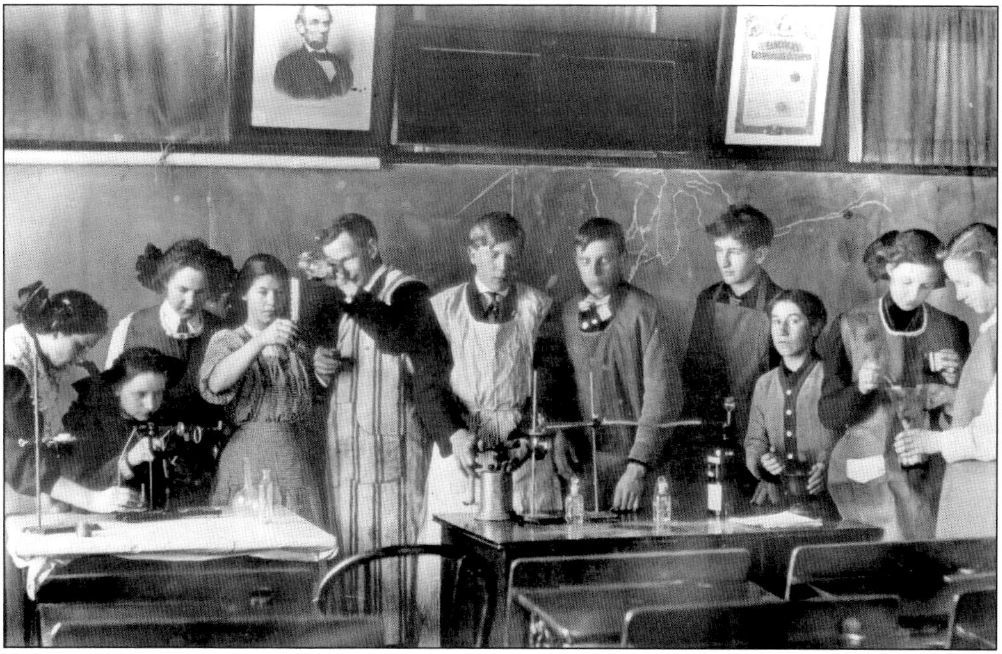

Pictured from left to right in this chemistry class at Fall Creek, 1910, are Clara Fuhrman, Adela Mehls, Odelia Bartz, Henrietta Kopplin, Mr. Hennessey (principal), Roy Quast, George Lindenthaler, Walter Schauer, Walter Emanuel, Selma Lindenthaler, and Caroline Bartz. (FCHS.)

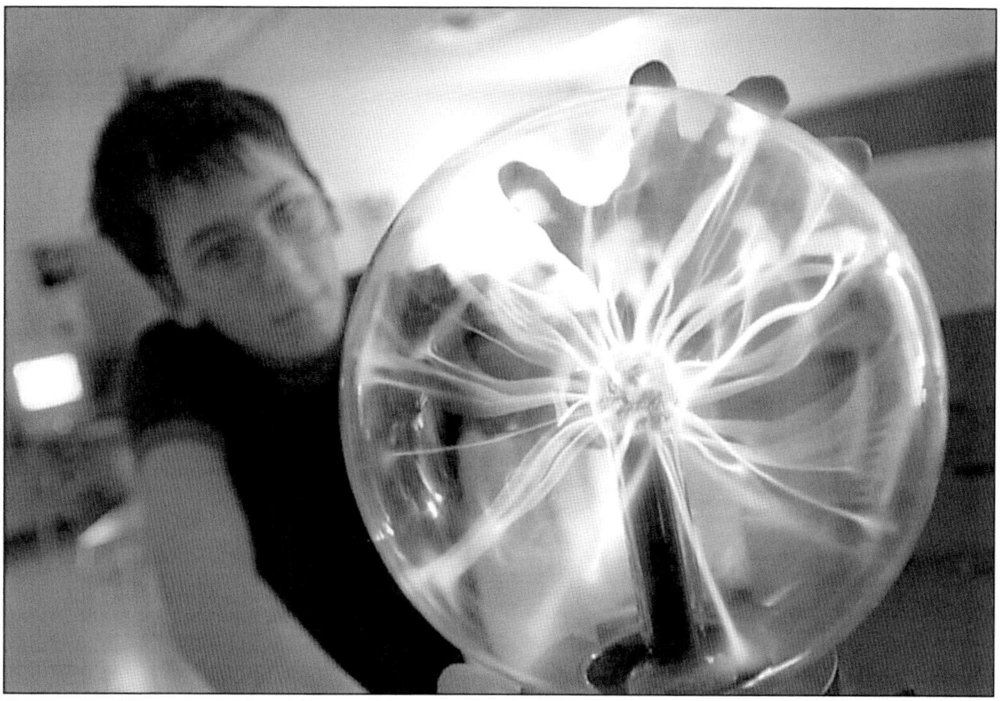

Sawyer Stubbe, a seventh grader at Augusta, is mesmerized by the electric lamp light that was used to demonstrate what the Manhattan Project looked like upon explosion during a "World War II Day" program, Augusta High School, May 2002. (Courtesy of the Eau Claire *Leader-Telegram*.)

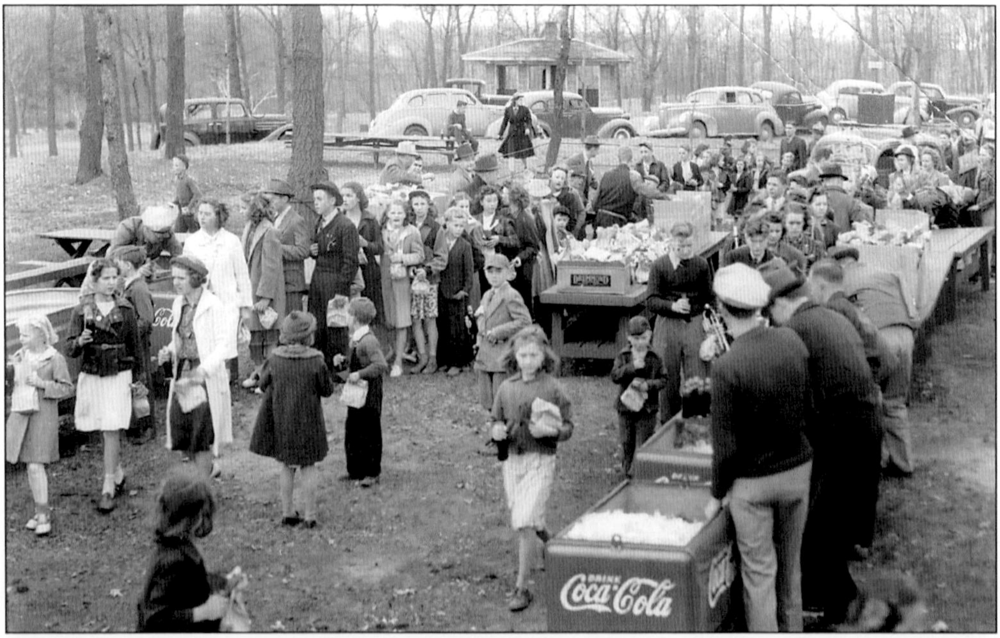

This school patrol picnic was held at Carson Park, Eau Claire, c. 1936. The U.S. School Patrol system was started in 1922, so that all children could cross safely at intersections. It now operates in more than 20 countries. As of at least 2003, Eau Claire school patrol picnics were still held in Carson Park. (CVM.)

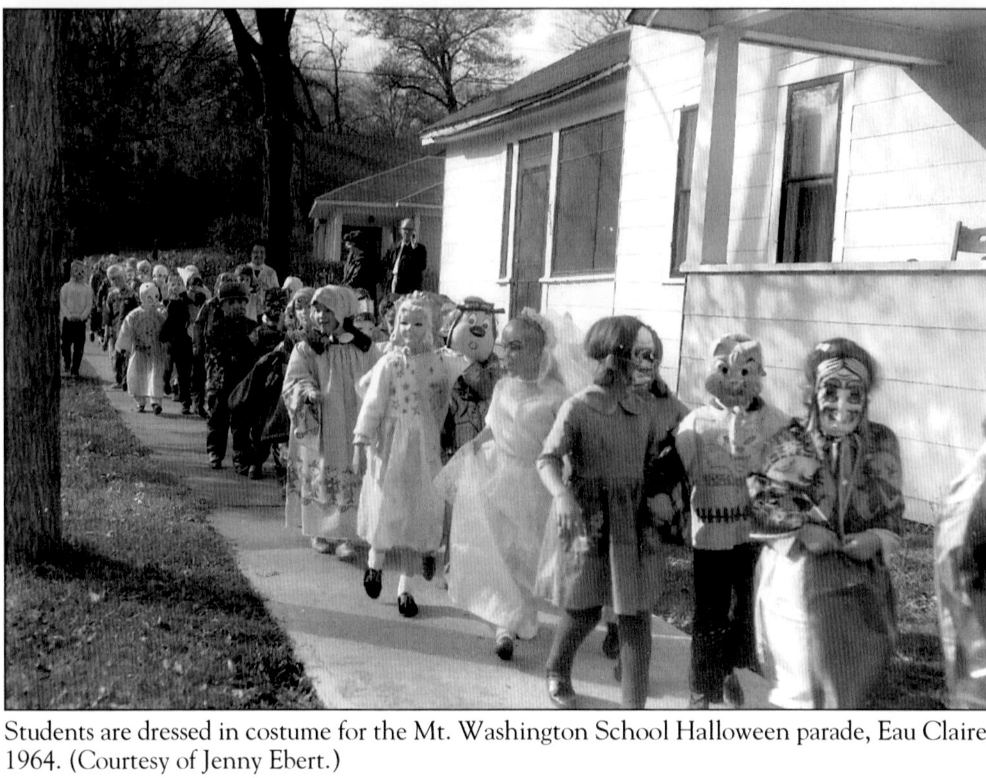

Students are dressed in costume for the Mt. Washington School Halloween parade, Eau Claire, 1964. (Courtesy of Jenny Ebert.)

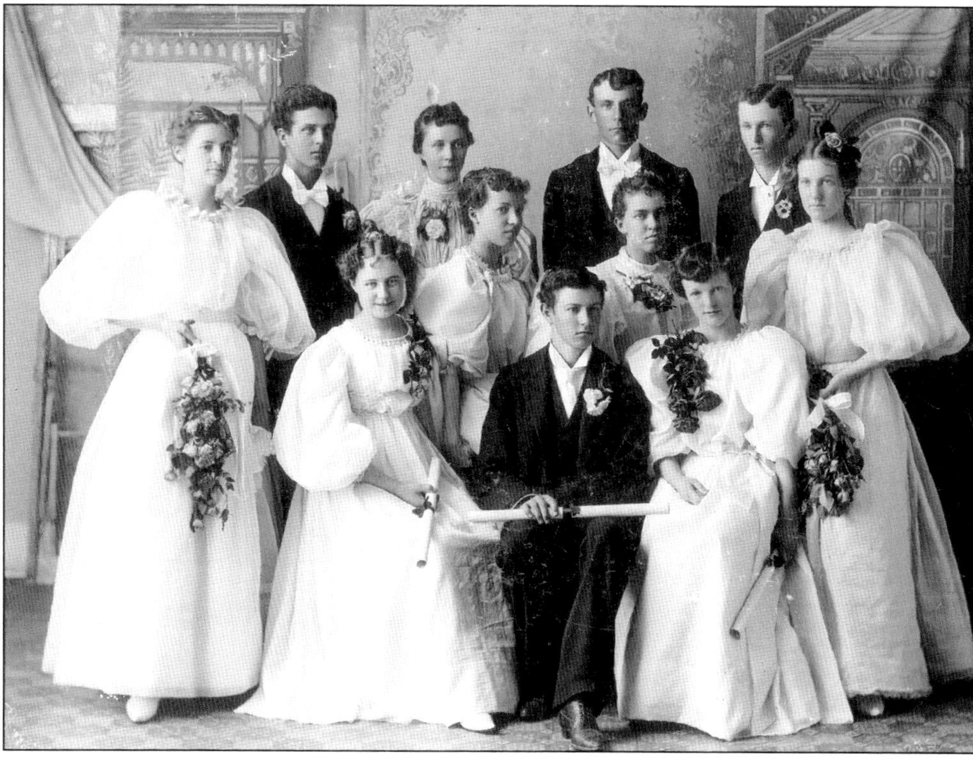

Pictured here is the Augusta High School Class of 1896. (CVM.)

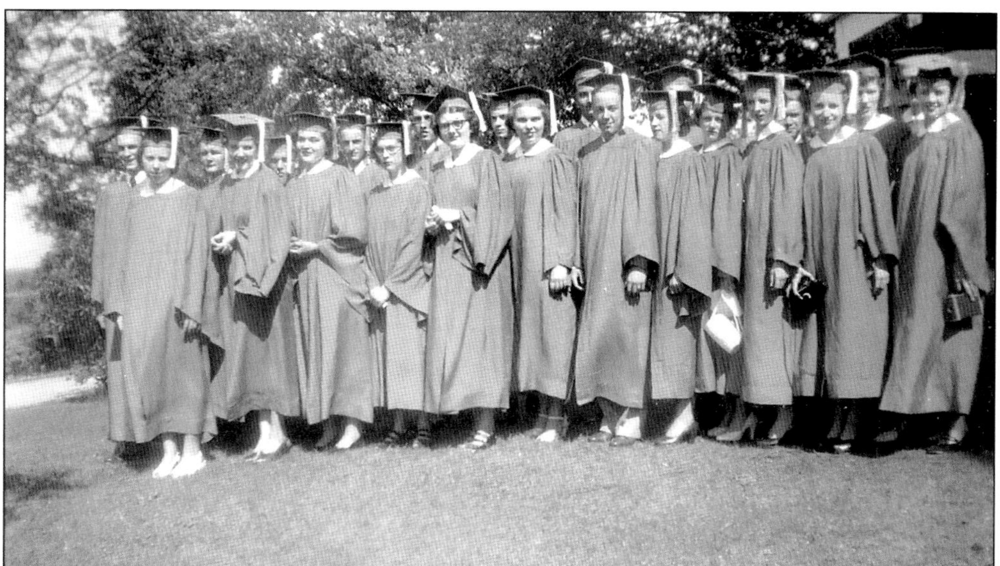

These graduates were part of the Fairchild High School graduating class of 1952. (Courtesy of Alice (nee Larson) Pingel.)

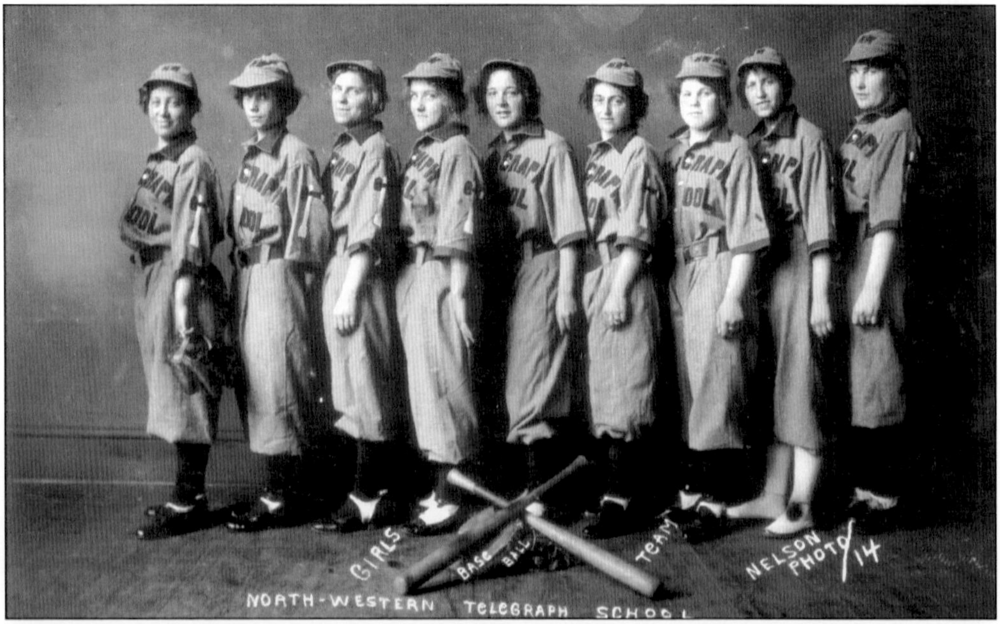

The girls baseball team, North-Western Telegraph School, near Eau Claire, posed for this photograph in 1914. (CVM.)

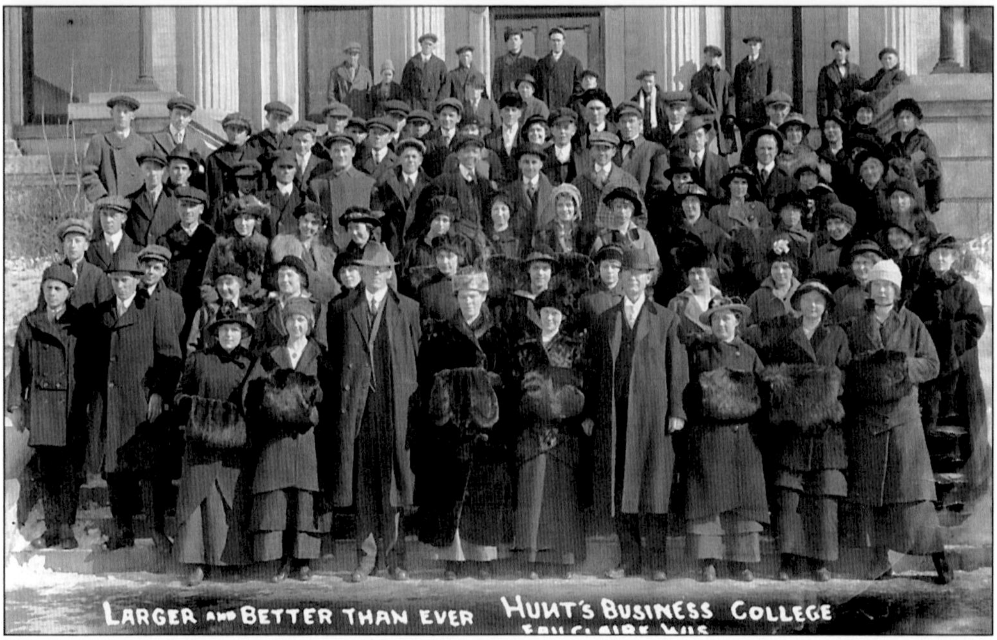

This gathering took place on the steps of Hunt's Business College, Eau Claire, c. 1915. According to the *History of Eau Claire County Wisconsin*, 1914, "Eau Claire can now boast of having a live, modern, up-to-date business school, known as Hunt's Business College, now permanently located in the Gas building in the quarters formerly occupied by the Eau Claire Commercial College [on South Barstow Street]. Professor D. L. Hunt is at the head of the institution. He is owner and business manager, also the principal of the department of penmanship and bookkeeping." The school operated for 20 years. Hunt died in 1928. (CVM.)

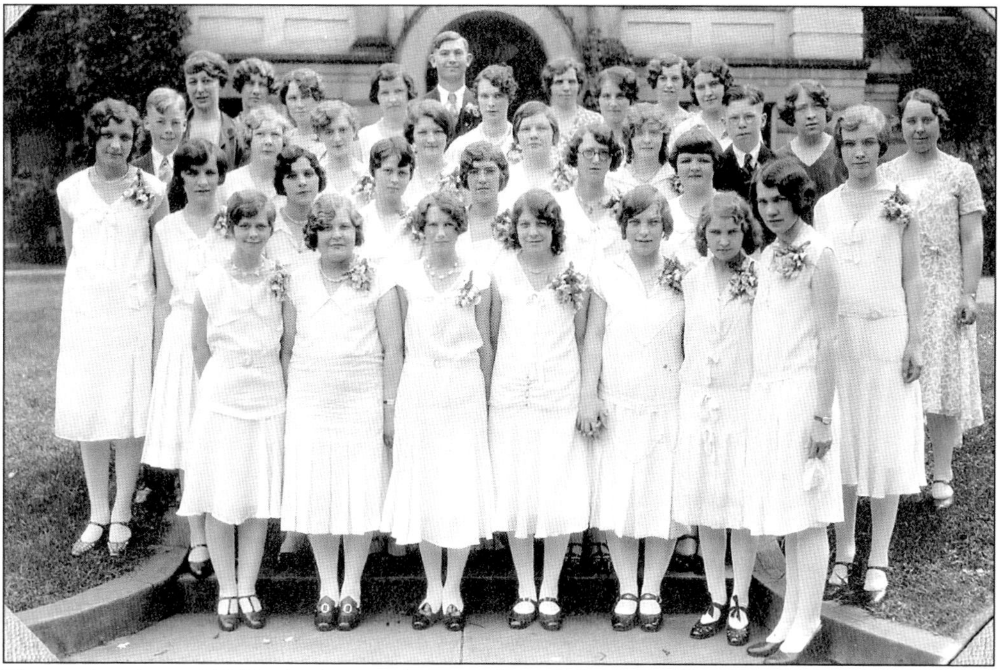

This is the class of 1930, the last graduating class of the Eau Claire County Training School for Teachers, Eau Claire. Pictured are, from left to right: (front row) Charlotte Bye, Nellie Johnson, Eleanor Bowman, Edna Curry, Ethel Durst, Esther Hoff, and Mary Vervooren; (second row) Sylvia Mickelson, Gladys Bergstrom, Helen Hickey, Marian Thompson, Hazel Erickson, Marjorie Kelley, Viola Christopherson, and Hazel Lee; (third row) Thomas Melville, Oleda Johnson, Eunice Clough, Irene Kurowski, Gertrude Oberle, Leona Olson, William Heideman, *Elsie Thompson, *Mildred Wilcox, *Elsa Nagel, *Hazel Vasey, unidentified, Hilda Erdman, John Ramsey, Lois Iorns, *Alma Anderson, Mayme Herman, Vera Wiese, and Fern Ross. Also known as the Eau Claire Rural Normal School, this school was not the same as the state-funded Normal School, also located in Eau Claire, which became part of the UWEC campus. (* denotes faculty. CVM.)

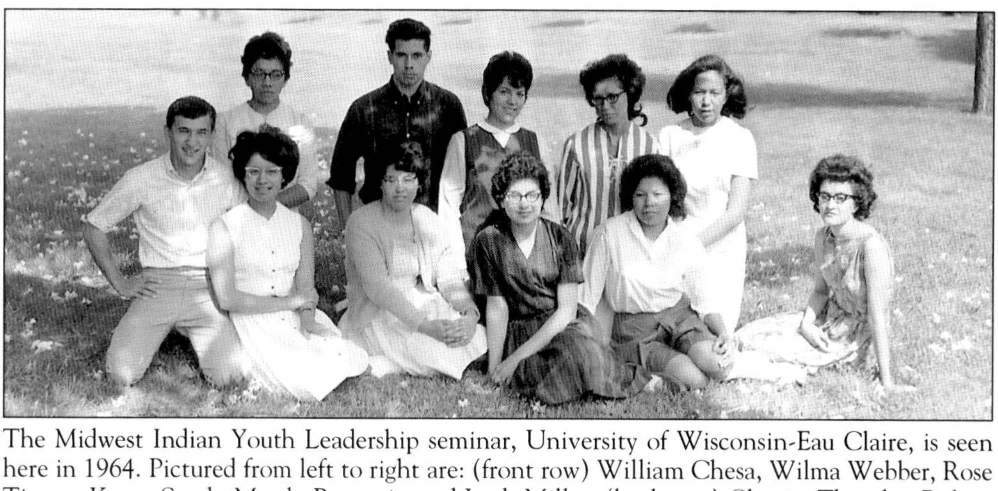

The Midwest Indian Youth Leadership seminar, University of Wisconsin-Eau Claire, is seen here in 1964. Pictured from left to right are: (front row) William Chesa, Wilma Webber, Rose Tipton, Karen Stack, Myrtle Pyawasit, and Leah Miller; (back row) Charity Thunder, Robert Deer, Jerilyn Grignon, Charlotte Brown, and Bonita Deere. (CVM.)

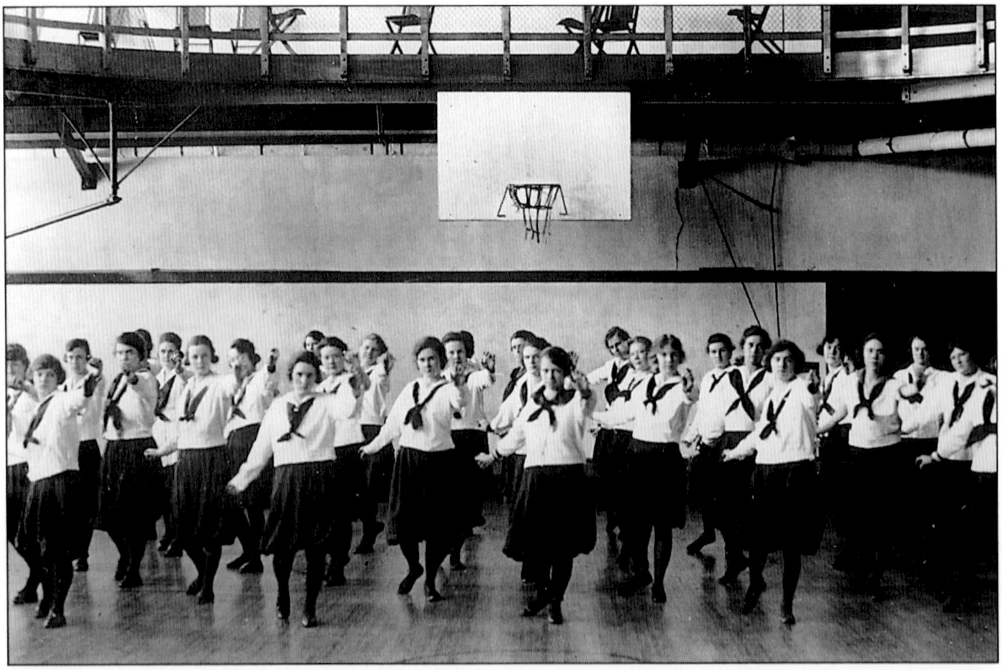

This is a women's physical education class at State Normal School, Eau Claire, in the late 1910s. (CVM.)

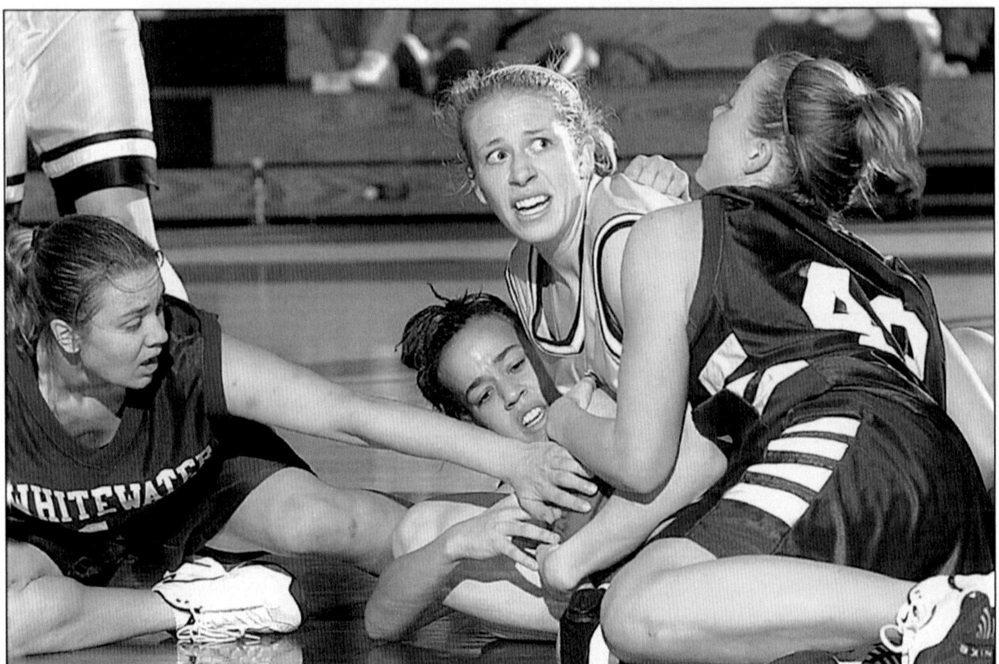

Division III basketball player UW-Eau Claire's Kristi Channing (in lighter jersey) fights for the ball on the floor at Zorn Arena, UWEC, January 2003. (Photograph by Steve Kinderman. Courtesy of the Eau Claire *Leader-Telegram*.)

Eight

A Place to Live and Play

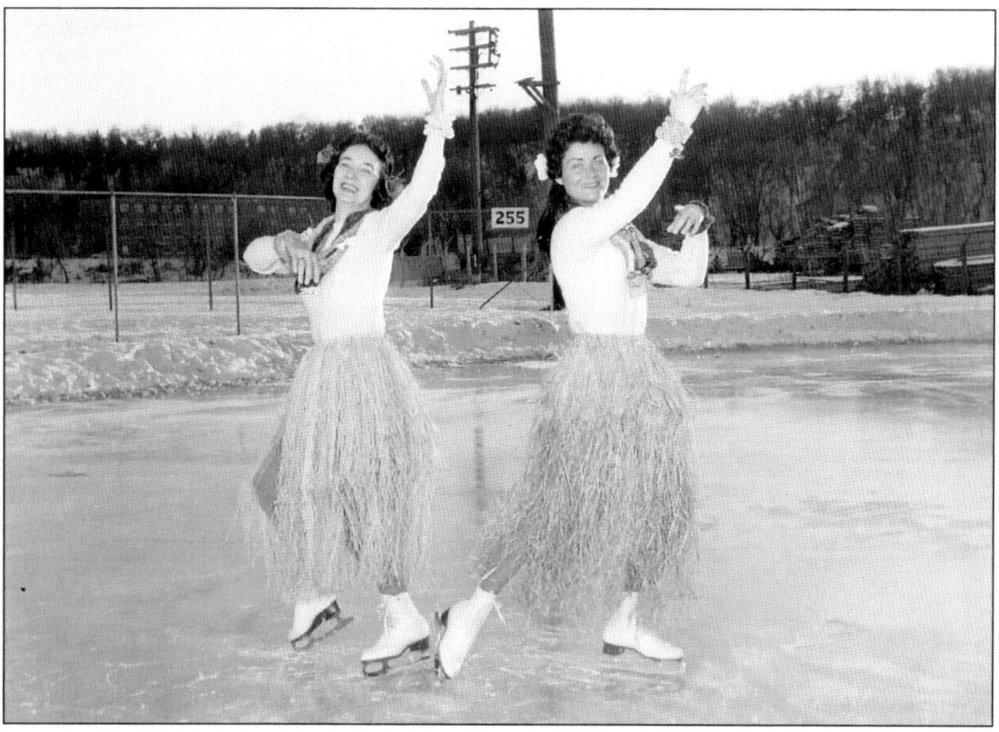

Ione Grilley and Eileen Krause show their figure skating moves in this 1957 photograph. They were members of the Eau Claire Figure Skating Club. (CVM.)

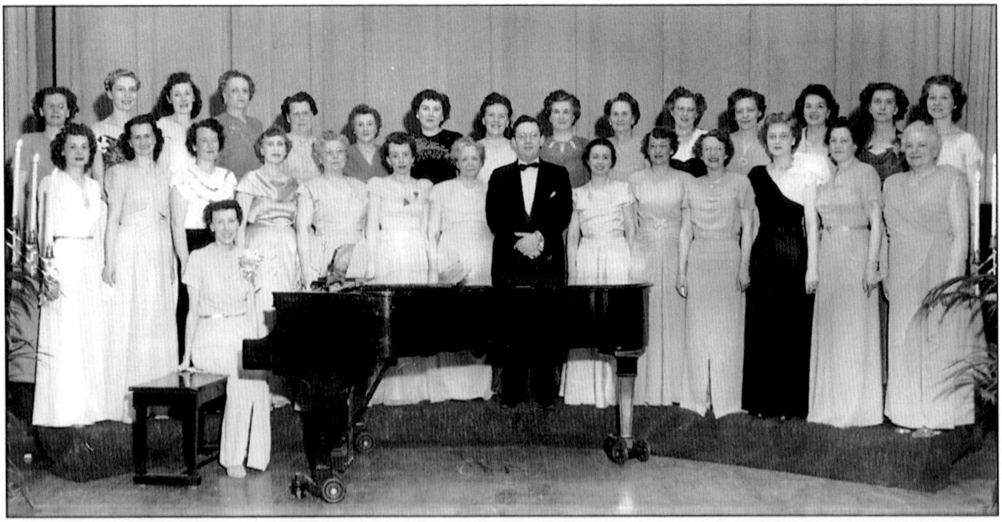

Eau Claire Woman's Club Chorus is seen here at a performance in the 1940s. Pictured from left to right are: (front row) Dorothy Demmler Haanstad, Dorthy Anderson, Mary Farr, Ede Timm, Vida Ferguson, Eileen Downs, Emma Erblang, Cecil Neubecker (director), Gladys Keith, Joan Horstick, Leone Risberg, Lucille Bilodeau, Sig Walsh, and Ethel Ellis; (back row) Tory Eggman, Mrs. Neubecker, Marion Ellenson, Olga Volkman, Mrs. Siggens, Mrs. Earl Packard, Ag Weiss, Jerry Crisp, Doris Burk, Sig Anderson, Margeret Aberg, Bernice Slagsvol, Lorraine Milward, Ag Finnessey, and Lucille Hinson. The accompanist is Esther Keith. (CVM.)

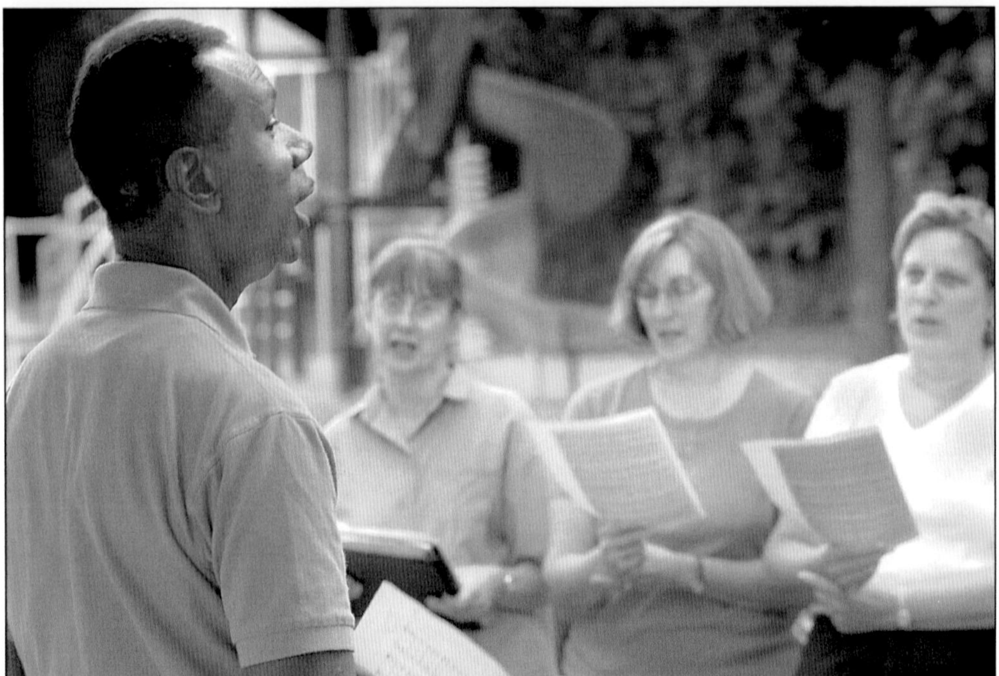

UWEC professor Dale Taylor conducts members of the Eau Claire Gospel Choir at the Juneteenth celebration, June 2003. (Photograph by Jason Tetzloff. Courtesy of the Eau Claire *Leader-Telegram*.)

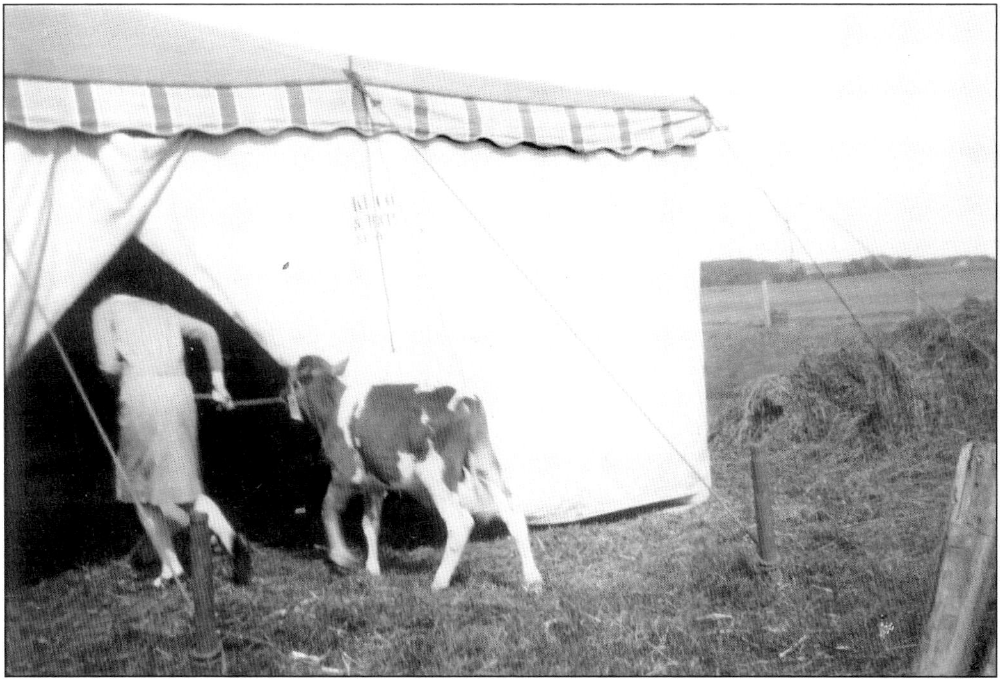

Margaret Russell leads her calf into a tent at the Eau Claire County Fair, Augusta, 1925. (CVM.)

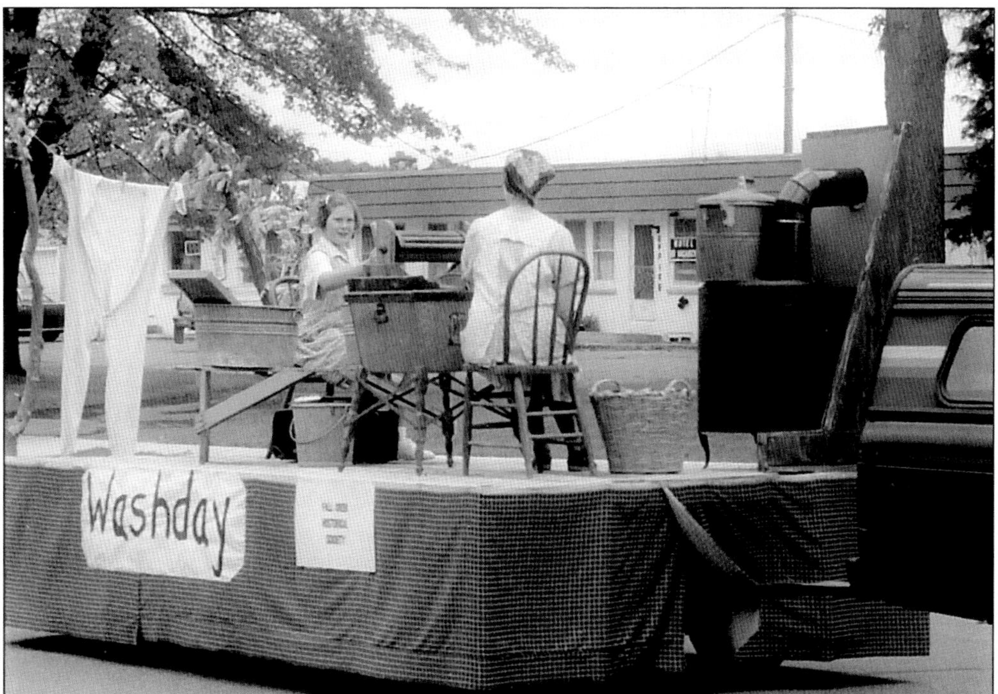

This Fall Creek parade float was created by the Fall Creek Historical Society in 1991. The society's original ideas have won it first-place honors most years that it has entered a float. (FCHS.)

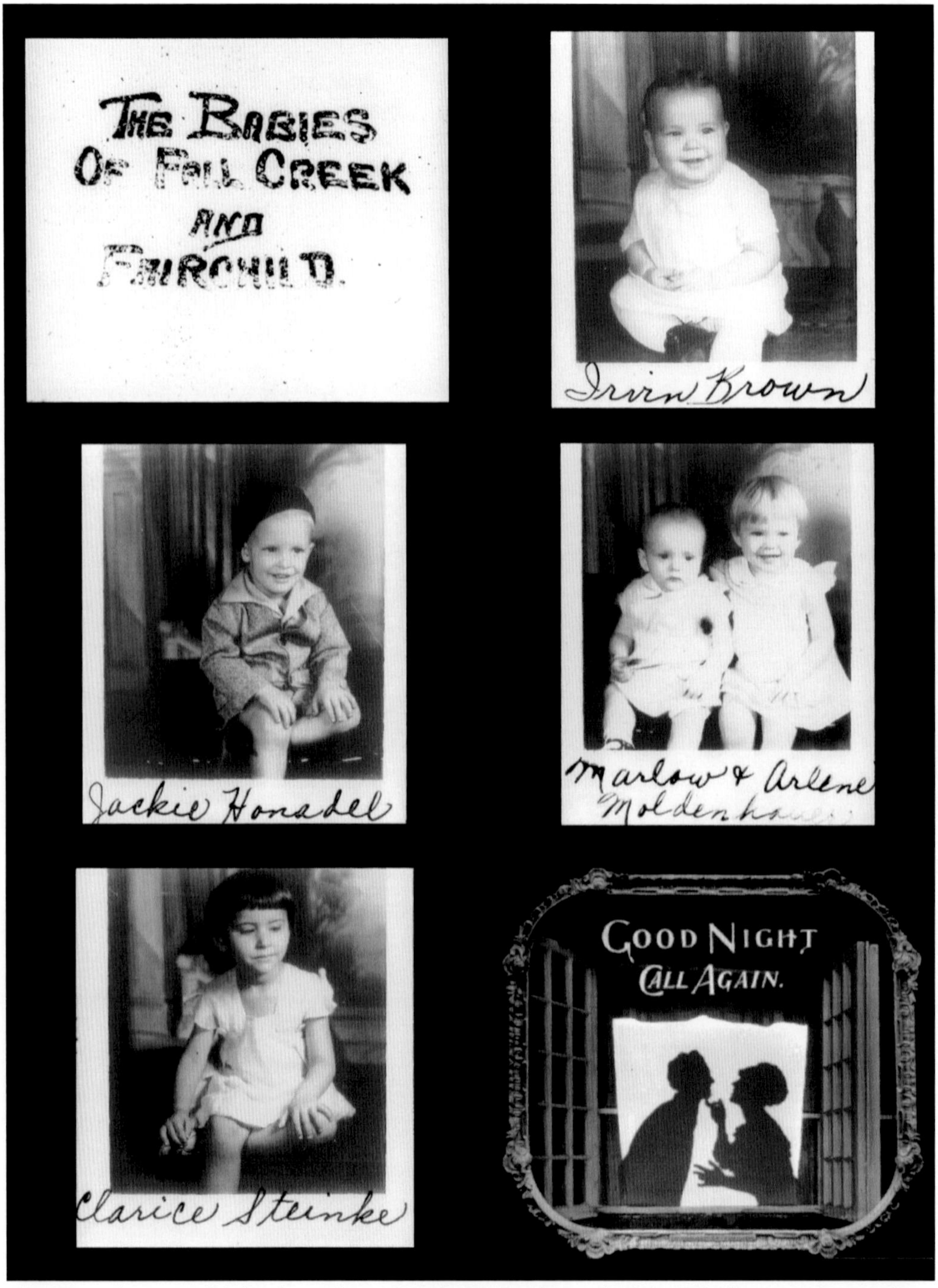

This is a selection of slides from the 1920s that were shown before and after a movie, perhaps at the Herman Emanual theater in Fairchild, or at a theater in Augusta. (Courtesy of the Roger "Buzzy" Hahn family.)

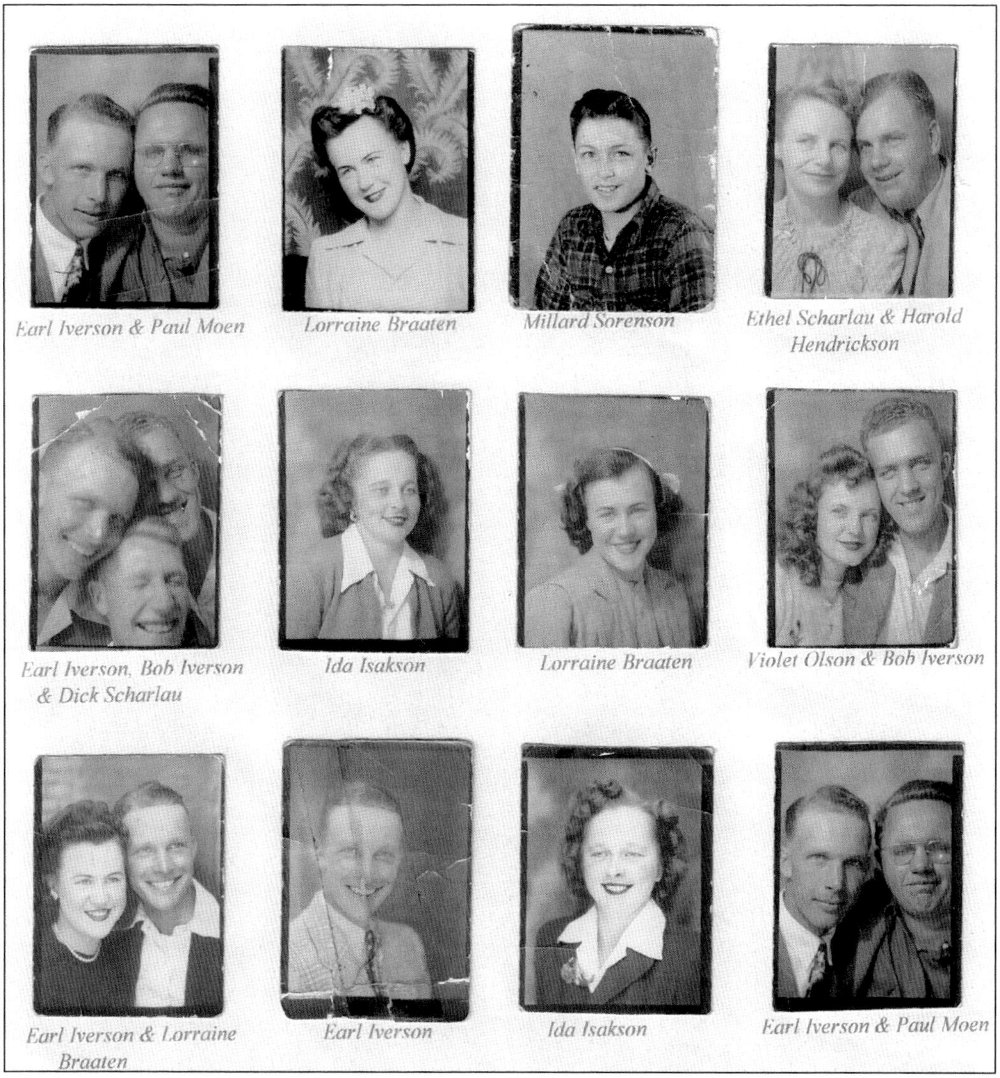

These snapshot portraits were taken at Fournier's Ballroom, Eau Claire, c. 1945. (Courtesy of Joan Scharlau.)

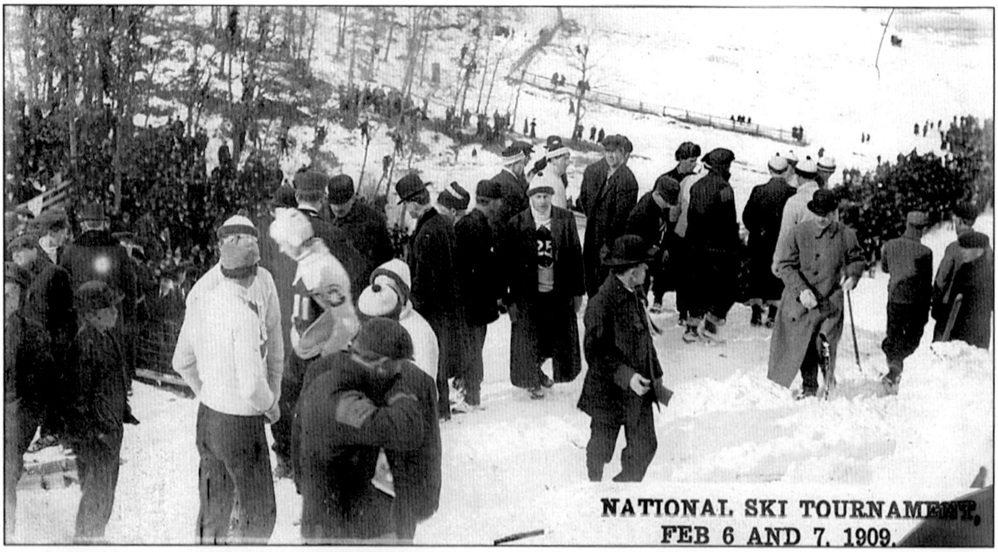

This National Ski Tournament was held at Mt. Washington hill, Eau Claire, February 6 and 7, 1909. Fifteen thousand people attended. Eau Claire's earliest ski contest was held at Mt. Tom in 1888; from there, contests moved to Carson Park during the 1890s, then to Mt. Washington. The city also hosted ski jumping at "Hendrickson Hill," named for 1930s-era U.S. team member Jimmy Hendrickson of Eau Claire, behind Sacred Heart Hospital. In 1969, the Eau Claire Ski Club opened the Olympic-sized Silvermine Hill in the Town of Union. (CVM.)

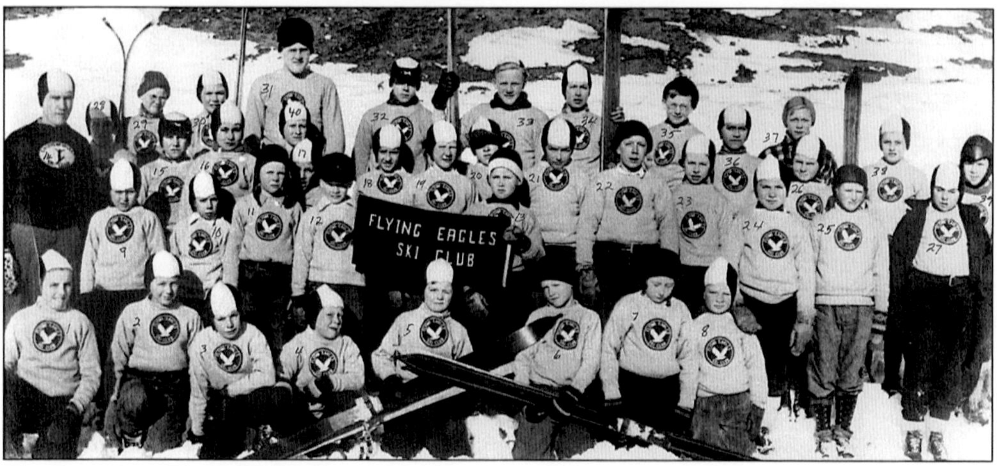

The Eau Claire Flying Eagles Ski Club is seen here in the 1930s. Pictured from left to right are: (front row) 1. Donnie Hovland, 2. Kerm Walker, 3. Harry Severson, 4. Allen Ellingson, 5. Harvey Ganong, 6. Derald Lahner, 7. Norma (Min) Roach, and 8. Billy Olson; (second row) 9. Oscar Severson, 10. Rodney Severson, 11. Robert Parker, 12. Ray Storlie, and 13. Eugene Bullis; (third row) 14. Jim Ellingson (coach), 15. Gerry Chamberlain, 16. Toby Melville, 17. Bob Lahner, 18. Fred Hefty, 19. Jack Moore, 20. Richard Krogman, 21. Paul Fleming, 22. Don (Sonny) Lahner, 23. Bobby Gault, 24. George Olson, 25. Bob Lawler, 26. Donald Dickson, and 27. Bussy Severson; (back row) 28. Orville Gynnild, 29. Bill Lawler, 30. Bob Donaldson, 31. George Hoff, 32. Garfield Jentlie, 33. Lee Hoff, 34. Norm Erickson, 35. Gordon Buckli, 36. Archie Walker, 37. Ingvold Hendrickson, 38. Marshall Mikesell, 39. Gilbert Gingras, and 40. Mickey Hotujec. (Photograph courtesy of Norma Severson.)

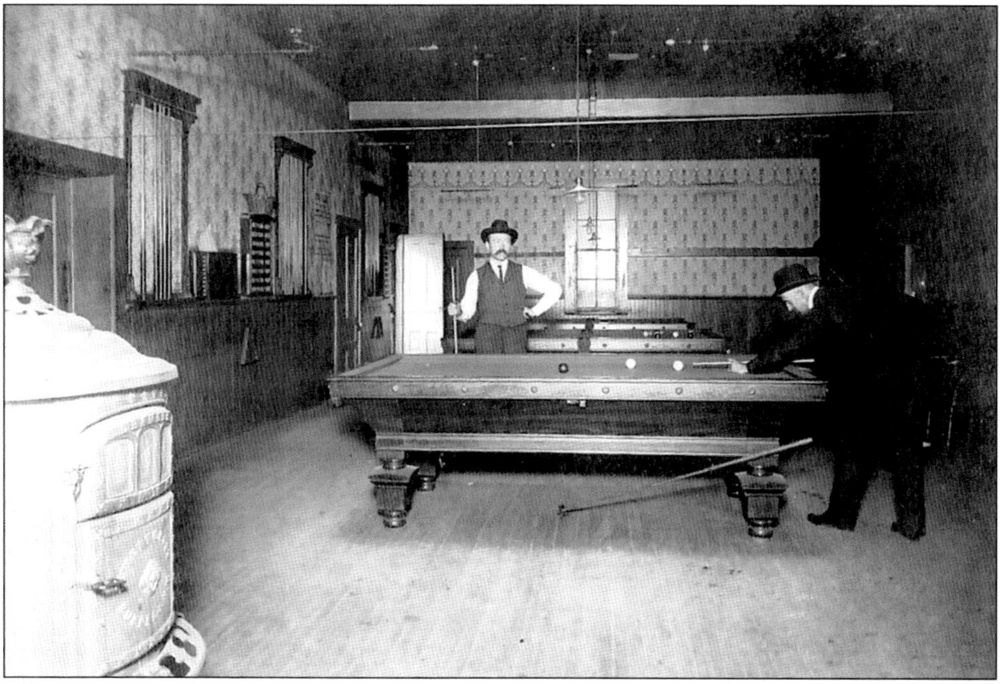

These two men share a game of pool at Severt Robertson's Pool Hall, Galloway Street, Eau Claire, *c.* 1905. (CVM.)

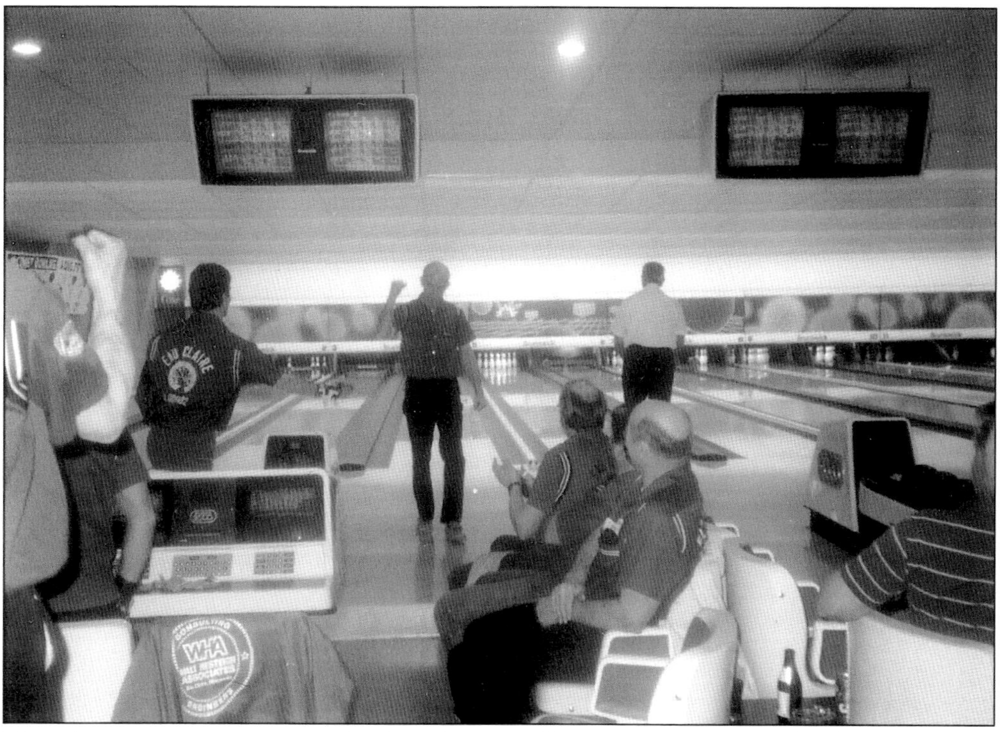

These bowlers comptete at the Elks State Bowling Tournament, Wagner's Bowling Lanes, Eau Claire, 1988. (Courtesy of Alice (nee Larson) Pingel.)

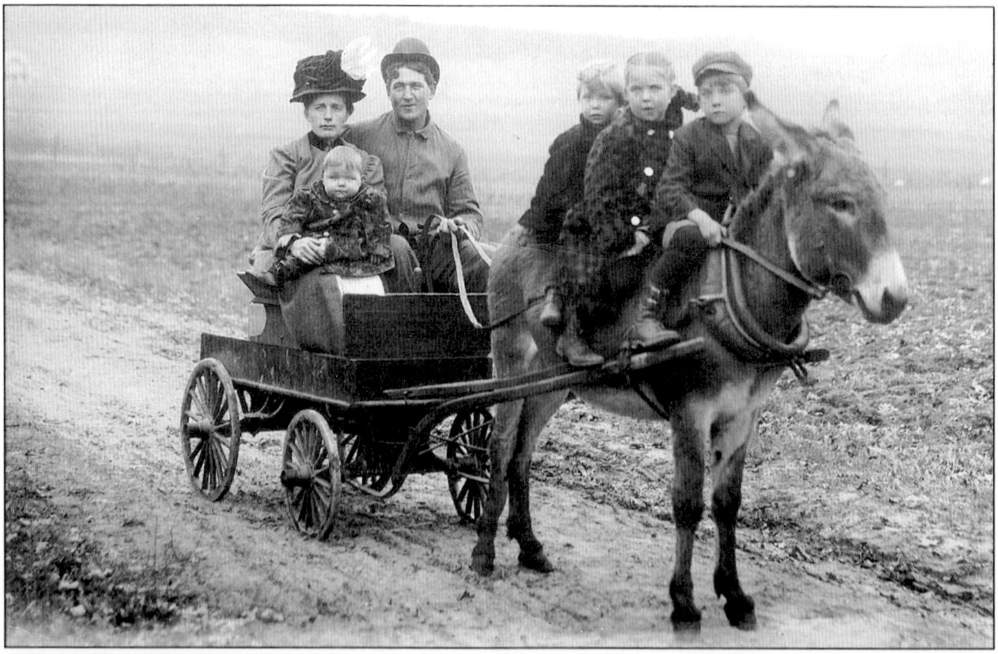

The William Welke family rides together with a donkey and cart, Cleghorn, Town of Pleasant Valley, 1913. (CVM.)

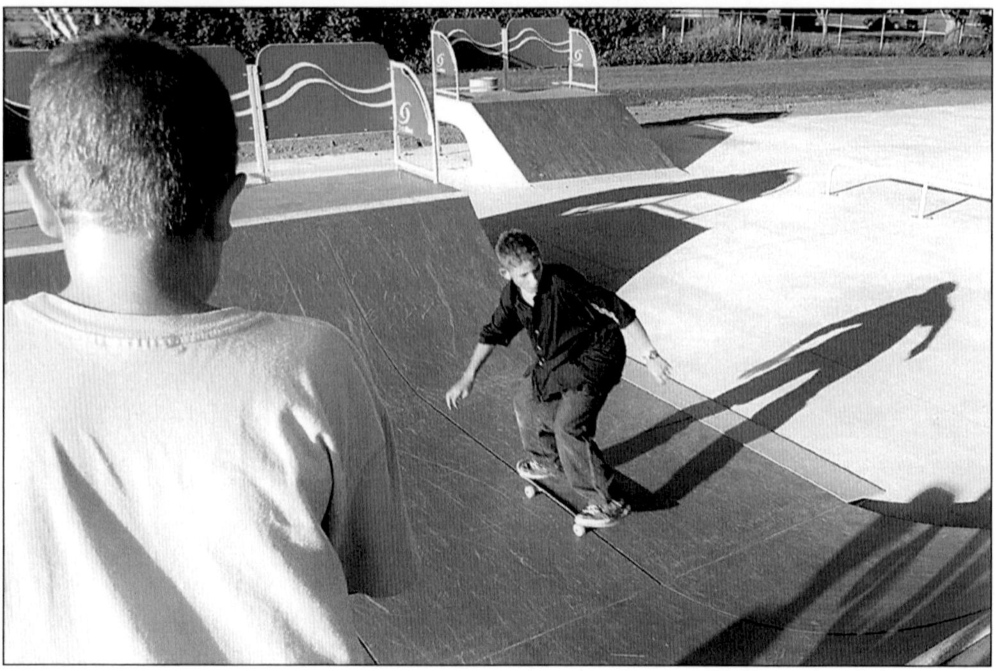

Kyle Dusso, 10, and Lyle Olson, 8, watched and waited their turns as Harley Kuberra, 15, showed his stuff at the new skate park in Augusta, September 2001. All three are from Augusta. (Photo courtesy of the Eau Claire *Leader-Telegram*.)

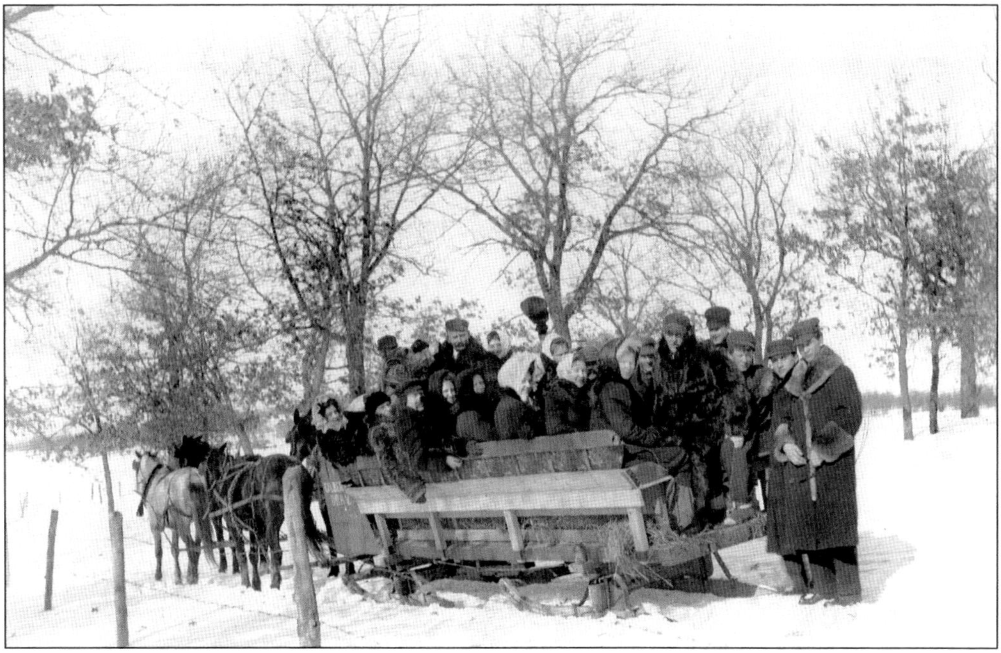

These people were at a sleigh ride party, Eau Claire County, 1911. Members of the Andrew Easterson, Severt Robertson, and Deitrick Nelson families all piled onto this dray for the ride. (CVM.)

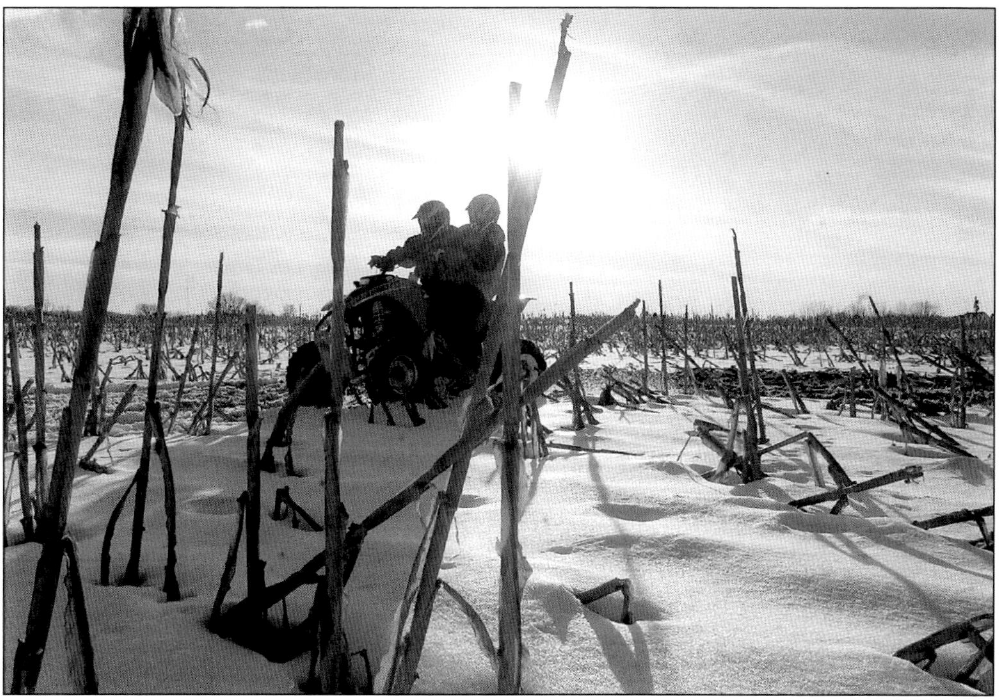

Dylin Steinke, 12, of Eau Claire gives his cousin Blake Cope, 12, of Altoona, a ride on his new Christmas present, a Polaris all-terrain vehicle (ATV), through a cornfield in the Town of Union, December 2003. (Photograph by Shane Opatz. Courtesy of the Eau Claire *Leader-Telegram*.)

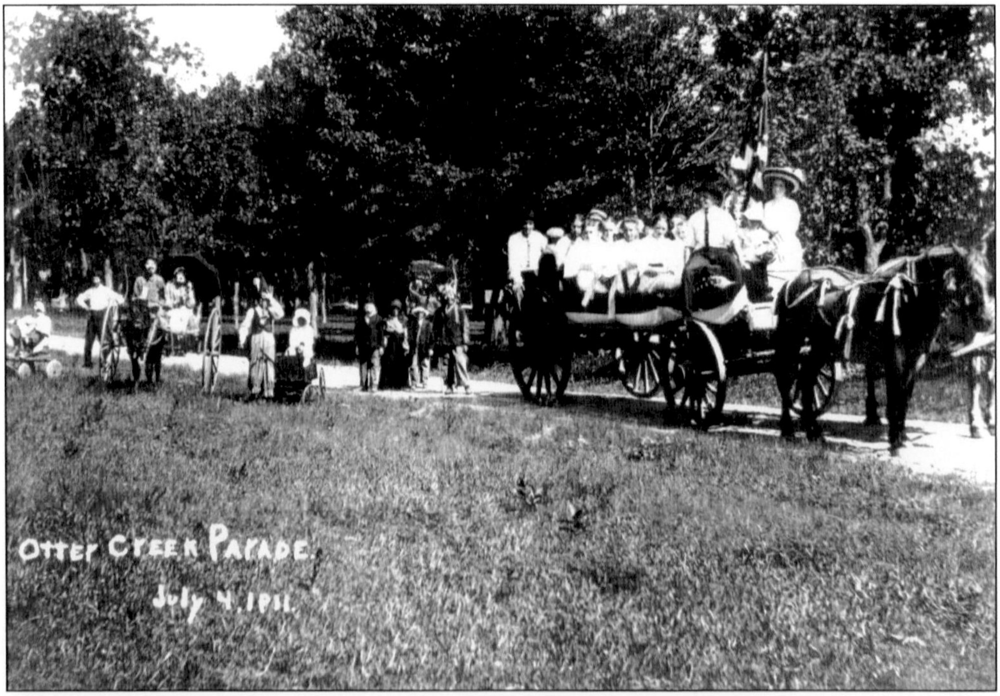

This is the Inependence Day parade at Otter Creek, July 4, 1911. (CVM.)

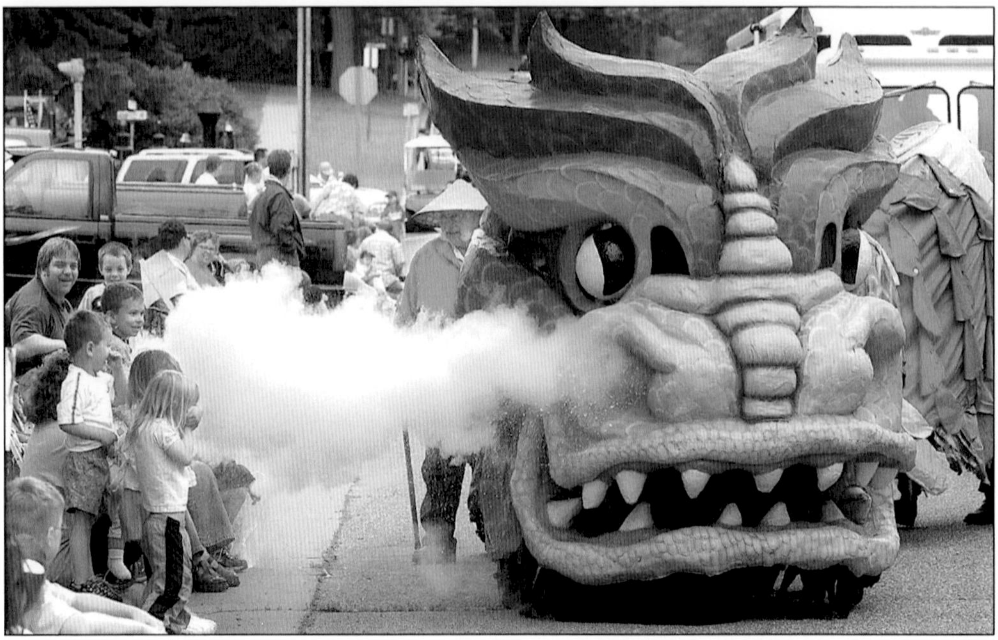

Spectators are surprised by a blast from "Chang" of the Osman Shrine Dragon Patrol of Rochester, Minn., Cinder City Days, Altoona, June 2003. Cinder City Days celebrates Altoona's railroad heritage. Steam locomotives spit hot cinders, which were partially burned coal or wood chunks, from their smokestacks. (Photograph by Steve Kinderman. Courtesy of the Eau Claire *Leader-Telegram*.)

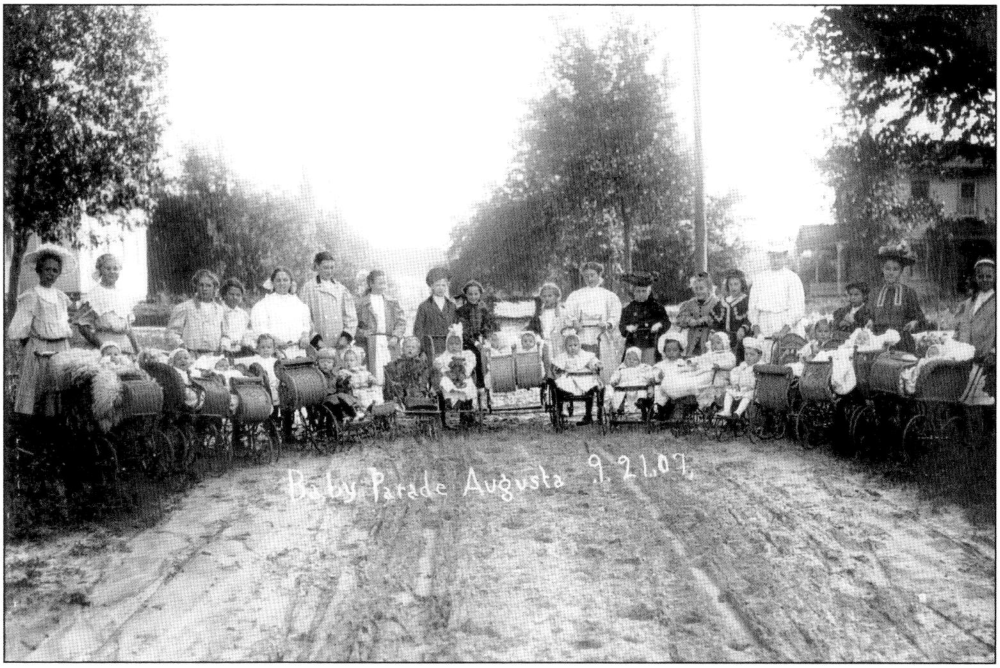

Parades were held for all kinds of occasions. This photograph shows the Baby parade, Augusta, September 1907. (CVM.)

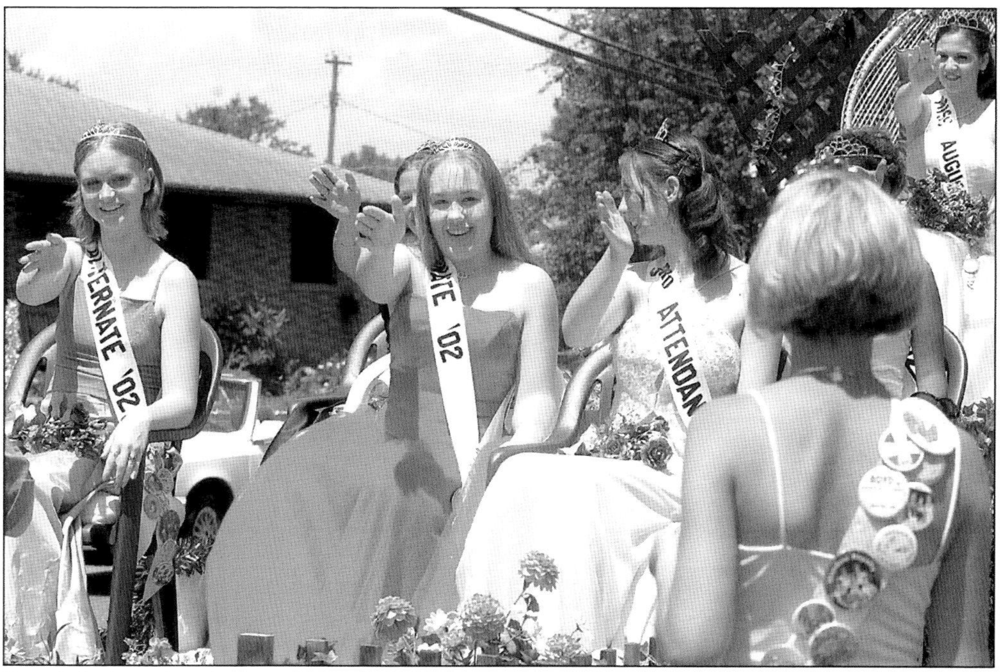

Teri Schulz, a fourth attendant of the previous year's court, teaches the new court the art of the "parade wave" minutes before a parade in Augusta, July 2002. (Photograph by Matthew Resenhoeft. Courtesy of the Eau Claire *Leader-Telegram*.)

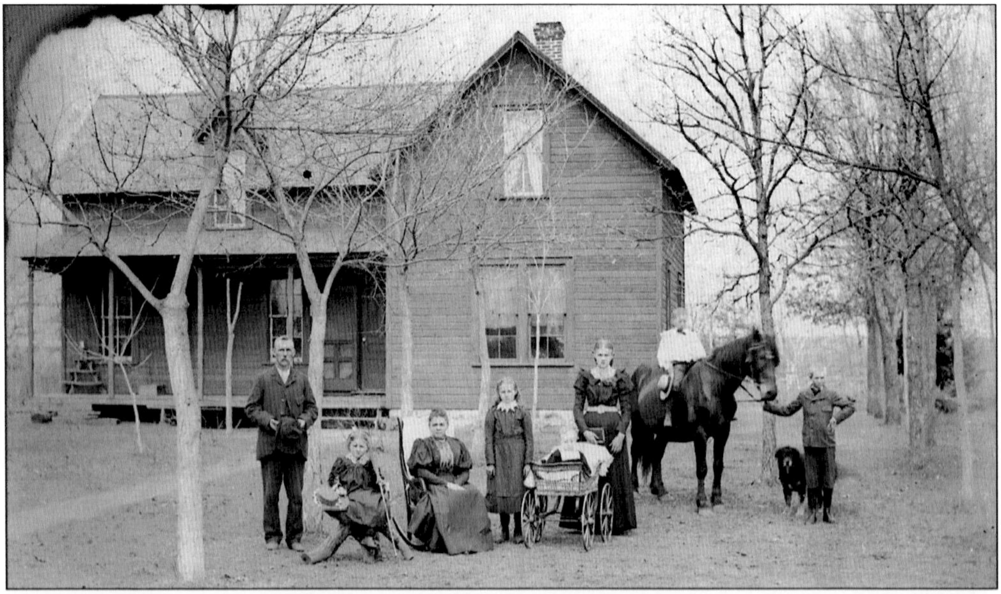

The Miller family poses for a photograph on their farm near Lowes Creek, Town of Washington, 1898. Pictured from left to right are Grandpa Miller, Martha, Grandma Miller, Pauline, Edna (in buggy), Anna, Albert on horse Nancy, dog Shep, and Henry. The photograph was made by C.R. Monroe, the "Traveling Photographer." From the 1860s until after 1900, scores of professional photographers traveled America, providing rural populations with family portraits, landscapes of their homesteads, and other photographic services otherwise unavailable except in larger towns. C.R. Monroe's work appeared in *The Photographer's Eye* by John Szarkowski (Museum of Modern Art, 1966). (CVM.)

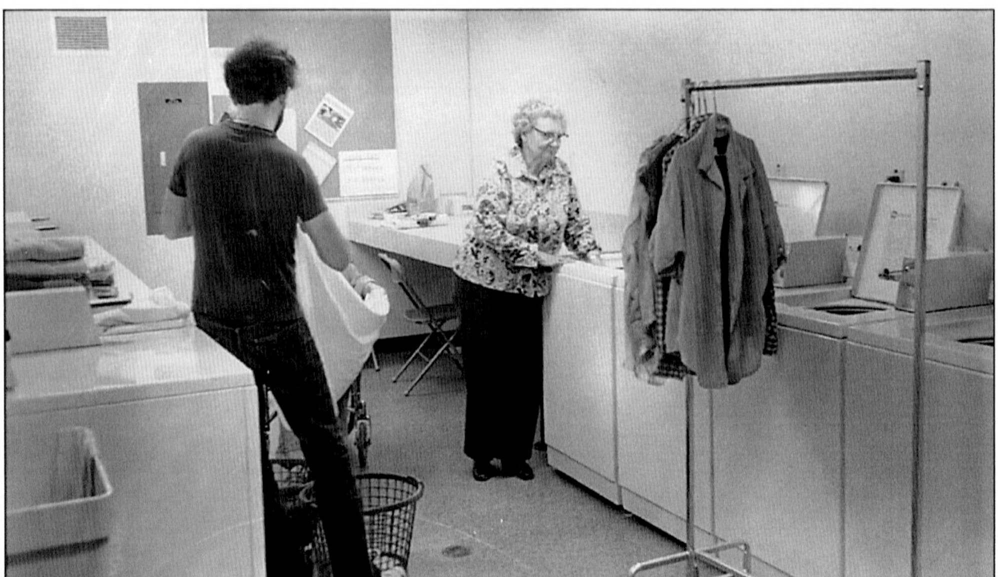

Pictured here is the tenants' laundry area, Park Tower Apartments, Farwell Street, Eau Claire, September 1980. Park Tower offers senior apartments, income-based rentals, and pull stations with direct links to city fire and ambulance services. (CVM.)

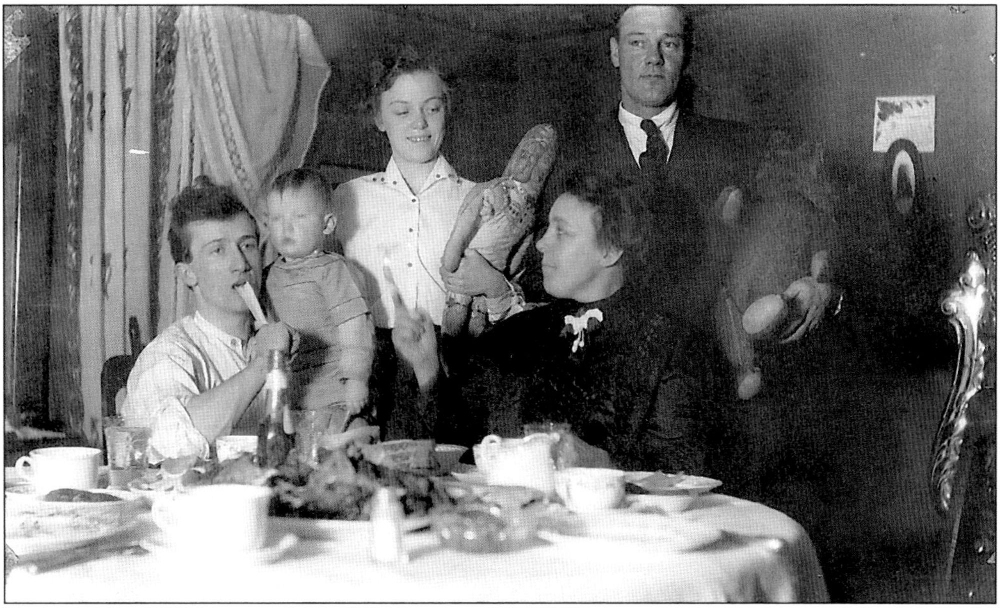

Fred, Dale, and Charity Deroin are pictured with Charity's parents, Clara and Ted Everson, in Eau Claire. (CVM.)

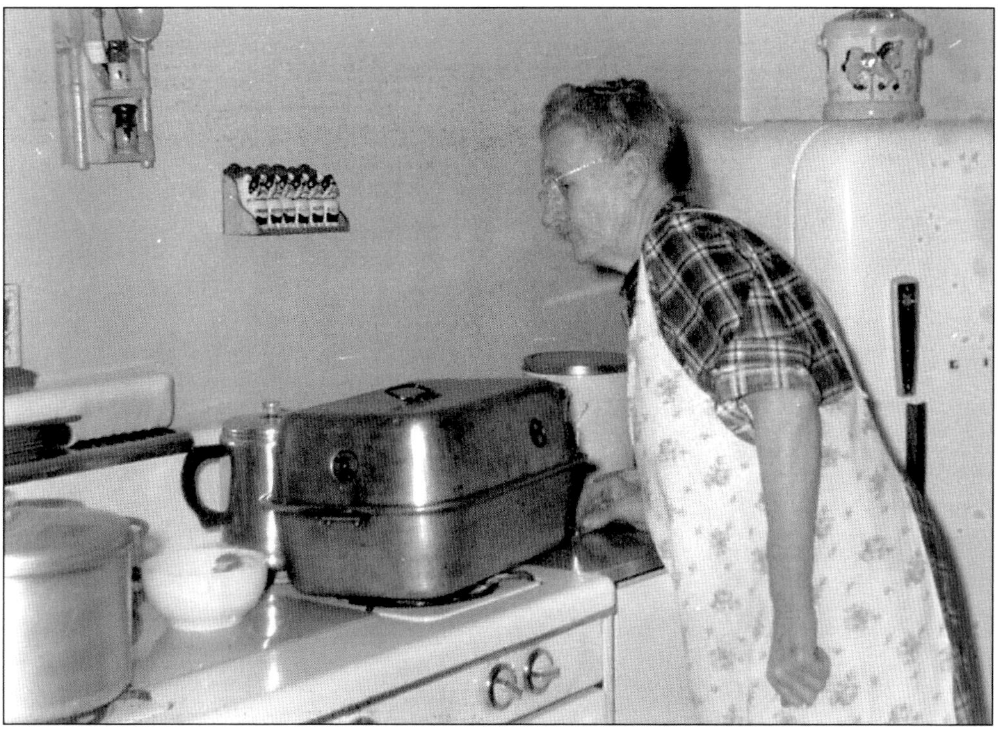

Florence Rushman cooks the Thanksgiving turkey, Eau Claire, 1960s. (Courtesy of Alice (nee Larson) Pingel.)

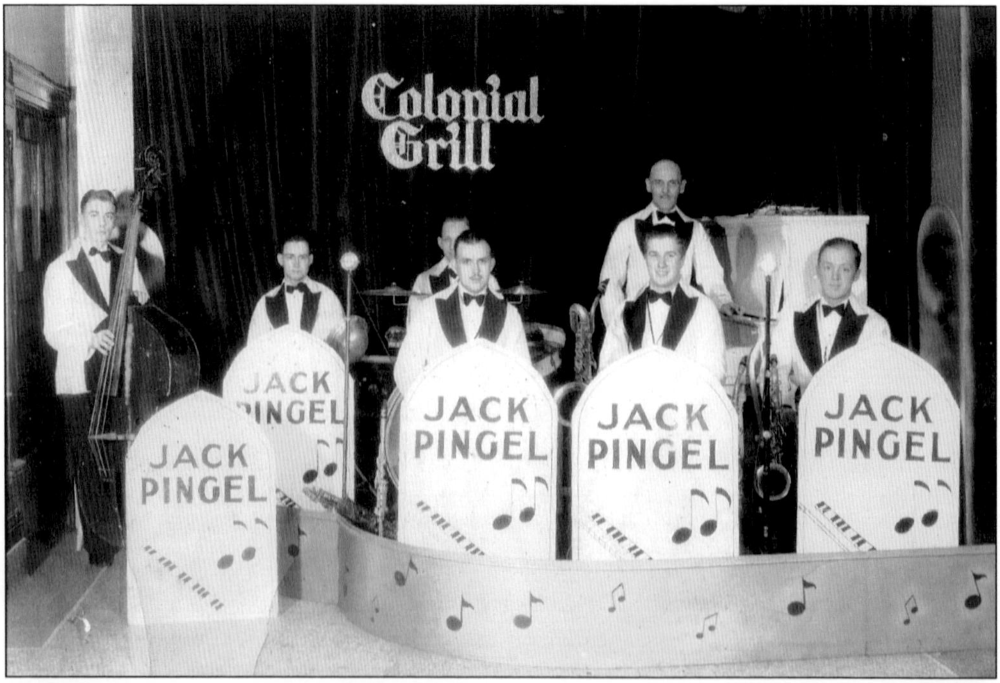

Jack Pingel and his orchestra perform at the Colonial Grill, Eau Claire Hotel, 1937-1938. Pictured from left to right are: (seated) Danny Torrance, Bill Larson, Jimmy Knight, Loren Pratt, and Alf Anderson; (standing) George King (bass), Jack Pingel. (CVM.)

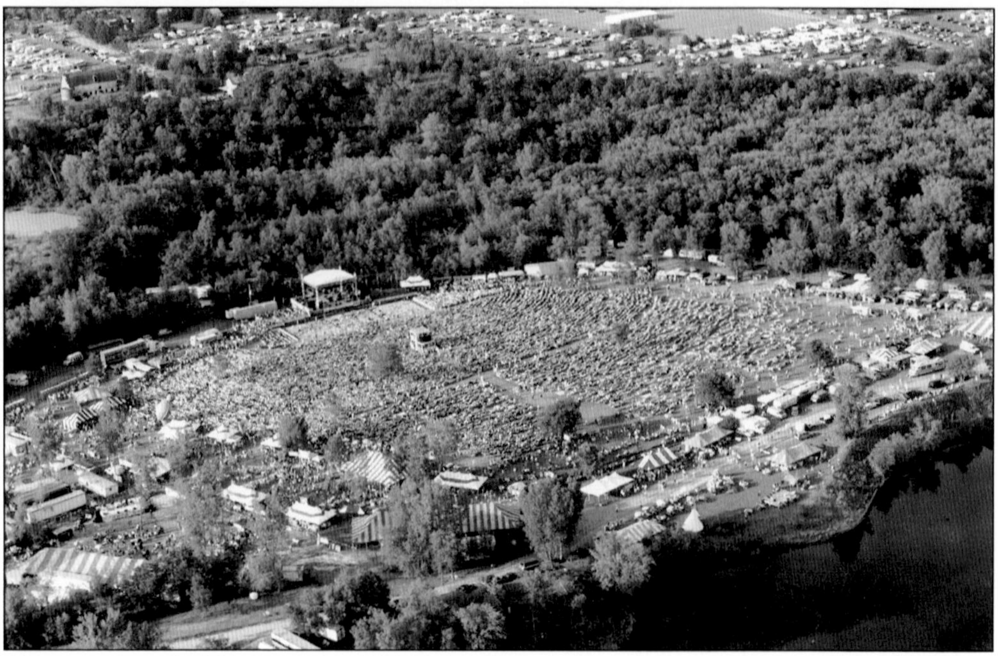

There was a packed house at the IGA Country Jam USA, Town of Union, 1990s. The three day country music festival attracts about 140,000 people to Eau Claire County each summer. (Courtesy of the Chippewa Valley Convention and Visitors Bureau.)

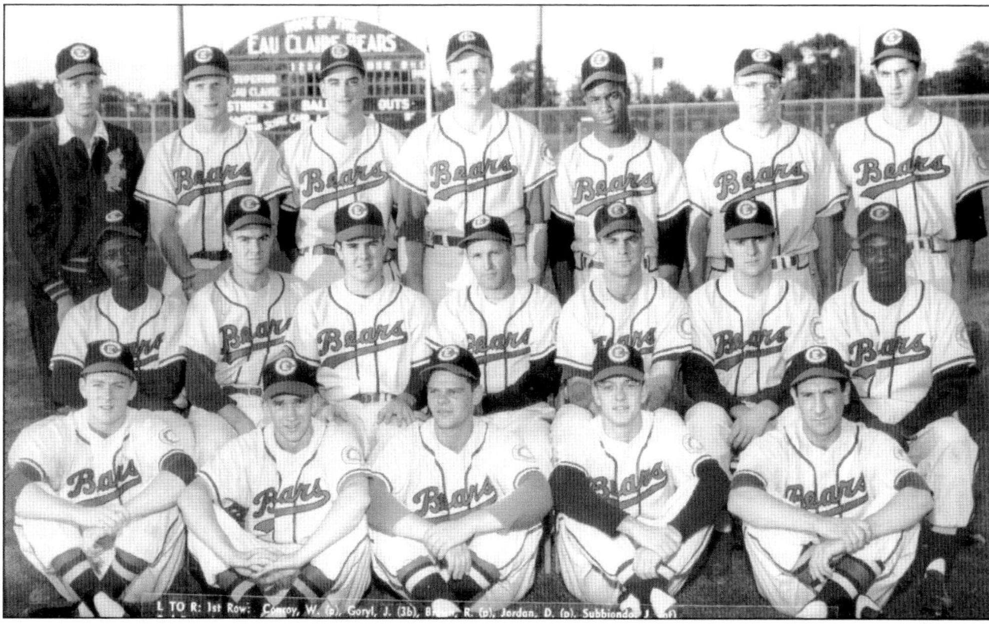

This is the Eau Claire Bears team photo from 1952. Eau Claire has a long and storied baseball tradition, which is chronicled in *Baseball in Eau Claire* by Jason Christopherson (Arcadia Publishing, 2003), and *A Summer Up North* by Jerry Poling (University of Wisconsin Press, 2002). (Photograph by Davis Studio. CVM.)

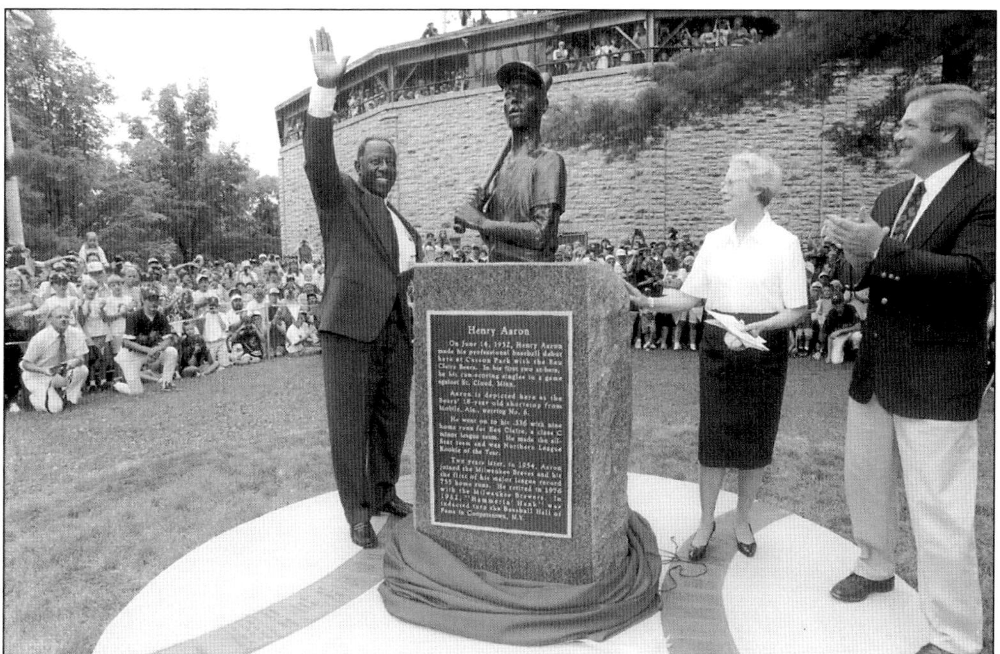

Henry "Hank" Aaron, Jane Campbell (widow of sculptor Ken Campbell), and Mark Lewis are pictured at the dedication of Aaron's statue in Carson Park, Eau Claire, on August 17, 1994. Aaron made his professional debut with the Eau Claire Bears in 1952. 30 years later, in 1982, the home-run king was inducted into the Baseball Hall of Fame. (Photograph by Dan Reiland. CVM.)

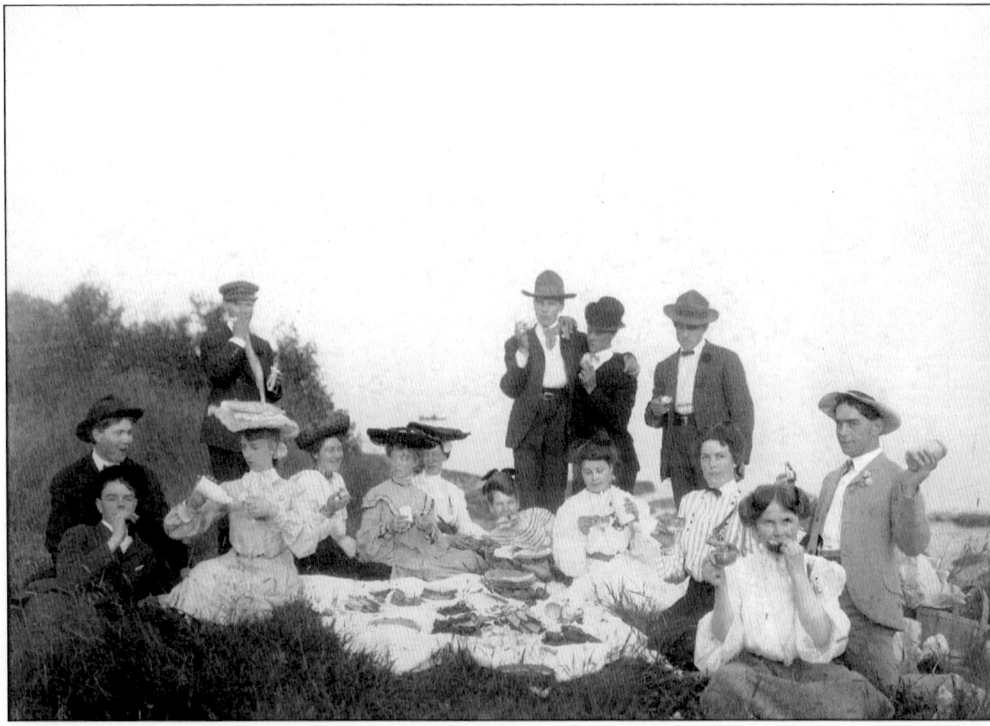

This picnic was held at Fairchild in 1901. (CVM.)

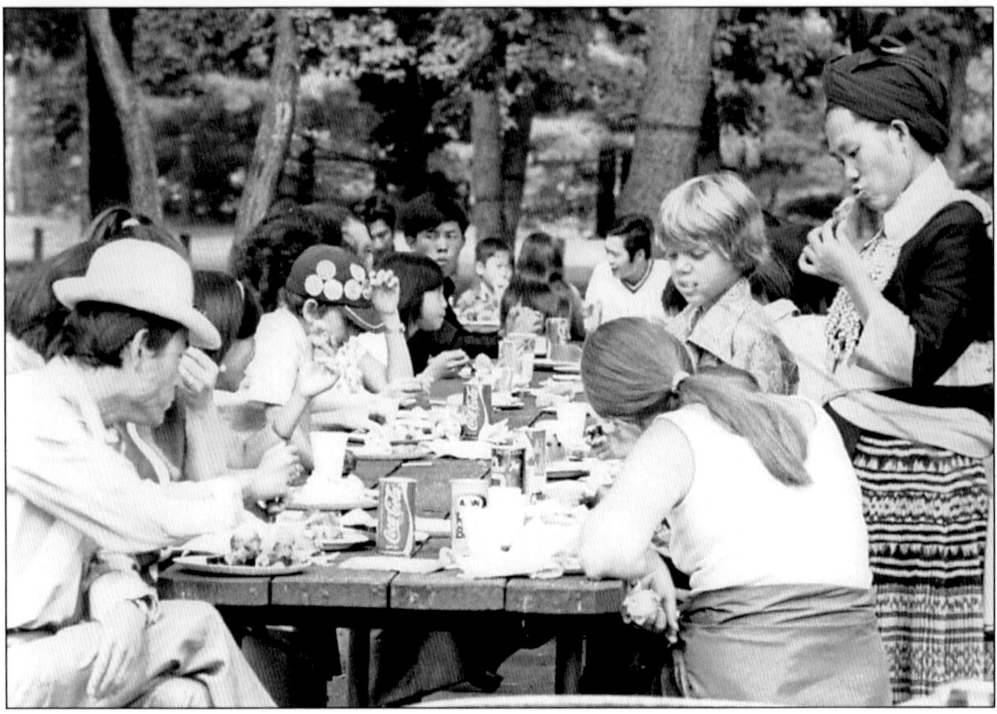

This picnic took place at Carson Park, Eau Claire, perhaps in the 1980s. (CVM.)

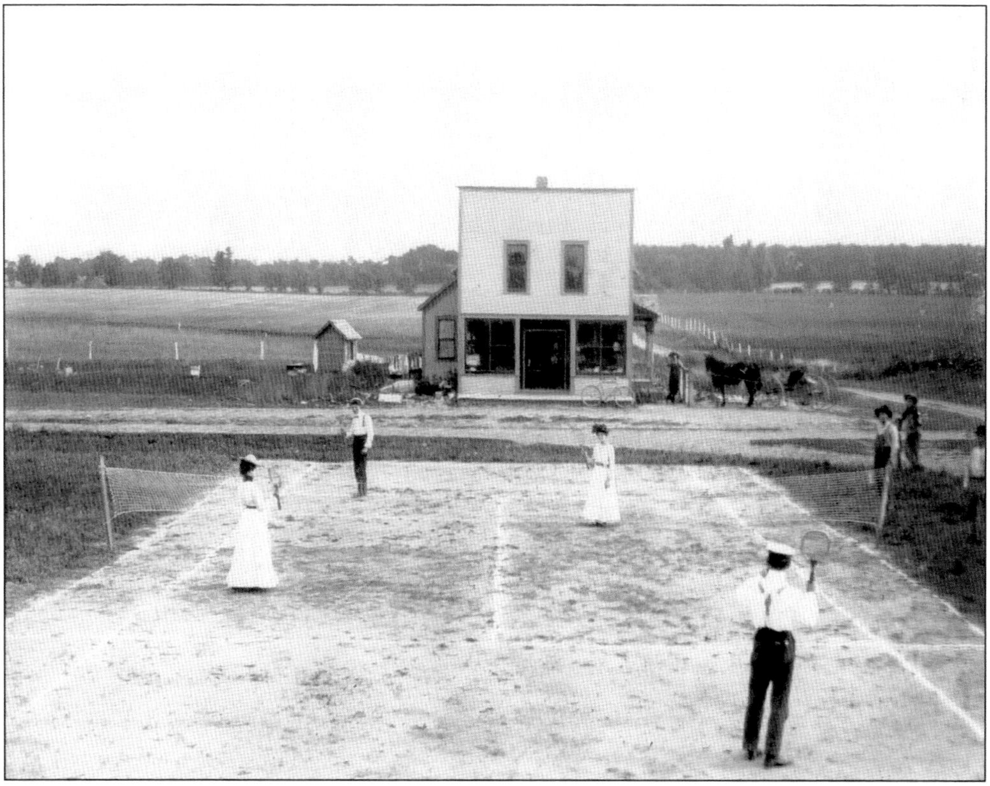

This mixed doubles tennis match was played near Cleghorn, Town of Pleasant Valley, *c.* 1900. Pictured are Mr. Kennedy, Matie Truax, Mabel Dunham, and Will Zeitler. (CVM.)

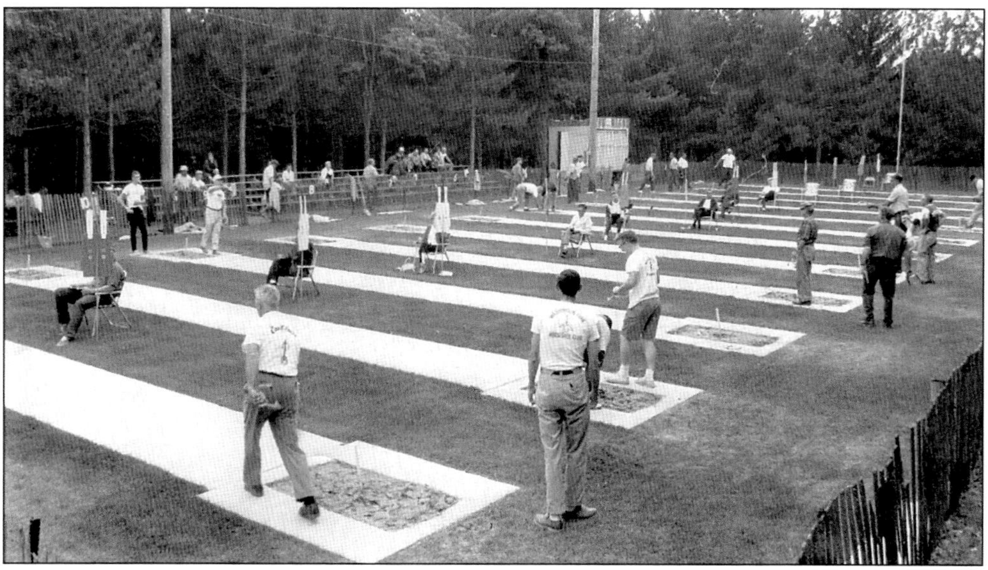

Horseshoes was obviously very popular, as seen in this photograph, taken at the horseshoe courts at Carson Park, Eau Claire, 1968. (Courtesy of Curt Bestul.)

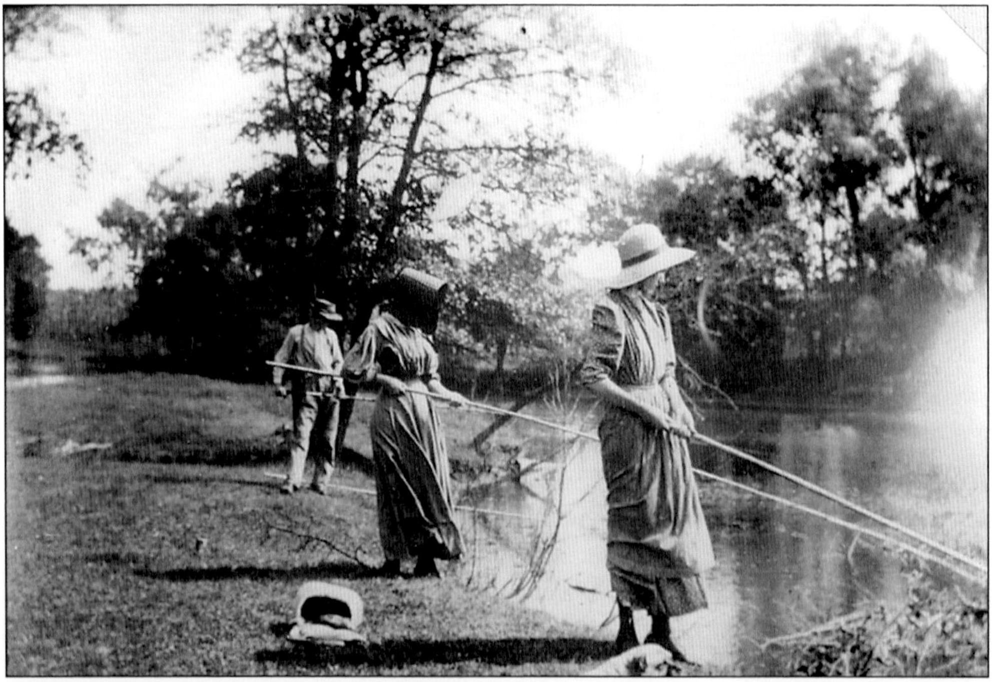

Fishing on Fall Creek mill pond. (FCHS.)

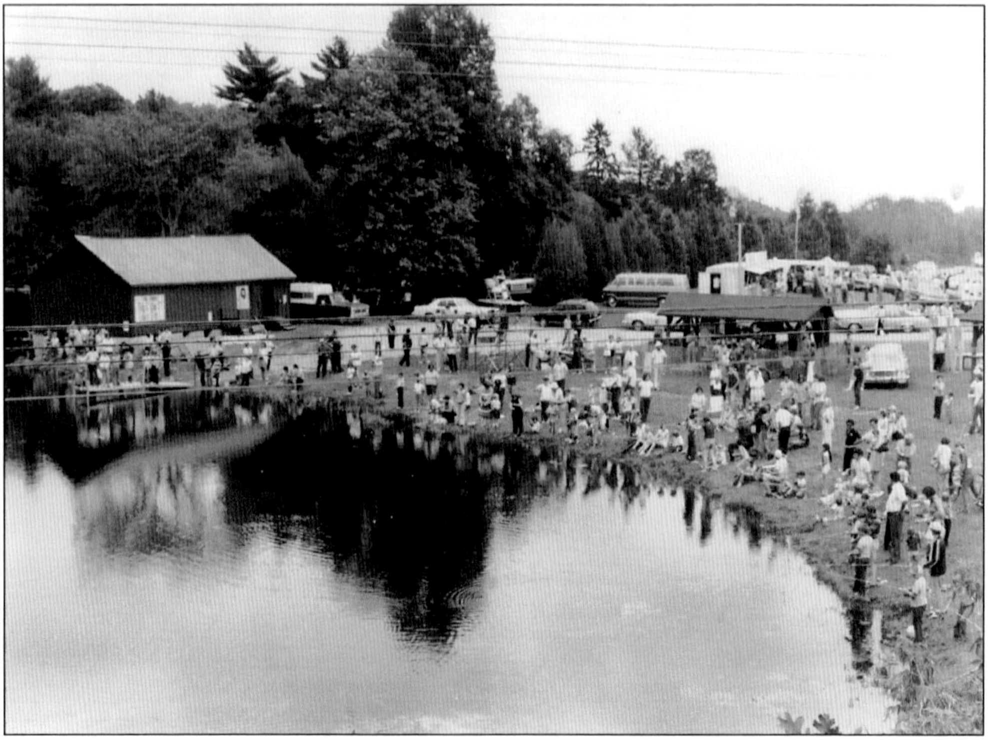

This kids' fishing contest on Fall Creek mill pond took place in July 1977. (FCHS.)

Nine

A Place for Friendship and Fellowship

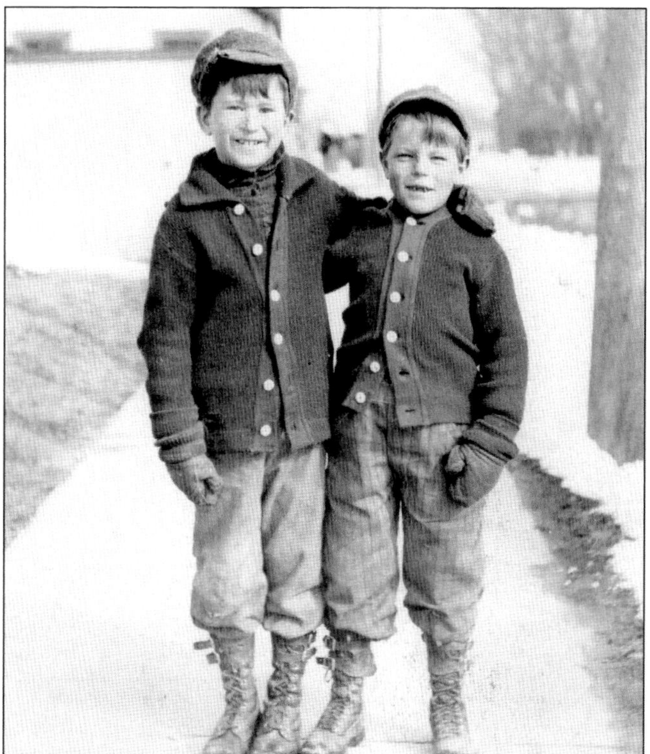

Edwin Livesey and Raymond Hammer were photographed in Augusta, *c*. 1911. (CVM.)

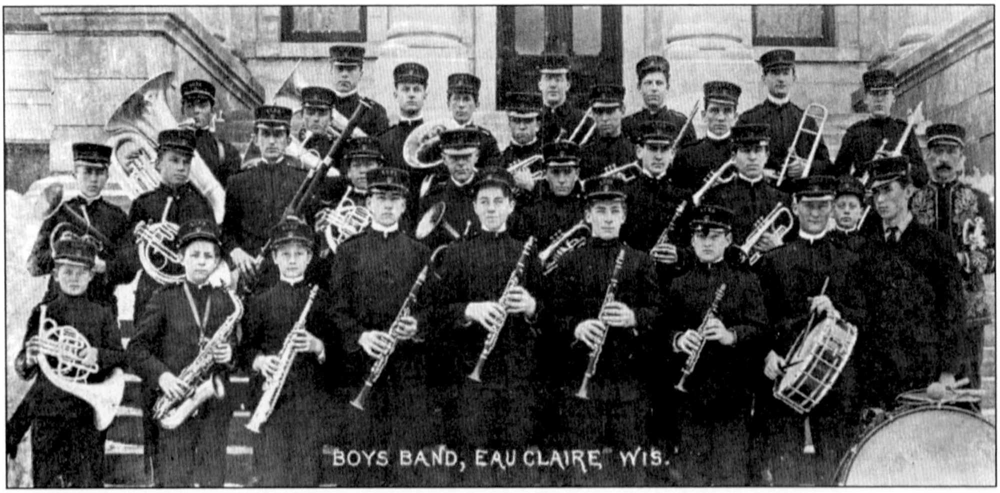

This Boys Band from Eau Claire was photographed some time after 1910. Boys Bands were organized as after-school activities. (CVM.)

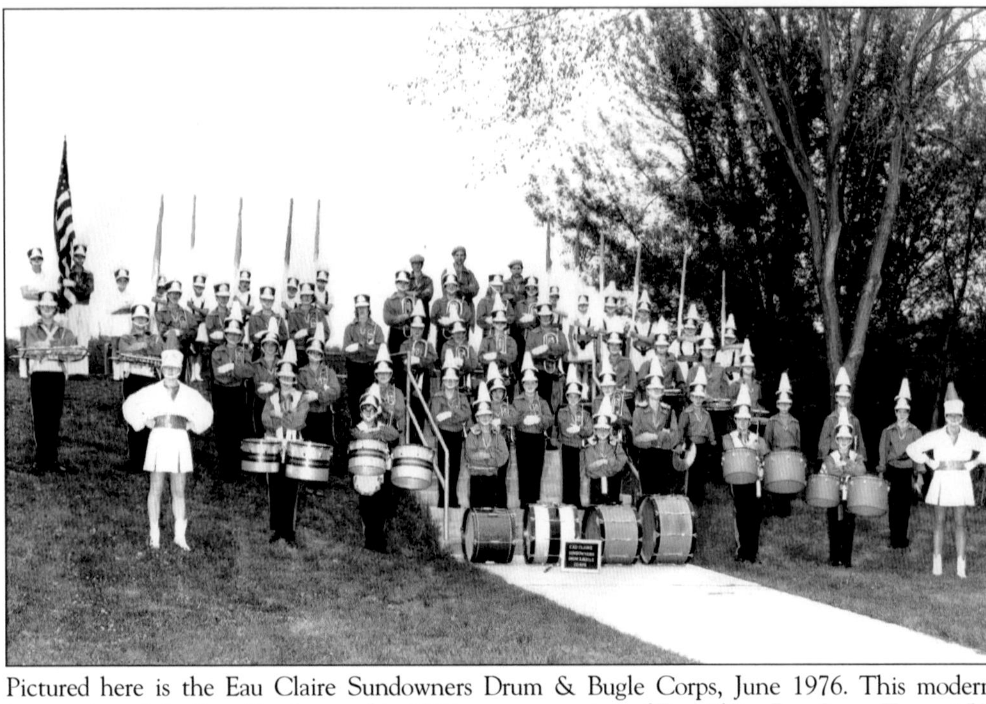

Pictured here is the Eau Claire Sundowners Drum & Bugle Corps, June 1976. This modern incarnation of the Boys Band started in 1952 as an extension of Eau Claire Boy Scout Troop 150. In 1959, the Scouts changed their name to Eau Claire Boys Drum & Bugle Corps. In June of 1970, the corps accepted girls into their ranks. They became the Sundowners in 1971. (CVM.)

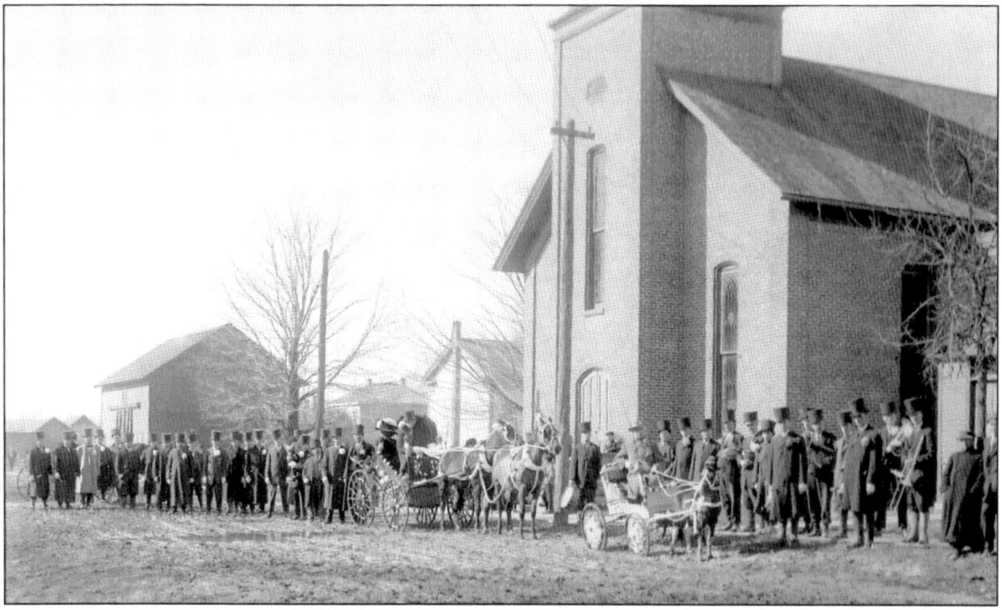

This is the Knights of Pythias minstrel parade, Augusta, September 1911. The Order of Knights of Pythias is an international non-sectarian fraternal order, founded in 1864. Minstrel parades were often held before circuses or other public entertainments. Minstrel parades were more often a southern U.S. tradition, although they were part of traveling shows. In this case, "minstrel" probably referred to the kind of music played, usually Southern standards such as "My Old Kentucky Home," "The Arkansas Traveler," and "Dixie." (CVM.)

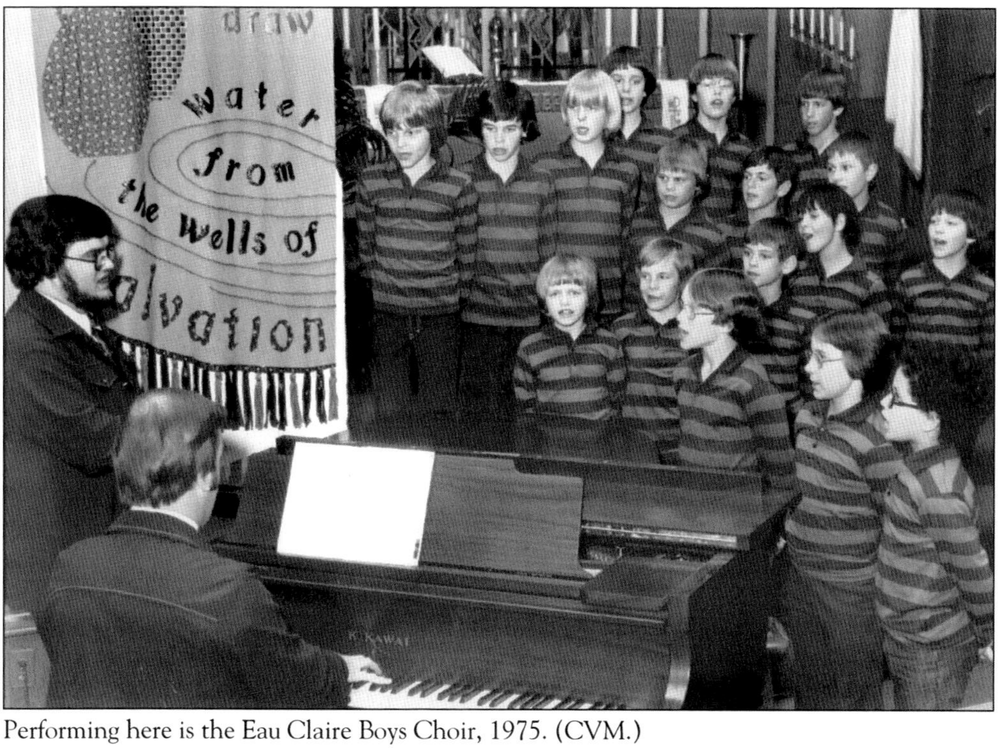

Performing here is the Eau Claire Boys Choir, 1975. (CVM.)

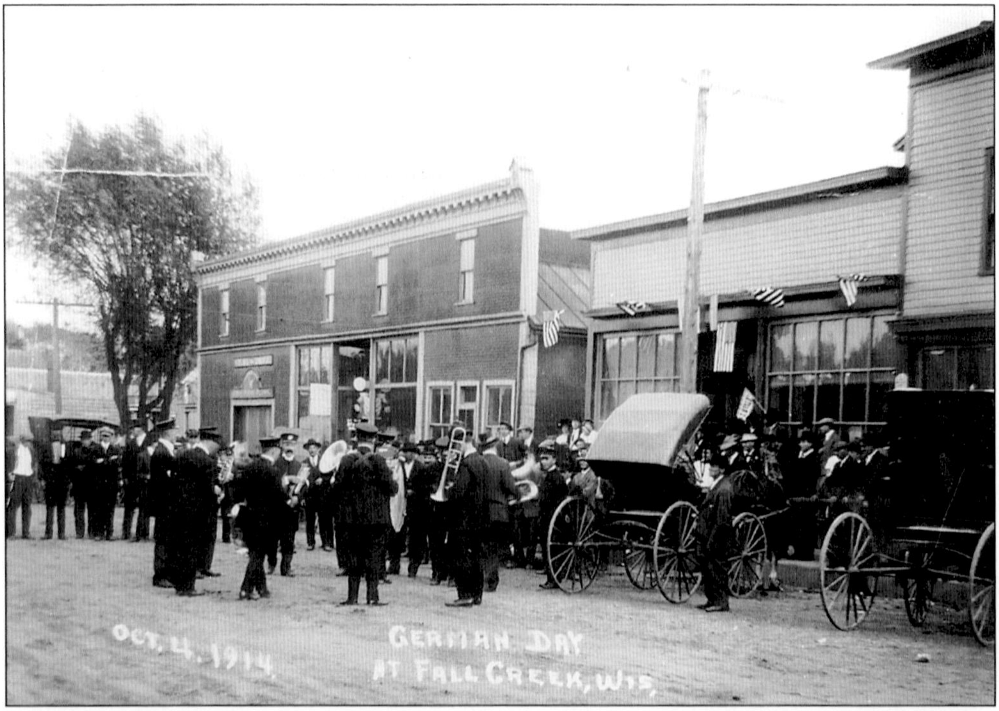

This German Day celebration is taking place in front of Emanuel's Hall and Roesler's Hardware, Fall Creek. (FCHS.)

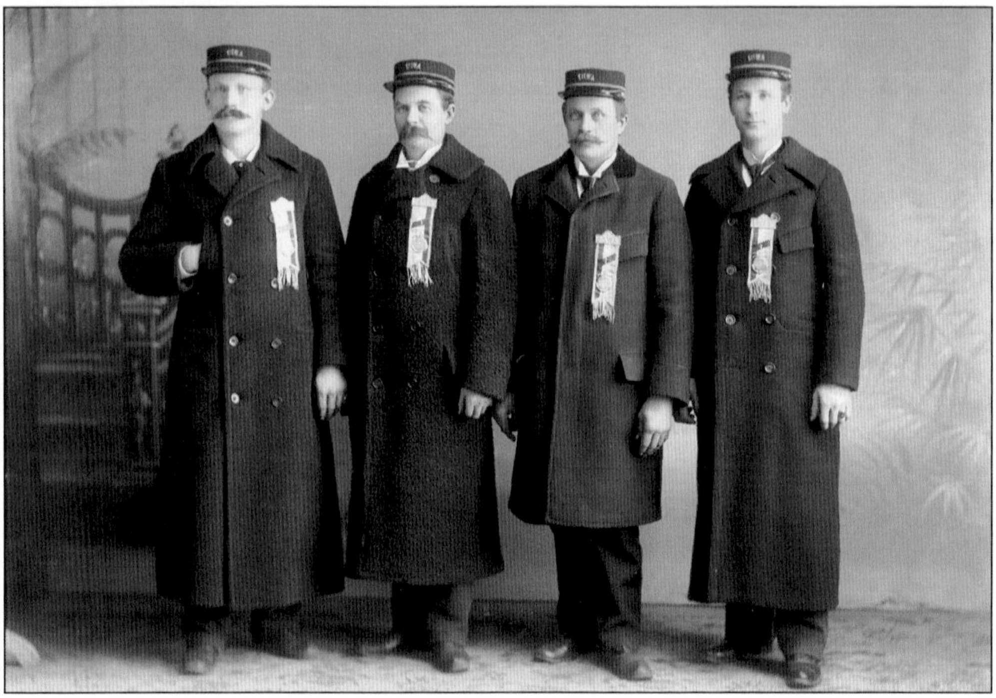

These four men were members of the Independent Scandinavian Workingmen's Association, 1900. (Photograph by R.G. Shaker, Eau Claire. CVM.)

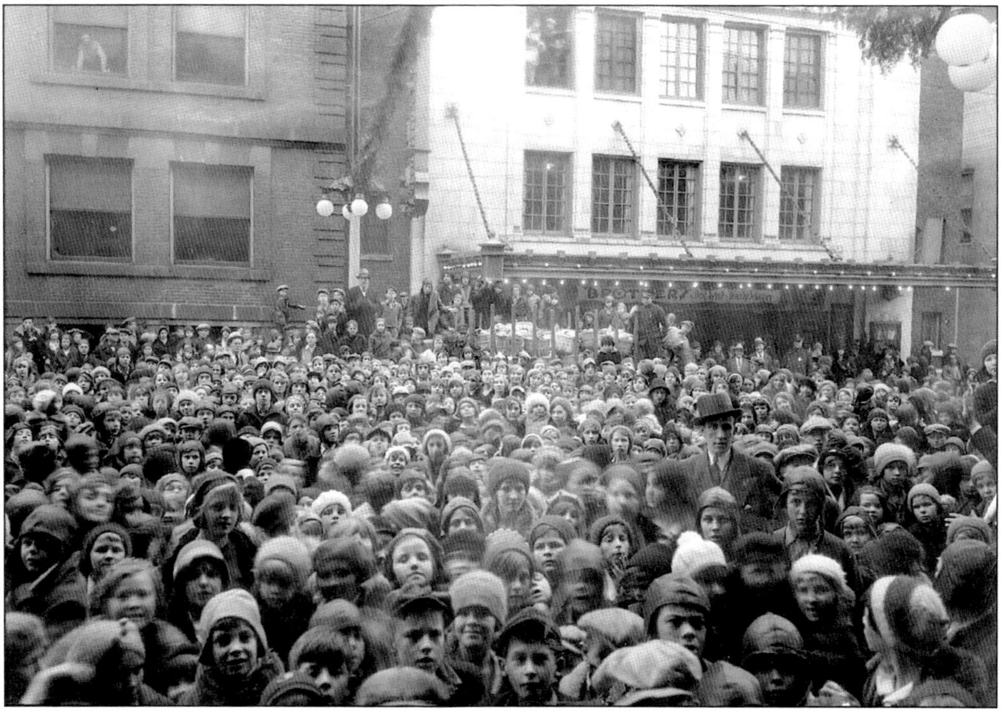

Pictured here is the Elks Club Children's Christmas party in downtown Eau Claire, 1930. (CVM.)

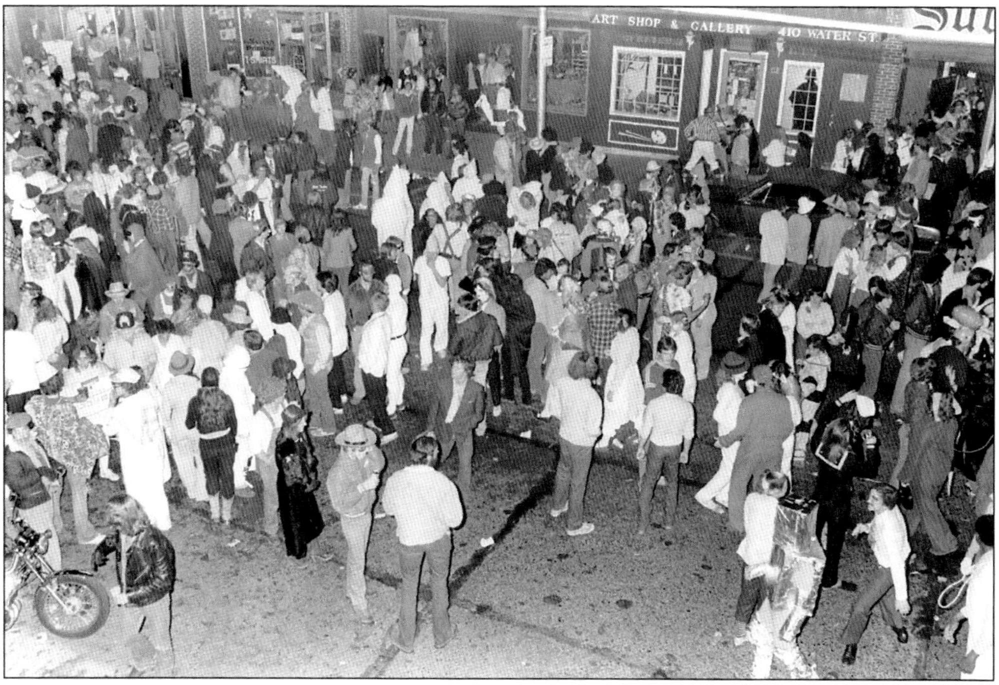

Pictured here are Halloween festivities on Water Street in Eau Claire, between 1980 and 1984. (CVM.)

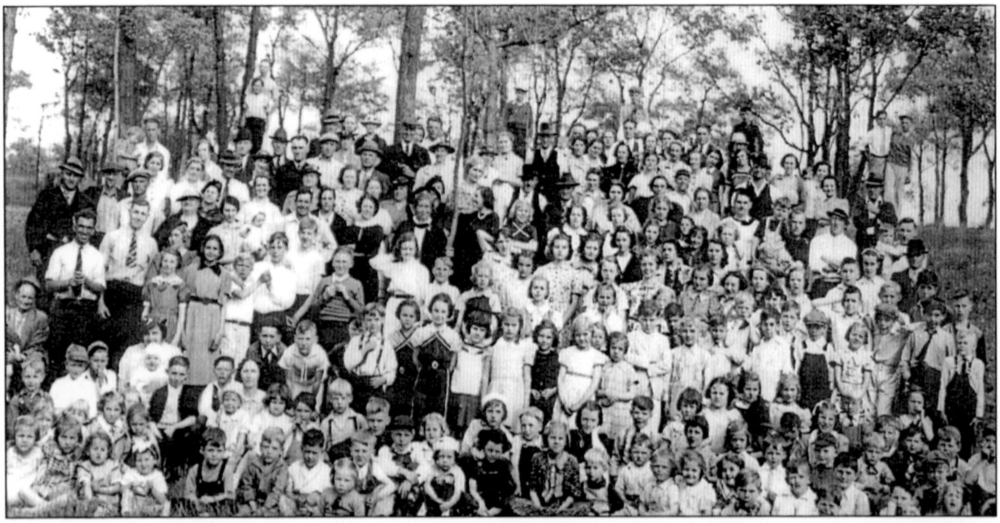

This crowd was attending the Shawtown picnic, Eau Claire, 1930s. The Shawtown neighborhood was named after the Daniel Shaw Lumber Company. Many of that company's workers lived there. Although the Shaw mill is long-gone, Shawtown retains its distinct identity and name. (Courtesy of Margaret Severson.)

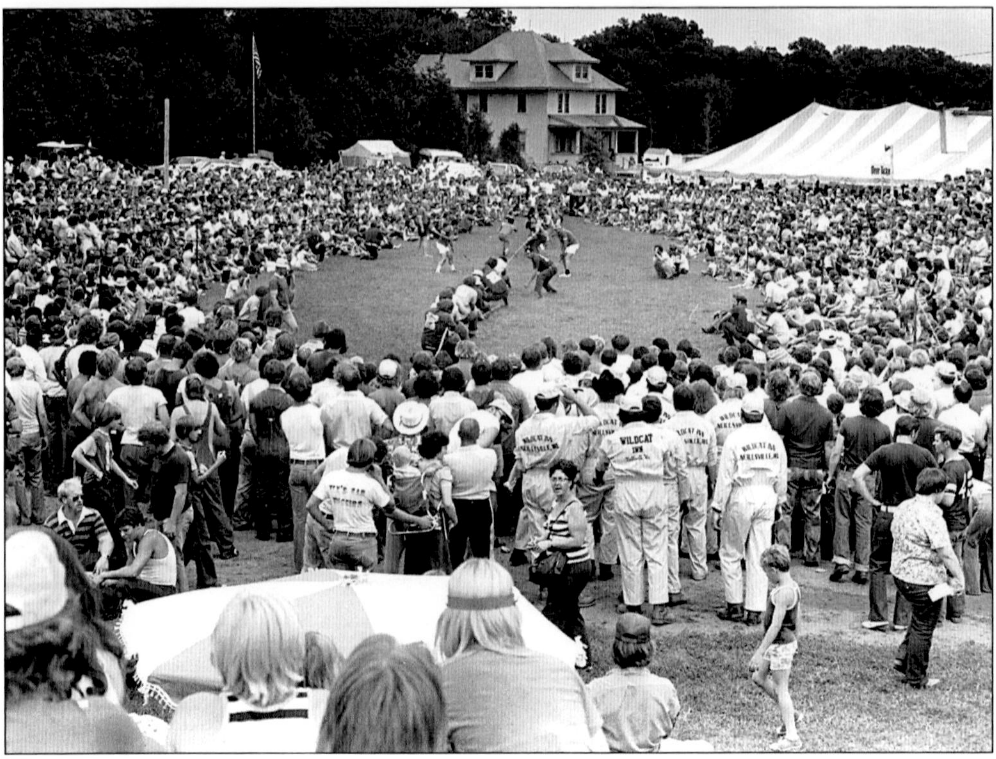

A large crowd watched the Fall Creek Tug-o-War, July 1977. (FCHS.)

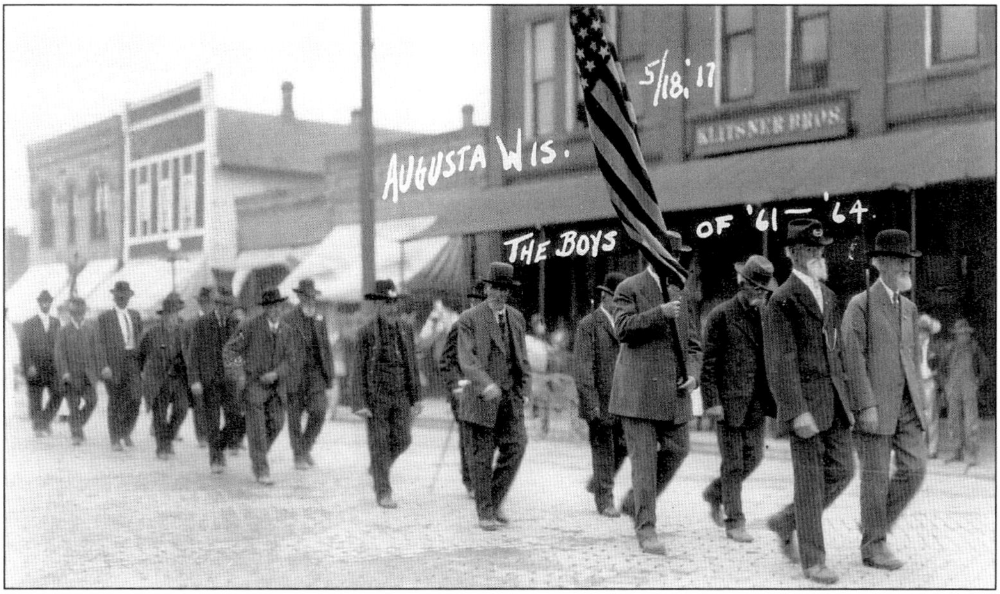

Civil War veterans marched in an Augusta parade, May 18, 1917. On that date, Congress passed the Selective Service Act, giving the President the power to draft soldiers. May 18th is also the anniversary of the beginning of the Siege of Vicksburg during the Civil War. (CVM.)

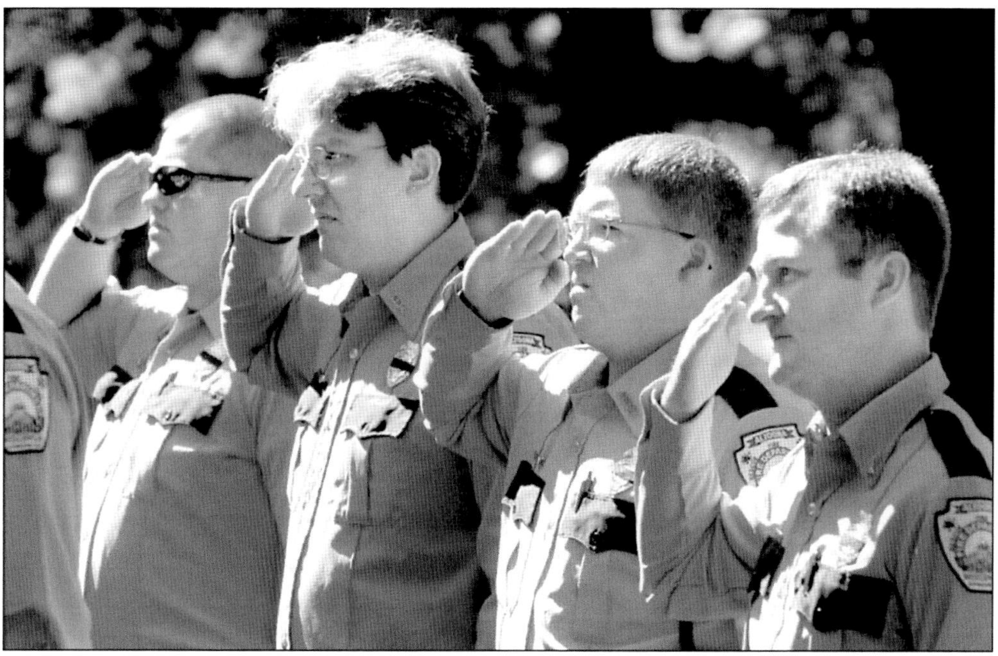

Pictured, from left to right, are Jason Knecht, Dave Daken, Andrew Doney, and Rodger Frye of the Altoona Fire Department saluting as the American flag was lowered to half mast during a September 11 commemoration ceremony, Owen Park, Eau Claire, 2002. (Photograph by Dan Reiland. Courtesy of the Eau Claire *Leader-Telegram*.)

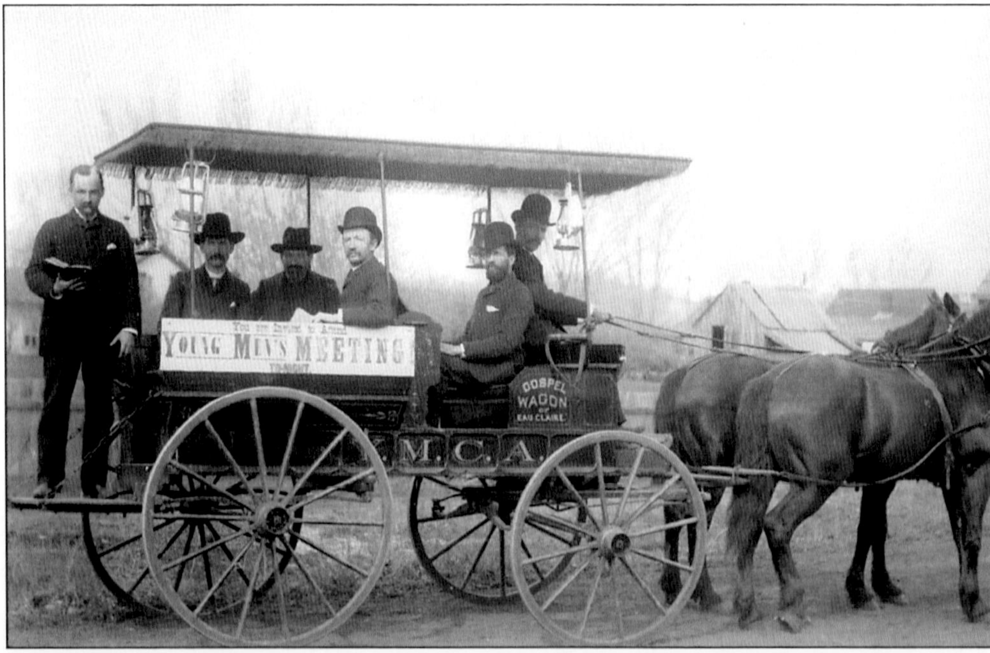

The YMCA Gospel Wagon of Eau Claire is pictured here before 1900. The local chapter was organized in 1881; members gave lectures, visited logging camps, and passed out literature. In 1961, the association built a multi-million dollar facility on Graham Avenue. The "Y" also maintains Camp Manitou, a summer camp near New Auburn. (CVM.)

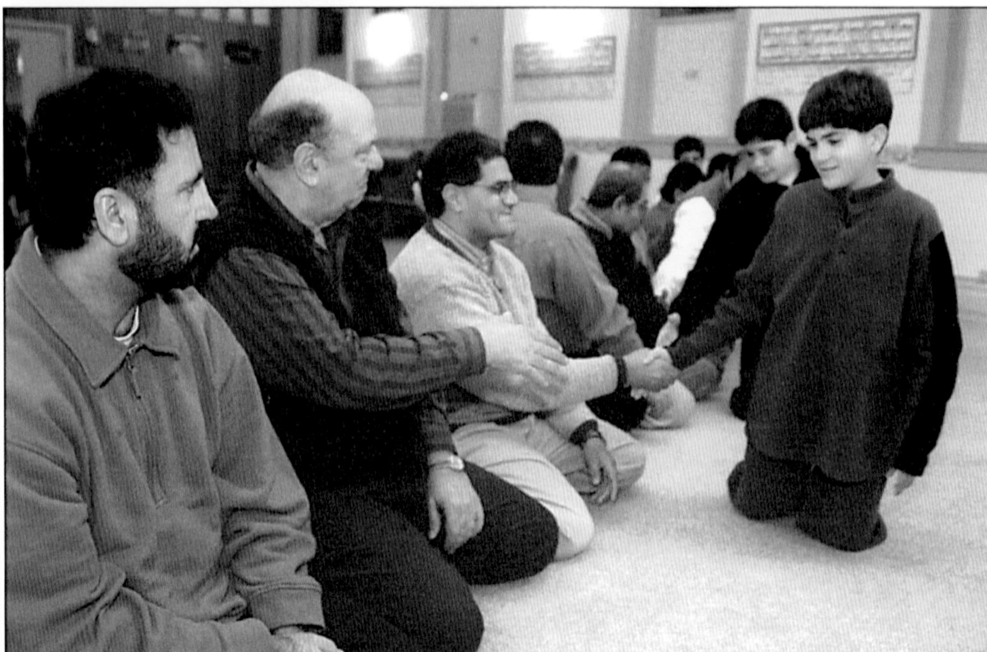

Yousef Ahmed and Tarek Elgindi, both from Eau Claire, show respect to their elders during a prayer at the Islamic Center and Mosque, Altoona, December 2001. (Photograph by Matthew Resenhoeft. Courtesy of the Eau Claire *Leader-Telegram*.)

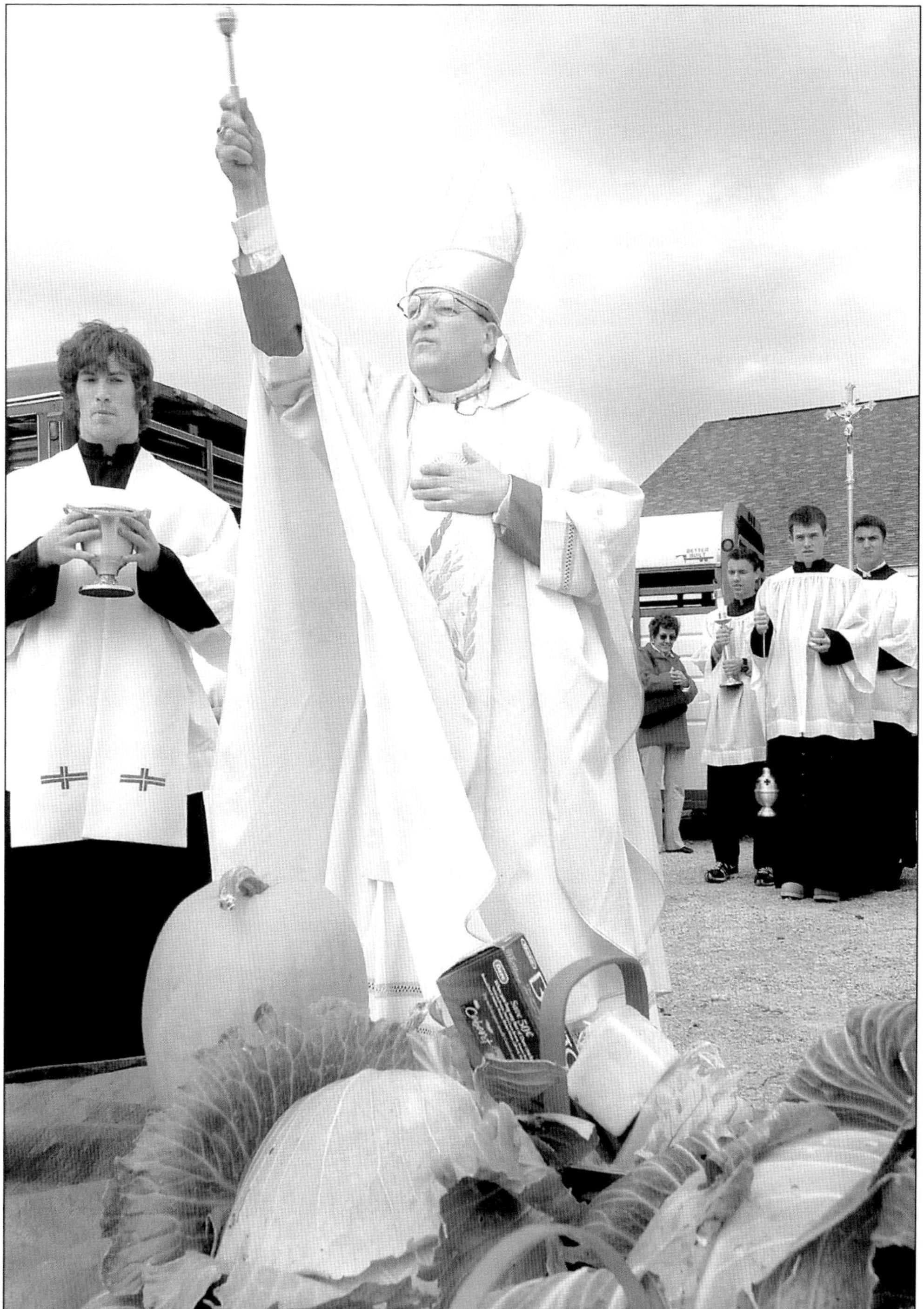

Bishop Raymond Burke bless the crops and animals at the Rural Life Day observance of the Diocese of La Crosse at St. Raymond of Penafort Catholic Church, Brackett, Town of Washington, September 2003. (Photograph by Dan Reiland. Courtesy of the Eau Claire *Leader-Telegram*.)

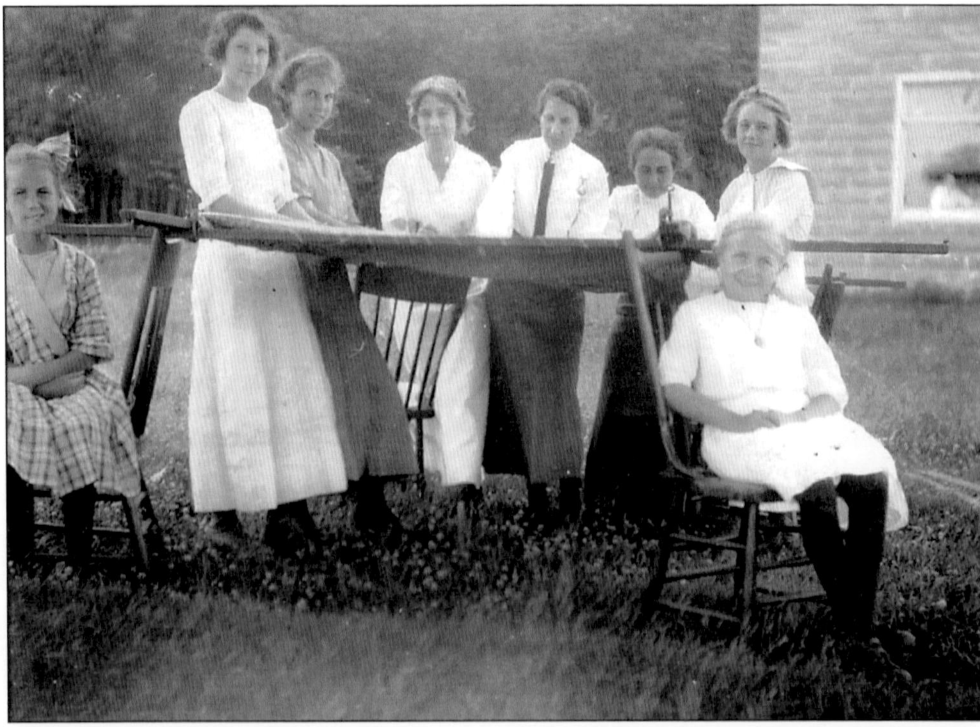

Mary Foster, third from left, and friends gathered for a quilting bee at the Foster family farm, Eau Claire County, *c.* 1910. (CVM.)

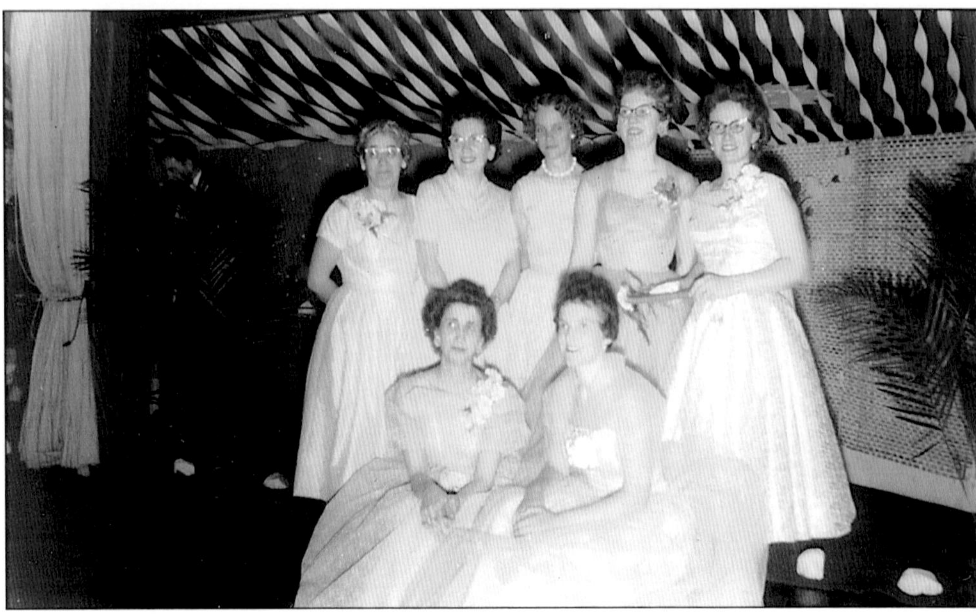

This photograph was taken at a dress-up dinner and party for the Homebuilders, an active young couples' fellowship group, First Baptist Church, Eau Claire, 1950s. Courtesy of Bev Peterson.

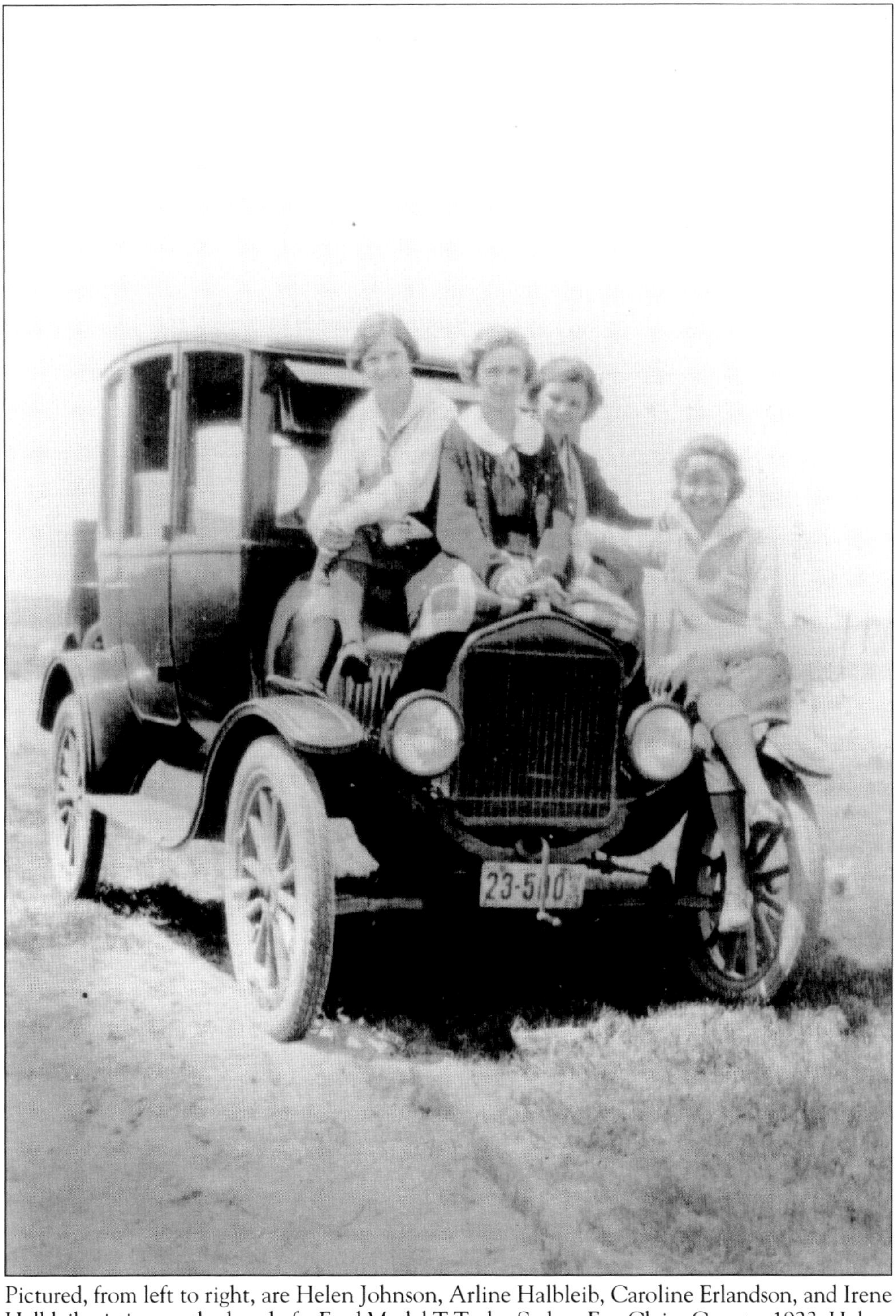

Pictured, from left to right, are Helen Johnson, Arline Halbleib, Caroline Erlandson, and Irene Halbleib, sitting on the hood of a Ford Model T Tudor Sedan, Eau Claire County, 1923. Helen, Caroline, and Irene may have been classmates; they were all born in 1897. This image is from the Lois Wilson collection. (CVM.)

Index